Go Native!

9/25/99

To Tom and Christine,
　　Native plants and wildflowers
are so wonderful — easy care,
undemanding, pretty & easy on
our fragile environment. What
more can we ask? Try a few
in your yard.
　　Its been great knowing
you — and having you as
good friends!

　　　　　Carolyn Harstad :"

Go Native!

Gardening with Native Plants and Wildflowers in the Lower Midwest

CAROLYN HARSTAD

PHOTOGRAPHS BY CAROLYN HARSTAD

DRAWINGS BY JEANETTE MING

Indiana University Press

BLOOMINGTON & INDIANAPOLIS

This book is a publication of

Indiana University Press

601 North Morton Street

Bloomington, Indiana 47404-3797 USA

http://www.indiana.edu/~iupress

Telephone orders 800-842-6796

Fax orders 812-855-7931

Orders by e-mail iuporder@indiana.edu

The paper used in this publication meets the minimum requirements of American National Standard for Information Sciences—Permanence of Paper for Printed Library Materials, ANSI Z39.48–1984.

MANUFACTURED IN THE UNITED STATES OF AMERICA

Library of Congress Cataloging-in-Publication Data

Harstad, Carolyn.

Go Native! : gardening with native plants and wildflowers in the lower midwest / Carolyn Harstad ; photographs by Carolyn Harstad ; drawings by Jeanette Ming.

p.   cm.

Includes bibliographical references (p.   ) and index.

ISBN 0-253-33561-2 (cloth : alk. paper). —ISBN 0-253-21302-9 (pbk. : alk. paper)

1. Native plants for cultivation—Middle West. 2. Wild flowers—Middle West. I. Title.

SB439.24.M629H37   1999

635.9'5177—dc21   99-11578

1   2   3   4   5   04   03   02   01   00   99

God blesses you as you enjoy nature.

—Aunt Ruth Fluegel, age 96, 1999

Dedicated to my dad and mother,
and to my grandchildren . . .
my link to the past, my hope for the future

Contents

What is love? One name for it is knowledge.
—*Robert Penn Warren, 1969*

Preface

I have had a long-term love affair with wildflowers. My tattered, well-thumbed Peterson's guide has been my faithful companion and teacher as I tromped through woods, along country roads, and on trails in our national parks. Wildflowers have been a major component in my own gardens since 1972. During the American Hosta Society's 1989 national convention, I was interviewed about my garden, one of six featured tour gardens. When the article appeared in the *American Hosta Journal*, the title read, "Harstad Confesses to Having a Wild Passion" and the interviewer, who referred to me as a *Waldfee* (Wood-sprite), wrote more about my passion for wildflowers than about my hostas.

Let me explain where I began, how I have traveled, where I am, and why I wrote this book. It is a journey that began long ago with a single step.

I think I was born with gardening genes, for it seems I have been a gardener forever. When I was very small, my mother gave me hollyhock seeds to plant next to the house for my "hollyhock dancers." I was amazed and delighted when bright red tulips grew in the spot where she and I had planted "those onions," and whenever anyone appeared with a Brownie camera, I always ran to the front of a flowering shrub, or my mother's pretty garden, even though the film was black and white.

I married a historian. I gardened wherever the moving van and my husband took me as he progressed from graduate school to college and university teaching positions and historical society administration in Wisconsin, Michigan, Idaho, Washington, Kentucky, Iowa, Minnesota, and Indiana. As we moved, many of my favorite perennials moved with us, waiting patiently in their plastic bags as I dug another new garden home for them.

In 1972, we moved to Iowa City with our five children. The ravine behind our new home was a jungle of poison ivy. After a long battle, I finally conquered this noxious weed and debated what to plant in its place. A new friend gave me a few spring ephemerals from her woods, and together we haunted construction sites for rescue possibilities. This was the beginning of my ongoing passion for wildflower gardening.

My interest in "native plants" began in 1993, when I became involved in the creation of the Indiana Native Plant and Wildflower Society. At the organizational meeting, I found myself—an ordinary, self-taught gardener—surrounded by professionals, botanists, and horticulturists. Up until that time, I regarded native plants as primarily shrubs and trees, or plants that most gardeners couldn't or wouldn't grow in their home landscape. I knew that some wildflowers were native and others nonnative, but if it was a wildflower and it was pretty, that was enough for me. I knew many gardeners who held similar reservations and beliefs, so I suggested that "wildflower" be included in the name of this new society to encourage these gardeners, who were eager to learn, but fearful of being deemed "uneducated." Did it help? I don't know, but I can happily report that the membership grew to over 500 statewide in the first four years, is still growing, and welcomes botanists, state employees, nursery owners, teachers, professors, horticulturists, professional landscapers, and, yes . . . a lot of ordinary gardeners, like me.

And why did I write this book? Because I love gardening and have always found it a solace for my soul. I never fail to get that childlike feeling of pure delight when I discover the first spring wildflower. Digging in the dirt, as I sit beside a beautiful flower garden, or under a tall tree amidst the sounds of nature, gives me incredible pleasure and peace. And I have always enjoyed sharing gardening tidbits and information about this "love of my life" with friends.

There are many arguments in favor of using native plants, not the least of which is concern for our fragile environment. In the past few years I have gained a deeper respect and appreciation for these incredible "citizens of the region." I hope that when you finish the last page, you will decide to *Go Native!*

It is not so much our friends' help that helps us as
the confident knowledge that they will help us.
                    —*Epicurus, 341–270 B.C.*

Acknowledgments

This book would never have germinated without the original inspiration, guidance, and skill of my special friend, e-mail correspondent, and editor, Bobbi Diehl. I also owe a particular debt of gratitude to Bill Brink and Ruth Ann Ingraham who got me involved with native plants in the first place; to the Indiana Native Plant and Wildflower Society (INPAWS) for keeping me focused; and to Ted Harris, who, through his unwavering zeal, contributed to my growing appreciation for our fragile environment.

As an avid gardener, I have become familiar with many native plants and the joy of using them. However, I certainly cannot claim to be an expert, so I have enjoyed consulting a wide variety of sources and people who are. Let me first acknowledge assistance from Alvin Bull, Colston Burrell, Michael Dirr, Ken Druse, Gordon Foster, Carrol Henderson, Samuel Jones, Margaret McKenny, Lawrence Newcomb, Roger Tory Peterson, Harry Phillips, Dean Roosa, Sylvan Runkel, Guy Sternberg, and Jim Wilson, and from the late Charles Deam, Leonard Foote, and Marie Sperka as well, whose books were of indispensable value as I read, researched, and learned.

I extend my sincere thanks to all who patiently and lovingly nurtured, counseled, and helped this "seedling writer" to grow. Dr. Rebecca Dolan, Director of the Friesner Herbarium at Butler University, suggested incorporating six recommended plants into each section; Kay Yatskievych, Missouri Botanical Garden; Ken Konsis, Executive Director, Vermilion County Conservation District, Danville, Illinois; and Patricia K. Armstrong, Prairie Sun Consultants, Naperville, Illinois, critiqued these lists. Jim Wilson autographed my personal copy of his *Landscaping with Wildflowers* with my chosen title, "Go Native!"

Acknowledgments

Thanks to Lee Casebere, Indiana Department of Natural Resources (IDNR), Division of Nature Preserves—a kind, gentle friend who has forgotten more about native species than I can ever hope to learn; to Spence Nursery horticulturist and INPAWS vice-president Kevin Tungesvick, a young man with an incredible knowledge of native plants; to Don Miller, who instigated and supervised the planting of over 27,000 native plants for Indy Parks in a single season!

Thanks to my husband, Peter Harstad, and to John Schaust, Director of nearby Holliday Park, for entrusting me with their rare, old books on uses of native plants; and to Gilbert and Emily Daniels for loaning me many books from their extensive personal horticultural library. Special thanks to Neil Diboll, of Prairie Nursery, Westfield, Wisconsin, and Mervin Wallace, of Missouri Wildflowers Nursery, Jefferson City, Missouri, who shared their insight, experience, and advice about establishing prairies; to Andy Wasowski for his concise explanation of "nature's envelope"; to Jim May, who helped me understand the construction details for water features; and to Roger Hedge and Mike Homoya of the IDNR Division of Nature Preserves for advising me about appropriate sedges to include in the book.

Particular thanks go to Dr. Gilbert Daniels, Dr. Rebecca Dolan, and Kathy Meyer, who read the final manuscript for accuracy; and to artist Jeanette Wong Ming, my loyal friend since our carefree high school days in a small town in southern Minnesota. Jeanette drew some of the initial illustrations from wildflowers that she ordered from We-Du Nursery in Marion, North Carolina, and nurtured on the window ledge in her apartment near Central Park in New York City! She also drove to Indianapolis, where she spent many hours in my gardens with sketchpad and pencil in hand.

And finally, I extend my thanks to my family—to my mother, Emma Frankson Schneider (1904–1976), who instilled in me a love of nature; to my dad and my sister, Walter Schneider and Joan Schneider Harstad, for their enthusiasm and encouragement as I wrote; to my brother, David Schneider, my nephew, Dan Schneider, and my son-in-law, Tim Vehling, for their computer expertise; to my five children, Linda Becker, Karen Scislow, Mark Harstad, Kristen Vehling, and David Harstad, for their insightful comments and helpful recommendations; to my sister-in-law, Grace Harstad, for editing suggestions; and above all, to Peter, my wonderful, loving, husband of 42 years, who spent many hours finding appropriate historical tidbits, reading, correcting, editing, and tightening up the manuscript, and was always there to give me a hug when I needed it.

This book was published with the aid of a generous challenge gift from
Helen B. Schwartz

Matching gifts from

Emily and Gilbert Daniels
Bobbi and Jim Diehl
Dow AgroSciences
Mark M. Holeman, Inc.
Marian Y. Meditch
Jill Perelman
Evaline and Harley Rhodehamel
Spence Restoration Nursery

Donations from

Pat and David Denny
Libby Frey

Climate rules, no matter what the hardiness zone
maps say.   *—Diane Heilenman, 1994*

Introduction

HOW TO BEAT
THE ZOMBIE ZONES

Native plants include trees, shrubs, vines, and
soft-stemmed plants, all of which take us back
into history to help explain our roots. They were
used for dyeing clothing, and for food and shelter;
they provided the medicines of the past, and many
are still used in modern medicine. Native
plants can create a small ecosystem
on our property to attract wildlife,
birds, and butterflies to our otherwise sterile
American lawns. They can help gardeners deal with
those pesky "Zombie Zones" of the Lower Midwest.
They are "environmentally friendly," less demanding than nonnatives, and once established will give
you more time to relax and enjoy your garden.

   Temperatures are generally more forgiving in
the states of the Lower Midwest than in some of
the more northern states. Ohio, Indiana, Illinois,
Missouri, Kentucky, the southern parts of Iowa, Michigan and Wisconsin, and the northern part of Tennessee are located in Zones 5 and 6. In these states, a mailbox seldom perches atop a snowbank all winter long,
as it does in Minnesota, where I grew up. In the Upper Midwest, everyone accepts the reality that snow
from the first snowfall may remain until the spring
thaws. In the Lower Midwest, school and civic events
may be canceled because of four inches of snow one

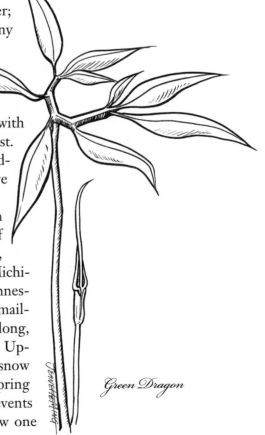

Green Dragon

week, and the following week residents may be able to wear a light sweater and enjoy a cup of coffee outdoors on the patio.

While these wild temperature swings may be pleasurable for people, they cause confusion for many of the plants we try to grow. The poor things never know whether to remain dormant under their cozy blanket of snow, or to begin sending out new buds in anticipation of spring. Diane Heilenman *(Gardening in the Lower Midwest)* refers to our area as the "Zombie Zones." Not only do our plants have to contend with temperature extremes in the winter, but the summer can be equally devastating. Pleasant days can suddenly become hot and steamy, then unpredictably swing back to chilly temperatures. It can rain for days on end like the deluge of Noah, then suddenly become so dry that the soil actually cracks. It is no wonder that so many plants have a difficult time surviving here. With natives, however, it's a different story.

I hope that you will find this book useful whether you are a beginning gardener, a wildflower aficionado, or a native plant guru. Using a simple question-and-answer format, I will try to answer some of the questions you may have about gardening with native plants and wildflowers, and explain methods of planning, site and soil preparation, garden design, plant selection, and propagation.

As I researched and wrote, I tried to focus on plants that are native to the Lower Midwest, but since this book encompasses nine states, there are obviously plants that are native to one state but not to another. Some plants may grow well in Iowa but languish in Tennessee. Others will thrive in Kentucky or southern Indiana but will not survive in northern Illinois or southern Wisconsin. I have tried to stress specific requirements for natives that may not thrive in all areas of the Lower Midwest. The six suggested species lists at the ends of chapters 4 through 12 are my own choices, and you may or may not agree. They are just a beginning, a stepping-stone, and I hope they encourage you to find your own favorites.

I was a teacher eons ago, and learned that repetition is an effective teaching tool. I use a variety of native plant terms in this book, and hope that by seeing these relatively unfamiliar terms over and over in context, you can incorporate them into your working vocabulary. The Glossary (see Resources) includes a number of these words, commonly used in the world of native plants.

Botanical names are often, but not always, included in parentheses after the common name. Botanical terminology is precise, and can be intimidating. Many gardeners with no formal scientific training are suspicious of those long "biblical names," as a friend calls them, and question why anyone would want to refer to Columbine as *Aquilegia canadensis*. What relationship do those words have to plants?

In recent years, I have become fascinated with these mysterious botanical names, because they tell so much about a plant in so few words. Once you understand the "lingo," the realm of native plants is not nearly so mysterious.

All plants and animals have a botanical name that consists of two words—Genus and species—printed in italics to let you know these epithets are foreign (usually Latin or Greek). Taken together, Genus and species make up the botanical name which identifies a specific species. *Genus* is first, is always capitalized, and identifies closely related plants or animals with common characteristics. For example, the genus name for dog is *Canis* (like canine). All breeds of domestic dogs are *Canis familiaris*, but a red wolf is *Canis rufus* and a dingo is *Canis dingo*. The *species* epithet always begins with a small letter and identifies a specific subclass of the genus; *familiaris* identifies "man's best friend."

And what a wealth of information you glean just from learning the meaning of those two words! The flower spurs of Wild Columbine *(Aquilegia canadensis)* are said to resemble the talons of an eagle. *Aquilegia* comes from *aquila*, the Latin word for eagle. *Jeffersonia diphylla* (Twinleaf) was named in honor of Thomas Jefferson; *diphylla* tells you it has divided butterfly-like leaves. Trilliums are in the lily family; *tri* means three and *lilium* means lily. *Trillium recurvatum* (Prairie Trillium) tells you that the sepals curve back, *T. grandiflorum* (Large White Trillium) has a large flower, and *T. sessile* (Toadshade) has no leaf stems or flower stalks.

A plant's botanical name is its only positive identification, so if I want to purchase a specific plant, I write down the botanical name and take it with me to the nursery. A beautiful wildflower with yellow bell-like flowers was used to treat throat problems in the Middle Ages. According to the Doctrine of Signatures of that era, the appearance or characteristic of a plant is the "signature" that reveals its medical uses. Bellwort's botanical name is *Uvularia grandiflora*—*Uvularia* because the flowers look like the uvula in the back of the throat, *grandiflora* meaning "large flower." Its common names include Merry Bells, Straw Flower, Wild Oats, and Strawbells, but if you specify *Uvularia grandiflora* in a catalog order, you can be assured of receiving Large-flowered Bellwort.

Chapter 1 presents the case for using native plants and wildflowers. There are a number of reasons, including their beauty, their historic interest, their value to the environment, and their ease of maintenance. I hope it is a convincing one.

Suggestions and recommendations for many gardening topics are similar whether you decide to plant only native plants and wildflowers, or prefer to combine them with your favorite nonnative annuals and perennials. There are general gardening tips in chapter 2 for planning, siting, establishing, and maintaining gardens, regardless of plant materials, to help you get started.

At a native plant conference in 1997, Andy Wasowski spoke eloquently about building within nature's envelope, and thoroughly convinced me of its merits. If you are building a new house, you may want to consider this exciting concept. In addition to reading chapter 3, I encourage you to read Wasowski's two convincing articles cited in the bibliography (see Resources) before beginning any building project.

As we delve into the world of native plants, I have elected to begin with native trees and shrubs in chapters 4 and 5. These are the bones of your garden, the framework that you need to establish first as you begin the landscaping process. After you have established the upper and middle layers of the landscape, next look to the lower level to complete the picture. Chapters 6, 7, and 8 cover vines, ground covers, and ferns.

Prairie and meadow gardens have become extremely popular. Recommended techniques for their preparation, establishment, and maintenance are found in chapter 9, as well as the culture and use of suggested native grasses and herbaceous plants with showy flowers called forbs. Because many sedges are major components of moist meadows, these small grass-like plants are also treated in chapter 9.

Chapter 10 will help you discover several ways to use water in the garden. Selections of plants that grow in water or near water, or that just prefer moist soil, are included. Chapter 11 discusses my favorite native plant garden—the woodland garden. Since woodland plants are not as readily available in the nursery trade, this chapter also addresses plant rescue where destruction of a natural area is inevitable due to development.

When you plant native plants, your landscape can restore an ecosystem and become a habitat so that wildlife will begin to reappear. Chapter 12 can guide you as you try to accomplish this. Chapter 13 deals with invasive exotics and their effect on our environment and on our native plants. In the very short chapter 14 are a few final thoughts about how our choices can influence our future.

The Resources section is a compendium of information: the Glossary, addresses of nurseries that sell native plants or seeds in the nine states of the Lower Midwest, State Forestry Departments, and native plant organizations in the Lower Midwest, and last but not least the References, which include my historical and technical sources as well as a variety of general and specialized gardening books.

Native plants have a rich history. In this book, I have included some nuggets of medical uses and plantlore, excerpts from pioneer letters and diaries, notes to help you understand why a particular plant got its botanical name, and other bits of information that I found interesting. I hope you do too. As we garden together, I will share stories and personal experiences as I try to entice you to add a few native plants to your own landscape. And if you feel compelled to visit the public library or a local bookstore to learn more about these wonderful "citizens of our region," then my efforts will have been worthwhile!

Go
Native!

In nature, there is no truly independent action
without impact.   —*Ken Druse, 1994*

1.

Why Use Native Plants and Wildflowers?

A friend in Iowa told me this story about her first native plant garden. One spring, while she and her sister were visiting their grandmother, they were each allowed to choose a plot of ground and plant a garden. They could plant anything they wished, anywhere on the property, so long as each cared for her own plot of ground. Her sister chose a sunny spot and planted colorful annuals, some perennials from her grandmother's beautiful perennial border, and a rose bush. My friend planted spring wildflowers that she dug carefully from her grandmother's woods. She chose a shady spot at the edge of the woods where she could take her favorite doll to sit under the trees, listen to the birds, and watch the squirrels chase each other.

Years later, when she was grown up, my friend had occasion to go there again in the springtime. Her grandmother had died many years earlier, the house had fallen into disrepair, and the yard was neglected. There was no trace of her sister's lovely sunny garden. Sadly, my friend

Rue Anemone

False Rue Anemone

walked into the woods at the edge of the property, and there she found her beautiful spring woodland wildflowers. They had increased and filled in a large section of the woods. "They were just as beautiful as I remembered them," she told me—and she smiled.

The use of native plants and wildflowers is one of the hottest topics to excite gardeners in recent years. Why has gardening with native plants suddenly become so popular? What makes this idea so attractive? Is it really such a new idea? Why are so many people suddenly interested in creating meadows, prairies, and wetland areas, or designing walking trails through adjoining woodlands? Why would you want to incorporate native plants and wildflowers into your landscape—and is gardening with native plants really that much different from any other type of gardening? What do you need to know in order to make good decisions about this "new" gardening concept?

Like many native plants, my friend's selections had survived on their own. When we choose native plants for our landscaping needs, we accomplish many things. These plants have adapted to the climatic swings of the Lower Midwest and are more likely to thrive and survive. Our maintenance is reduced because these plants need less artificial watering, less fertilizing, less chemical maintenance, less of the forces currently degrading our environment.

When plants become readily available, they become more widely known and used by gardeners, by landscape architects, and by the public in general, so that by requesting plants and seeds from nurseries and garden centers, we help to increase the supply. As more and more gardeners request and plant native plants, nursery owners and seed production managers begin to take note, and respond accordingly. Regional seed production and simple propagation can help to keep these various species alive and abundant, and as a result, conservation is assured.

I enjoy watching a bevy of tiny hummingbirds make frequent visits to the Cardinal Flower and Royal Catchfly, two brilliant red native perennials planted just outside my kitchen window in a border garden among red and white begonias, parsley, oregano, sage, rosemary, and thyme. These fascinating little birds always choose the red flowers first, before visiting the hummingbird feeder that hangs on the tall evergreen Arborvitae. Royal Catchfly is currently on the threatened or endangered species list in several states, but is easily propagated by seed, and multiplies readily in the more forgiving habitat of a home garden. Using it in this way may prevent its disappearance.

Perhaps I am an idealist, but I would also like to believe that one of the reasons for the recent interest in native plants and wildflowers stems from a growing national awareness of our environment—an environment that is constantly being compromised as we build hundreds of new homes, businesses, parking lots, roads, and highways, cut thousands of trees, bulldoze hundreds of acres, and cover fertile land with concrete and asphalt. Once-blue skies are changed to leaden gray smog as we scurry about in our private automobiles, and we wink when industry does not comply with clean air regulations, so that weather forecasters find it necessary to report reasons to stay indoors. We drain wetlands and marshes and cut forested areas in the name of progress, changing ecosystems, destroying wildlife habitat, and threatening species including our own. As a result of disregard for our environment, we experience flooding, landslides, health problems, and the disappearance of many varieties of plants, birds, and animals.

Am I against progress? Absolutely not. I firmly believe that we need to develop new and better ways to accommodate our ever-expanding population, to use scientific advances and discoveries, and to learn how to make our lives better, easier, and more productive, but there are alternative ways to accomplish this. Using native plants in the landscape can actually help in the total scheme of things by cutting down on watering, fertilizing, and the use of chemicals. And once a native plant garden is established, it will also save us time.

There is widespread concern over the devastation of the world's rain forests and the subsequent loss of a multitude of plants which may have untapped value for medical purposes. Our native plants have similar value for current and future generations. The yew tree that is native to the Pacific Northwest *(Taxus brevifolia)* is a source of Taxol, a powerful medical weapon in the fight against cancer. The familiar garden perennial known as Purple Coneflower *(Echinacea purpurea)* is native to the Lower

Midwest. Parts of this plant are available in an herbal preparation which reportedly strengthens the immune system. Mayapple *(Podophyllum peltatum)* is being studied for use in cancer chemotherapy preparations, and the Pawpaw tree *(Asimina triloba)* provides a new experimental cancer-fighting extract that is reputed to be even more powerful than Taxol. The battle to preserve our heritage might begin right in our own back yard.

By using native plants we can assist in the preservation of a centuries-old ecosystem, and in so doing, increase the survival rate of multitudes of birds, butterflies, and wildlife. Common Milkweed *(Asclepias syriaca)* is necessary for the Monarch butterfly to complete its metamorphosis. As urban development increases, the numbers of this plant diminish. Ingesting Common Milkweed gives Monarch caterpillars a nasty taste which is unpalatable to most birds. Monarch caterpillars also feed on other species of milkweed, such as Swamp Milkweed and Butterfly Weed, which are not as effective in producing this "taste test" protection, but do assist in the proliferation of the Monarch.

In the only sunny area behind my home, I planted a small oval prairie garden with native grasses such as Indian Grass, Prairie Dropseed, and Little Bluestem, surrounded by Swamp Milkweed, White Turtlehead, Black-eyed Susan, Liatris, Cardinal Flower, and some nonnative annual Blue Lobelia. Swamp Milkweed *(Asclepias incarnata)* has an upright form, large beautiful rosy-red flowers, and interesting silk-filled seedpods. During World War II, this silky fluff was used as a substitute for kapok in life jackets. Schoolchildren felt proud to help the war effort by collecting milkweed seedpods.

Last summer I observed five Monarch caterpillars devouring the leaves of the milkweed in my small prairie patch, and on the recommendation of my grandchildren, I captured one of the fat caterpillars and confined it in a large glass jar. It quickly evolved into a beautiful lime green, gold-studded chrysalis. In

Twinleaf

the allotted nine days, the chrysalis darkened and I saw the markings of the butterfly within. On that beautiful Sunday afternoon, time stood still as I sat fascinated on the ground under the Sugar Maple tree and watched the butterfly emerge with tiny, damp, wrinkled wings. I carefully removed the small stick to which it was clinging and placed it upright in the garden. The new little Monarch pumped its wings, and as I watched in awe, the wings expanded to full size. After a few hours, it climbed from the stick to a nearby flower, where it poised, opening and closing its wings, and then soared into the blue sky.

Did "my" Monarch make it to Mexico? Will this butterfly, or one of its offspring, return to these latitudes next summer to complete the life cycle? I shall never know. I do know that without the milkweed plant in my yard I would never have experienced a wonder of nature. By planting native milkweed, we can help to ensure the continuation of this miracle.

Why should you incorporate native plants and wildflowers into your landscape? Most gardeners have purchased beautiful, healthy plants at the nursery or garden center, only to have them succumb to the ravages of the first winter, or, even worse, to die before the growing season ends. Suitably placed or selected native plants and wildflowers grow on their own, thriving where many nonnatives (exotics) fail, because native plants have adapted to that particular area. Once established, they can survive without constant care. If you were to leave town for two or three months in the summertime, how would your untended garden look when you returned? What if you left a garden area for over a year? How about five years? Or more? As my Iowa friend discovered, native plants and wildflowers have the ability to thrive and survive on their own, and even increase, because they are a part of our particular environment, unlike hostas, roses, or chrysanthemums.

The common misconception that native plants and wildflowers are weedy and that a native plant garden will look scruffy and unkempt is far from the truth. It is possible to design a garden using native plants that is every bit as beautiful as any perennial garden you have seen. Many well-known garden perennials such as Great Blue Lobelia, Black-eyed Susan, Coreopsis, and Purple Coneflower are native plants.

When the pioneers came to the Lower Midwest, they wrote glowing reports in their diaries of the colorful flowers that made the land through which they were traveling look like an immense flower garden. In 1853,

Frederika Bremer described the succession of color, "in spring white, then blue, then purple, and now mostly of a golden yellow." She told of tall sunflowers, "frequently four yards high," towering over the heads of all, and described the sight as "an ecstasy in the life of nature. It was bathed in light . . . sunflowers sang praises to the sun."

I do not claim that a native plant garden is a no-maintenance garden, or that it will become established in an instant, or even in a single season. Like any beautiful garden, it takes thought, time, and above all . . . patience. And yes, it requires maintenance. But with proper planning and preparation, your native plant garden can be a less demanding garden over the years.

Am I against the use of nonnative plants? Again, absolutely not. My garden has over 300 varieties of hostas, native to Japan. I use a combination of native and nonnative plants in most of my gardens, and often recommend beginning by adding native plants to an existing garden border. However, it is imperative in choosing any plant to consider its impact, including its growing habits and requirements.

While some use the words "wildflower" and "native plant" interchangeably, others insist there is a great difference. In general, "wildflower" and "native plant" both include flowering herbaceous plants. Native plants also include trees, shrubs, vines, ferns, and ground covers. The Glossary has a more complete list of plant terminology, but let's briefly discuss a few terms like *native plant, provenance, wildflower, alien,* and *exotic.*

Native plants are those that greeted the settlers when they arrived; plants that grow on their own regardless of climatic extremes. This is their natural range, their chosen environment. These plants have weathered many winters, survived drought, heat, rain, and the ups and downs of temperatures and wild growing conditions which characterize the area we designate as the Lower Midwest. When we have a severely cold winter, many nonnative flowering trees and shrubs fail to flower or are winter-killed. A native plant is adapted to the local growing conditions, survives, and generally flourishes regardless of the extremes we experience in the area.

Provenance means that the seeds originated in a particular locality. For example, if you live in Missouri or Ohio, a plant that originated from seed raised near your home will be more likely to survive than one originating from seed raised in Texas or Maine.

Webster's Dictionary's definition of a **wildflower** is a plant that can survive without cultivation. Native flowering plants are often referred to as wildflowers. A wildflower may also be a flowering plant brought over by European and Asian settlers. Many nonnative plants, also called exotics or aliens, have escaped from cultivation to the wild and become naturalized, and are able to cope with the conditions of the local environment. These include Queen Anne's Lace, Dandelions, Chicory, Dame's Rocket, Japanese Honeysuckle, and the orange Asiatic daylilies that grow along the edges of country roads. Many wildflowers have been here so long that we assume they are native plants when indeed they were introduced from some other part of the world.

Both **alien** and **exotic** can be defined as foreign, which means that they are not indigenous, or, in more simplistic terms, did not originate in a particular location. Some alien wildflowers are lovely additions to our gardens, while others become "invasive exotics" and can cause terrible problems in our environment. When we choose wildflowers for our gardens, we need to educate ourselves about their habits before introducing them to our landscape. Garlic Mustard (*Alliaria petiolata*) is an attractive little wildflower with pretty four-petaled white flowers and scalloped leaves that exude a faint smell of garlic when crushed. This wildflower was originally brought as a potherb to this country. It escaped cultivation and is currently threatening our native wildflowers (see chapter 13). In Germany, it is still cultivated and used, but evidently the natural checks there are not present in the United States.

This book is not meant to be a case against nonnative plants, but rather an invitation to expand your gardening horizons, as well as to encourage personal education and individual responsibility. By planting native plants, we can do ourselves and our environment a favor. An ancient Chinese proverb says, "The journey of a thousand miles begins with a single step." Planting native plants in our own small space may be that first step in the ever-present challenge of preserving our precious environment. Since only one plant can occupy one space, we need to choose wisely.

Thousands of acres of prairies, woodlands, and wetlands have disappeared in the name of progress since the arrival of the first settlers, changing ecosystems and altering habitats. In 1973, Marie Sperka wrote in *Growing Wildflowers*, "The native flora of our prairies, mountains, and woodlands are a living part of the American heritage, as valuable and irreplaceable as any we have. But daily our wilderness and woodlands are vanishing, and with it the plants they nurture. Unless we act quickly, our wildlings will disappear." As we become more knowledgeable about native plants and their use in the landscape, and begin to use them in our own area, we will help to preserve a part of our heritage for future generations. Perhaps it is time for each of us to consider taking that single step. I invite you to take that step with me. Now, how do we begin?

Mother Nature was, and still remains, my
mentor.   —*C. Colston Burrell, 1997*

2.

How Do We Begin?

Planning the Garden

A wise old gardener once told me, "You don't have to garden all of your yard all of the time." As you plan your landscape and plant your gardens, you will find that each season brings a particular beauty to different parts of the landscape. Our woodland garden lifts my spirits in early spring with its pastel display of spring flowers, but then retreats in summer to become a quiet, serene space, filled with the cool green leaves of Wild Geranium, Celandine Poppy, and lacy ferns. In summer, the slumbering prairie perennials awaken to brighten another section of the yard, followed by the brilliant fall foliage of surrounding trees and shrubs. The waving, soft green grasses of the summer prairie garden change to dried russet-brown and gold in autumn, and as winter progresses, a stark landscape is enhanced by deep green evergreens.

The historical prairie began at the western edge of Indiana. Fire perpetuated prairies by destroying young saplings and shrubs. Generally, prairies did not exist in

Side Oats Grama

the eastern part of America. A large proportion of the Lower Midwest was once woodland, with meadows and oak openings. In 1835, a farmer named Patrick Shirreff wrote, "In America, trees vary in number on a given space, from the dense forest to the oak opening, with half-a-dozen of trees to an acre."

If civilization disappeared from the Lower Midwest, much of the original vegetation would return through natural succession. The easiest kind of habitat to recreate is the habitat that existed when the settlers arrived. Ohio, Kentucky, Tennessee, Wisconsin, Michigan, and eastern Indiana were originally woodlands with meadow and oak openings. That certainly does not mean that the residents of these Lower Midwestern states can't have a prairie, but initially it may take a little more effort to create the proper soil and moisture required by that prairie than it will for residents of Illinois, Iowa, or Missouri.

Take a moment to think about how you decide what to plant in your yard. Do you have an existing space designated as "garden"? An area of dirt around the foundation? A place drawn on paper? Or a garden that is still just a figment of your imagination? Are you starting with a new home and an empty yard to design? Or with a large generic area behind an existing home? Was your property originally a woodland, a prairie, an "oak opening," or a meadow? It might be fun to find out! Perhaps that little bit of research may encourage you to recreate a piece of history in your own yard. To begin your planning, go into the house.

Go into the House! Why?

In 1843, Dr. Thomas Steel settled in southern Wisconsin and wrote to his father in England, "I have left a few trees near the house [including] two noble oaks which cannot be less than three or four hundred years old. From my house the view is splendid. I wish you could see it." When you decide to plan a new garden, whether your home is brand new or you are just adding to an existing landscape, the first thing to do is to follow Dr. Steel's example and go into the house!

Since we spend more time indoors than outdoors, we should take into consideration the view from our windows. Most people plant gardens against the foundation of their houses—gardens that can be enjoyed only when they walk outside to view them (or to maintain them). People driving past see these gardens more often than their owners do. Locate gardens where you, the gardener, can enjoy them—from inside or out. So go inside and look out the windows. Where could you place a garden so that you can see it from your kitchen? As you relax in your family room? From your screened porch? You get the idea. Just don't fight the site.

Don't Fight the Site . . . What Does That Mean?

Gardening is easier, more energy efficient, and consequently more enjoyable when you match the plants to the site. Assessing the site, taking the time to plan, and preparing the garden properly before you plant will save you money, time, and frustration both now and in the future.

Many gardening decisions are obvious. If your yard is wooded, it does no good to plant prairie plants unless you chop down all the trees. Prairie plants will be happiest in a sunny location with well-drained soil that allows their roots to reach deep into the earth. Butterfly Weed likes well-drained soil, but rots in heavy clay. Fire Pink will tolerate light shade and is often found at the edge of the woods, whereas Royal Catchfly needs full sunlight to bloom properly. If conditions are dry and sandy, moisture-loving Cardinal Flower and Queen-of-the-Prairie will not survive. Azaleas and rhododendrons need an acidic soil and will become weak and chlorotic if the site is alkaline.

Plants found growing together naturally in the wild are referred to as plant communities. Similar requirements for moisture, light, and soil dictate these natural communities. In planning a garden, identify the existing site conditions and try to choose members of the plant community that is appropriate for the type of environment you have.

Tall silphiums like Rosinweed, Compass Plant, and Prairie Dock are part of a prairie community, as are warm-season grasses such as Indian Grass, Little Bluestem, and Switchgrass. All need full sun, well-drained soil, and annual mowing or burning.

Aquatic plants grow in water. These communities contain

Fire Pink

plants like arrowhead, cattails, and rushes. Marsh or bog plants, such as Blue Flag Iris, prefer consistently moist soil. Moisture-loving plants, like White Turtlehead, Buttonbush, and Joe-Pye Weed, can be found growing in the transition zone that occurs between wet, moist, and dry areas.

Spring Beauty, Toothwort, Prairie Trillium, Wild Geranium, and Jacob's Ladder are examples of a community of spring wildflowers often found in beech-maple forests. These woodland plants typically grow in loose, fertile loam that has been amended for years by the decomposition of fallen leaves in the forest.

Large-flowered Trillium

"Work smarter, not harder" by determining which plants will love your existing site. Where their light, moisture, soil, and nutrient requirements are naturally met by existing conditions, plants will thrive. Know the requirements of the plants you want to grow. If the chosen site doesn't meet them, stop and think about what changes are needed, and whether those changes are feasible, if the garden is to be successful.

What Do I Need to Know about Requirements for Light?

Check the available light where you plan to locate the garden and try to choose plants accordingly. "Full sun" means at least 6 hours each day. Sunlight filtered through trees is considered "light shade"; less than 6 hours of dappled sunlight is "moderate shade." If no actual sunlight reaches the ground below, you have "deep shade."

Shade-loving woodland wildflowers and ferns may burn in too much sun, or require inordinate amounts of moisture to stay alive. Several ferns, like Ostrich Fern, will grow in full sun, but without additional moisture will begin to look bleached and tattered and go dormant earlier in the season than when grown in a shady, moist setting. Ground covers that require shade will burn and die in too much sun. Most prairie and meadow plants need full sun. Many sun-loving plants can exist in shade, but may be stunted, become leggy and need staking, not bloom as well, or languish and die.

Of course, there will be times when you simply want a garden that doesn't fit the site and are willing to take the consequences. Plants in my small prairie garden have to be tolerant of light shade, and the Indian Grass does not grow as tall and handsome as it does in my friend's sunny yard. My Black-eyed Susan is recumbent rather than upright, but the Great Blue Lobelia loves the site. The milkweed and goldenrod species flourish and attract lovely butterflies. I don't mind a short clump of Indian Grass, and the Black-eyed Susan looks almost like a bright yellow ground cover. Sometimes you may choose to work a little harder in order to incorporate plants with special needs. Just make those decisions with your eyes wide open!

What about Moisture Requirements?

Once established, most native plants will tolerate some drought. If drought becomes too severe, some will simply go dormant. However, every living thing needs water, even cacti, so don't expect your native plants to survive without it. During extremely dry periods it may be necessary to provide a welcoming drink until the next rainstorm comes. Let the hose run and water deeply rather than lightly sprinkling the garden daily.

Some plants require more moisture than others. In *Landscaping with Wildflowers*, Jim Wilson recommends using bricks laid flat and close together at the base of the planting hole for these moisture-lovers. He writes, "The roots grow around and between the bricks to reach the moisture that accumulates beneath them." Other authors recommend using "potato-sized" rocks to accomplish the same purpose. You can also plant water-loving plants in a large buried tub or in a hole lined with plastic sheeting. Punch small holes in either for slow drainage. Good drainage is critical for most plants, although some tolerate—or even prefer—"wet feet."

How about Soil?

Do you know the composition of the soil on your property? Is it heavy clay? Friable loam? Sandy? Composition is easy to determine by digging an orange-size sample from the planting area about 5–6 inches deep.

Squeeze the slightly moist soil in your hand to compress it into a ball.

1. Clay: The small particles in clay soil stick together, hold moisture and nutrients, and will keep the soil in a firm ball that doesn't break apart easily. Clay soil is fertile, but can crack and dry rock-hard in a drought; it can be a hostile environment for plants with moisture-loving roots.

2. Sandy: Sandy soil will not maintain a ball shape regardless of how hard you compress it. This type of soil drains well, but moisture-loving plants need to be watered more frequently. Sandy soil is not as fertile as clay soil.

3. Loam: Soil that will compress into a ball but can easily be crumbled apart is loam, generally considered the optimum planting medium. Friable garden loam is the preferred soil for most plants.

How Do I Make Sure My Plants Have the Proper Nutrients?

Nitrogen (N), phosphorus (P), and potassium (K) are well known nutrients, always listed in order on a fertilizer bag (10–10–10, 46–0–0, etc.), indicating the concentration of each of these elements. In addition, soil is composed of a multitude of trace elements, including minerals such as copper, iron, magnesium, etc. The availability of these nutrients to a particular plant is determined by the pH of the soil. Acid is 7.0 and below; alkaline is above 7.0. Most plants prefer soil with a neutral to slightly acidic pH between 6.0 and 7.0. If the pH is not compatible with the needs of the plant, the nutrients will be bonded to the soil particles and will not release themselves to that plant. This explains why acid-loving Pin Oaks cannot take up the available iron in alkaline soil and get yellow (chlorotic) leaves. Just like humans, plants need proper nutrition in order to grow and remain healthy. Therefore, pH is important.

How Do I Test My Soil?

If you don't know whether your soil is acidic or alkaline, you may want to have it tested. Many county extension agencies will test the pH of your soil for a small fee. Generally you are asked to gather samples from several parts of your yard and mix them together for this test.

There are also commercial kits available for purchase that you can use to test the pH yourself. The "do-it-yourself" method allows you to determine the actual pH of different parts of your yard with a minimum of expense. In the December 1998 issue of *Fine Gardening* magazine, Keith Davitt reports on his experience testing pH with three moderately priced soil-test kits. He concluded that fancy packaging or high price does not necessarily guarantee quality, but commented that "regardless of the test, the most important things that you can do are to use the same test on a regular basis, to note the effects on your plants of applying the recommended amounts of fertilizer, and to keep track of those results so you have a history to refer to."

If you don't have a source to test the pH, or are simply not interested in bothering with this step, there are ways to "eyeball" the site. Clay soil is generally alkaline; sandy soil tends to have a neutral pH. Soil in acidic sites tends to be more loamy, although a loamy soil may also be neutral. You can determine a lot about soil conditions by simply taking a walk through the neighborhood to observe what grows well. If acid-loving plants like rhododendrons and azaleas are doing well, the pH is probably low. If the Pin Oak on the neighbor's lawn is yellow and chlorotic-looking, the soil is apt to be alkaline.

Most woodland wildflowers, native trees, and shrubs will grow well in a neutral garden loam. Try to choose plants that can obtain the proper nourishment from your existing soil conditions to avoid ongoing, labor-intensive soil amendments. In addition to rhododendrons and azaleas, Bunchberry, Partridge Berry, and Wintergreen require a highly acidic environment. Decide how important it is to you to include these acid-lovers in naturally alkaline soil that must be intensely amended each year to lower the pH. One of the reasons you find particular plants growing together in nature is because each member of that community needs a similar soil pH, so study the cultural requirements of each plant before you custom-mix a plant community.

However, as I said, there may be times when you simply yearn to grow a particular species that does not fit the site. In a perennial bed where I planted hostas, astilbe, ferns, and Pink Turtlehead, a clump of acid-loving Wintergreen remains as a specimen plant rather than spreading as a ground cover because I did not amend the neutral soil. I enjoy the glossy, thick leaves and the pretty berries, and even though my Wintergreen is not flourishing, it is surviving. But for most gardens, the ideal planting medium is garden loam.

How Do I Amend the Soil to Create Garden Loam?

Amend clay or sandy soil before planting by adding large amounts of humus such as well-decomposed compost or sphagnum peat moss. In the fall, incorporate organic matter such as sphagnum peat moss, finely shredded leaves, straw, well-cured weed-free manure, animal bedding chips, ground bark, sawdust and wood shavings, or even shredded paper. Add up to half the volume of the soil to be amended and spade or till thoroughly. Since the organic matter actually takes nitrogen and other nutrients from the soil in order to break down, sprinkle the area liberally with a balanced fertilizer like 10–10–10 (about one pound for 50 square feet). If you prefer to use only nitrogen, purchase 46–0–0.

How Deep Do I Have to Amend the Soil?

Large plants such as trees, shrubs, or deeply rooted meadow and prairie plants need to have the soil amended and rototilled 18–24 inches deep. Most woodland plant roots grow within the top 4–12 inches of soil, so in those areas where rototilling is impossible, I spade in compost and sphagnum peat moss in the top 6–12 inches. It is best to amend the entire planting bed rather than just the planting hole, lest you create a "basin effect" and drown your plants. But sometimes this is impossible. At a minimum, score the sides of a planting hole and dig the hole at least twice as wide as but no deeper than the root ball, and amend the soil.

If your soil is hard clay, take extra time before you plant to amend the soil, especially if you plan to plant woodland wildflowers. Your basic task is to break up the sticky clay particles and try to recreate the loose, loamy soil where most spring ephemerals and woodland wildflowers grow. I have gone through bales of sphagnum peat moss and compost. Pine needles can be added if you need to increase the acidity of the soil. Amendment also helps to create well-drained soil, which can spell the difference between life and death for many woodland and prairie plants. Ideally you should use equal parts of sphagnum peat moss, compost, and soil. Add a balanced fertilizer such as 12–12–12 or 10–10–10 at the rate of 10 pounds to 100 square feet. To promote good drainage, add an inch or two of coarse sand. Be sure the sand is coarse, not fine, because fine sand plus clay equals cement!

Sandy soil tends to drain too quickly, depleting the soil of necessary nutrients and leaving the roots of your plants thirsty. By amending sandy soil with compost and sphagnum peat moss, you can improve its fertility and bring it closer to ideal garden loam.

What about Using Manure?

Manure is an excellent composting addition and loosens most soils, but, contrary to general belief, does not provide many nutrients. Its primary function is to recreate loose, friable soil. Be sure it is aged and well-rotted rather than fresh, because it takes time and the heat of composting to kill the weed seeds in fresh manure. Fresh manure may give you great loamy soil, but it will probably produce a healthy weed crop as well.

When Should I Bring in Additional Soil?

Consider mounding the soil to change the "lay of the land." Think about nature. Landscapes with high and low spots are more interesting than flat ones. A raised area can create an element of surprise as you round the path, draw attention to a specimen plant, or give wildflowers like Wild Ginger and Mayapple a rare chance to show off the flowers normally hidden under their leaves.

In heavily wooded areas where the tree roots may be too tightly inter-laced to dig, you can add up to 6 or 7 inches of amended soil over tree roots (more than that may suffocate the tree). Maple roots are notorious for filling all available space. Lay a piece of spun-fiber garden barrier cloth (not plastic) on the ground before adding amended soil. Eventually the persistent maple roots will sneak through, but this will slow them down.

How Do I Decide "What Goes Where"?

Before you start digging a new bed or border, take a garden hose and several buckets, pots, or even chairs out to the area to use as markers. Outline the proposed new garden with the hose, position the buckets, pots, and chairs to represent trees, shrubs, and plants, and then look at the proposed site from both inside and outside the house to evaluate your handiwork. You can use spray paint to mark the outline of the garden if you need to remove the hose. Continue to relocate, rearrange, and re-check until you have everything satisfactorily sited from both inside and outside the house. It is much easier to move a chair than to move a tree! In chapters 4 and 5, there are more details on siting, planting, and maintenance.

In an existing lawn, cut the sod next to the line if you are planning to remove it. Slice about half of the roots of the sod by pushing the spade in at an angle just below the soil level. The sod will make a good addition to your compost bin. It is also possible to place 8 sheets of newspaper over the sod, cover with 8–10 inches of topsoil amended with compost or mulch, and plant. The newspapers will decompose. You can actually plant in the topsoil the first season if you wish. However, with a healthy crop of aggressive weeds and undesirable plants, you may first want to let this covered area lie undisturbed for a growing season.

What if I Want to Plan a Meadow or Prairie?

The beautiful grasses of a meadow or prairie, waving and undulating gracefully amid brightly colored sun-loving flowers, are a visual treat that you don't

Big Bluestem

want to leave behind when you go indoors. Make sure it is visible from several windows in your house before you turn over the first spadeful of dirt. Even though this type of garden is generally much larger than a typical flower bed or border, it is still helpful to place some large markers in strategic spots and return to the house to determine if the size and location you have outlined are satisfactory. You will be surprised how your perception changes from outside to inside.

Once you have determined the size and location of your meadow or prairie, the next step is to examine the site and identify existing desirable and undesirable plants, trees, and shrubs. In chapter 9 there are detailed instructions about site and soil preparation, plant propagation and selection, and descriptions of recommended plants for prairies and meadows.

Do I Need to Use These Markers to Plan a Woodland Garden?

Wooded areas already have the framework of trees and shrubs in place. Most woodland wildflowers are best viewed and enjoyed as you stroll through the woods, rather than from within your house. Your initial tasks will be to decide where your paths will be, remove unwanted vegetation from the paths, and then determine what steps to take to successfully relocate any plant material you want to save. After the paths are sited, remove any additional unwanted trees, shrubs, or plants that will interfere with your planting scheme, and relocate desirable vegetation in accordance with your plan. Further instructions, plus recommended plants, will be found in chapter 11.

How Do I Design my Gardens?

Gardening, like interior decor, is a reflection of one's personality. However, your home's interior is private and you don't have to invite anyone inside if you don't want to. Gardens are outdoors, and even though they are personal, they are also public. So before you dig up a huge area to Go Native! think about the location of that area.

The front yard, like the formal living room in the house, is where you "greet the public." Woodland gardens, such as the one in front of my home, are calm and restful. Since none of the native woodland plants are oversized (as are some of the prairie grasses), woodlands tend to look natural and civilized. A woodland garden does not generally "threaten" the neighbors regardless of where it is located.

Prairie and meadow gardens can be beautiful and relatively carefree. Many new native plant enthusiasts want to dispose of their turf lawn and install a natural lawn complete with a variety of grasses and forbs. However, remember that this type of garden can take up to five years to become established.

I believe the most consternation in our American lawn-worshipping society is caused by prairie and meadow plantings, particularly those incorporating native grasses. If this is the style you plan to start with, let me encourage you to start small, or practice in the back yard, especially if you have a neighbor who hates "ridges" at the property line and consequently expects you to mow your lawn each time he mows his. City officials will tell you that the "weed patrol" is generally called by a disgruntled neighbor, so have a plan and explain it to your neighbors. If you live in a typical suburban neighborhood, try to keep those lines of communication open. It pays.

Consider designing a curving border garden to attract butterflies or hummingbirds with brightly colored native perennials and perhaps a representative grass or two, rather than rototilling the entire front yard and scattering prairie seed. Edge the border to make it look neat and tidy, do some research, and choose interesting native trees or shrubs to complement your public area. Next year, increase the size of the border garden, adding a few more grasses in a civilized fashion as you continue to research, educate, and learn. By the time your turf grass is totally replaced by a native meadow, perhaps your neighbors will be ready to follow your lead. This approach will be more manageable and less frustrating to you as well.

The back yard could be compared to the family room, the place where you "live," so consider planting a biohedge—a hedge of a variety of shrubs and small trees around the back to encourage wildlife, create a living privacy fence, and provide color and interest in all seasons. Chapters 5 and 10 have more information on this concept. If you allow enough space between trees and shrubs so that each can grow and mature to its natural size and shape, you can forget about shearing, shaping, and stunting.

If a meadow or prairie is still what you yearn for, rototill a manageable section of the back yard that can be seen from inside the house. Prairie plants require at least two or three years to settle in. If you decide to seed this area, consider purchasing enough plants for a 4- to 5-foot border of prairie plants around the perimeter. Borders and edges are particularly important when you first begin because they give a planned look from the start and will be more pleasing for you to view out of your windows as you wait for the seeded area to catch up.

Black Chokeberry

Since the back yard is more private, do your experimenting with color, size, shape, plant selection, and design here. The back meadow can also serve as a nursery to grow perennials that can be moved to other gardens after a year or two. Start some plants from seed, and try cuttings or layering to increase the stock. You can afford to wait in the back yard, and if the border is attractive you won't become impatient.

To get from the front yard to the back, hallways or "corridors" are necessary. What is planted here depends on the space available, on the existing conditions, and also on the view from inside. If you can't see the area from inside the house, use low-maintenance native shrubs or ground cover, rather than perennials.

The windows of our living room face the corridor between our house and the neighbors, and I have planted a massive ground covering of Ostrich Ferns near the path. Native evergreen hemlocks form a curved line through the area. A small pond amidst a ground cover of Japanese Pachysandra accents the outside atrium area. With shade-tolerant annuals, airy wildflowers, assorted native ferns, and spring bulbs, I enjoy this garden as I walk from the front yard to the back, and it also creates a pretty scene out the living room windows.

Every yard needs a work area, just as every home needs a utility room. There should be a spot on your property for a compost pile, a holding or "nursery" bed for newly acquired plants, a trash area, and a place to pot plants.

It All Sounds So Overwhelming . . .

As you plan your landscape, take the concept of "rooms" seriously. This concept is an old one, familiar to most gardeners, but I am not using it in quite the same way here. Instead, think in terms of dividing a large project into pieces or "rooms" in order to make the task manageable.

Earlier in this century, spring cleaning was a traditional activity. Winter-weary people flung open their storm windows to shake the dust mop, emptied, sorted, and rearranged drawers and closets, washed and aired draperies, curtains, and bedding, vigorously scrubbed walls and windows, and after hanging their rugs over the wire clotheslines, used their metal carpet beaters with a vengeance. Modern-day homeowners clean one room at a time, spread out over a longer time period, making the task more manageable and less overwhelming. The thought of thoroughly cleaning the whole house in a single day, or even in a week, is mind-boggling to most of us.

When you mow paths through a woodland or prairie site, cut the sod of your lawn into a desirable shape, or designate a certain area as a meadow, you are creating small individual gardens, or rooms, which are each part of the total garden. Prepare and plant one "room" at a time, instead of trying to redo the entire "back forty" in a single growing season. If you undertake too much at once, you will find the preparation, planting, and maintenance more than you can manage, and you will probably give up in frustration.

After clearing one "room" of perennial weeds and replanting with wildflowers of your choice, mulch it well and move on to the next. It took several years of this routine to work through our entire acre of property. When I began, there were only a few areas which looked like acceptable garden spaces; the rest of the site was filled with weeds that I mowed once or twice during the summer and again in fall. As time went on, the garden spaces grew larger and larger and the weedy areas decreased. After about five years, I finally began to achieve the effect I wanted.

How Shall I Begin?

Inventory the site as you "walk your property." Mentally divide the property into front, right side, back, and left side of the "footprint" of the house, and using these four divisions, simply list the vegetation in each section on a sheet of paper, including trees, shrubs, plants, and existing gardens. If you do not recognize the various types of vegetation on your property, invite a knowledgeable friend, or hire a professional. Invest in a good field guide for identification of leaves and flowers. Gardening is more fun if you can identify what exists on your own property, including the trees and shrubs.

Next, make a rough drawing, showing the location of existing plants. Don't let this step frighten you. You don't have to know how to draw a landscape design. This is only a working tool to help you determine what already exists on the property. It need not be drawn to scale. However, just putting the information on paper will help as you begin to plan your gardening areas. I use a clipboard and a spiral notebook with a separate sheet of paper for each side of the house. To be more precise, you can transfer your rough drawing to graph paper with one square equaling one foot, but that is not essential.

1. Indicate directions, with north at the top of the first page, and draw the approximate shape of your property. Is it long and narrow? Wide and shallow? Wide and deep? Some lots will have equal dimensions on each side; others have uneven dimensions. Some lots are square with the directions of the compass, but most are not. Don't worry about precision. This is a rough plan; "approximate" is the buzz word for this first step.

2. Enter the "footprint" of the actual or proposed house on the same page to show the size, shape, and amount of space on the front, right, back, and left sides of the house, as well as the approximate distance between the house and the property lines. This page will show the total picture of the property.

3. The next four pages should give a close-up view of each side of the house. Begin with the front and work counterclockwise around the footprint of the house. Use a separate page for each side of the house, because a larger rough sketch is easier to draw and understand. A single line is adequate to designate the location of the house on these pages. All you really want to know is where gardens, trees, shrubs, or other plantings already exist on each side of the house, in order to determine where to change or incorporate additional planting areas.

4. On each of the four pages, outline the approximate shape of existing gardens, as well as driveways or other permanent features. Draw circles to designate trees and show the canopy spread. Use smaller circles to designate shrub dimensions, X for sun-loving plants, O for shade plants, or use numbers for any plants that are smaller than shrubs, and then key

those numbers to a list at the bottom of the page. Continue to keep each rough sketch directionally oriented with North at the top of the page. This is important for future plant selection.

What Shall I Do Next?

After you pick a spot to develop into a garden and complete a site inventory, your next task is to establish a path. Wander through the area, noting existing vegetation. A path or trail should lead you through the site to make it easier to view plantings, to weed, water, and maintain them, and to help make guests feel welcome. Even if your shady woodland, prairie, or meadow is relatively small, a path will be an asset. It creates a specific place to walk and saves the rest of the precious woodland loam from becoming compacted. It makes your prairie or meadow a little more civilized-looking and provides an opening for you and your friends to wander leisurely among those historic plants.

Is the area filled with what look like weeds? Try to identify as much of the existing ground-level vegetation as possible to determine if it should be destroyed, relocated, or left alone. Dig and remove any trees, shrubs, or plants in the path area that you want to save before clearing the path. Soak these plants in a solution containing one tablespoon per gallon of a rooting hormone compound, such as Hi-Yield liquid Vitamin B–1, for several hours or even overnight. This will prevent wilting, minimize transplant shock, and help to get the relocated plants off to a good start. Plants can remain in the water for 24–36 hours, but if more than 36 hours will elapse before you are prepared to move these plants to their permanent location, take them to a holding area and temporarily heel them in to protect the roots and prevent rot until you are ready to replant them.

Many shrubs have shallow root systems and are easily relocated. Moisten the soil around the plant. Then dig as wide and as deep as possible in order to save as many of the roots as you can. Slide the shrub onto a tarp or a piece of plastic and pull that material up around the root ball to hold as much of the soil in place as possible as you transport it to its new location. Dig a planting hole twice as wide as, but no deeper than, the root ball. Place the shrub in the hole, fill the hole with water, and when the water has drained out, refill with the soil you removed. Amending the soil with compost and sphagnum peat moss before replacing it in the planting hole will give your relocated shrub a better start. Water again and keep it well watered for at least three weeks, as well as during any extended periods of drought.

When you transplant, you need to remember to place the tree, shrub, or wildflower at the same depth at which it was growing. To plant it deeper can weaken the plant. If a plant's roots are too shallow, they may dry out.

You will generally need to remove about a third of the branches, otherwise the roots will have a difficult time sustaining the transplanted specimen. Giving a shrub a "crew cut" encourages witches' broom growth on the ends of the stems, which is unattractive and encourages disease. It is better to cut at soil level. Remove older, larger branches to encourage new growth.

After the plant rescue is completed, remove all unwanted vegetation, including the roots, if possible. In order to curtail regrowth of the mowed path, you can use either nonchemical or chemical methods. Either will accomplish your purpose.

Nonchemical methods: Place 6–8 layers of newspapers over the path, or black plastic, and cover with wood chips, pine straw, or some other type of available mulch. You can also use 4–5 inches of coarse sand to hold the newspapers or plastic in place. Any vegetation that sneaks through this barrier is generally easily hand weeded.

Resprouting of unwanted trees and shrubs can be discouraged by cutting and removing the bark 3 to 4 inches (girdling) below the soil. Patrol your paths often, removing any resprouted vegetation immediately.

Chemical methods: Sprinkle the path with a pre-emergent such as Treflan or Preen to keep seeds from sprouting. (Some gardeners report that pre-emergents can adversely affect tulip or daffodil bulbs. Experiment with this chemical to determine its effect in your garden, or limit its use to paths where no vegetation is wanted. I have used a pre-emergent on many of my flower gardens with no problems, perhaps because I rarely apply the chemical until the bulb foliage is up. Of course, I never use chemicals on areas containing wildflowers; I want them to reseed and spread, so I hand weed.)

To kill existing vegetation, use a watering can or a small sprayer to drench it with glyphosate herbicide. This herbicide is inactivated by contact with the soil, is not residual in the environment, and dissipates in a few days. It is sold commercially under various trade names, including Round-up, Ranger, and Kleen-up (or Rodeo, used primarily for wetlands).

I fill a spray bottle, or a small bottle with a pointed tip (like a hair tinting bottle), with a 50% solution of glyphosate herbicide and water. This concoction, a pair of sturdy garden clippers, a small sharp saw, and rubber gloves are all you need for a good one-two punch. Cut off the unwanted vegetation close to the ground and immediately drip or spray the mixture onto the fresh cut. The chemical will seep into the open wound, go to the roots, and kill them. It is an excellent way to get rid of any unwanted shrubs or tree seedlings with extensive or deep roots without jeopardizing surrounding vegetation.

You can also spray this herbicide onto the leaves of a plant and it will eventually translocate to the roots. Don't expect the plant to die immediately. It may take several weeks to eradicate a treated plant.

Glyphosate will work any time the plants are actively growing. However, it is most efficient in early fall. In the spring, most of the added fertilizers, chemicals, or killing agents go to the leaves or top growth, while in the fall nearly everything goes to the roots. (For this reason, fall is the best time to rid your lawn of dandelions!)

Another possibility includes herbicides such as Scythe or Sharpshooter, which are made from soap-based fatty acids that disrupt plant membranes, causing the plant to dry up and die. These herbicides quickly break down once they are in the soil and affect only the plants you have treated.

Any time you use chemicals, be sure to read the labels, follow directions explicitly, and dress to protect yourself in a long-sleeved shirt, long pants, stockings, and moisture resistant boots, and wear good, heavy rubber gloves. Shower and wash your clothing when you have finished.

Mulch the treated path with wood chips, gravel, sand, or pine straw to keep down regrowth and deter weed seeds from sprouting.

Will Neighbors Object to My Non-Traditional Landscape?

Typical suburban landscapes are composed of large expanses of turf-grass lawn, shrubbery pruned into boxes and balls and velcroed to the foundation of the house, a straight driveway, and a token tree or two in the front yard. Flowers, if any, are generally found near the foundation, in a container by the front door, or around the mailbox. This is the type of landscaping considered acceptable and desirable by the majority of the American public, so before you rip up your entire front yard to plant a prairie, it might be wise to talk to the neighbors about your plans. Because of widespread disagreement over the definition of a lawn, some cities and municipalities have enacted laws in order to maintain control within their boundaries. For example, homeowners in Madison, Wisconsin, who want to replace a conventional lawn with grasses taller than eight inches must apply for a Natural Lawn permit. Applicants are required to submit a written plan to the city with the legal description of the property, a statement of their intent and purpose for the area, a list and description of proposed vegetation, and proposed management and maintenance. Grass plantings must be maintained no higher than 8 inches in the 4-foot strip along the street and along the 3-foot strip at the property line, unless the neighbor waives the latter restriction. Neighbors within 200 feet of the proposed natural lawn must be given a copy of the application, and these names submitted to the Director of the Inspection Unit. If more than 51% of these homeowners file written objections within 15 days, the application is referred to the Urban Design Commission for hearing and decision.

The City of Madison distributes an inexpensive booklet detailing many aspects of the Natural Lawn concept, which can be ordered from the Department of Planning and Development Inspection Unit, 215 Martin Luther King, Jr. Boulevard, Madison, WI 53710. For further information call (608) 266–4907.

As I said above, you can avoid frustration by not planning too many gardens at first. Gardening is relaxing and fun if it is kept within the limits of your time and energy. Start small and increase your gardens as time and resources permit. Even native plant gardens require some maintenance, so try to create a few beautiful areas rather than a huge weed patch that becomes overwhelming and unmanageable. A transition between lawn and woods, or between prairie, meadow, and woodland areas, is important. Look at nature and try to design the transition zone to look as if it has always been there. Try to keep any native plant sites looking attractive, tidy, and relatively civilized, especially at the outset.

And now it is time to begin . . .

Take your time as you plan your new gardens. Determine what you want to accomplish. Select plants to provide color, foliage, and texture, to attract birds or butterflies, or to create a wildlife habitat.

Choose the right plant for the right spot, and don't fight the site! Combine plants with similar growing requirements. Planting a Prickly Pear cactus next to a moisture-loving Cardinal Flower spells disaster. Common sense tells you not to intersperse sun-loving prairie plants with woodland wildflowers. Do some research on each plant to determine its needs. By studying its native habitat, you can determine what kinds of conditions it needs and with which plants it normally grows. Prepare the site and thoroughly amend the soil to mimic the plant's natural environment as closely as possible.

Then after all your hard work, take time to sit among the flowers as you enjoy the beauty of nature and the joy of native plants.

You don't have to destroy the natural landscape
to build on it.   —*Andy Wasowski, 1997*

3.
Building a New Home

Inside Nature's Envelope

For those about to design landscaping for
a new home, consider protecting what you
have just purchased—the building lot.
Lecturer, photographer, and author Andy
Wasowski bemoans the loss of a sense of
place through disregard for indigenous
vegetation and topography, calling traditional developments "Anywhere USA" and
extolling the virtues of building within
nature's envelope. In the premiere issue of
Wild Garden, Wasowski wrote, "One
benefit of the nature's envelope approach
is that a true sense of place is maintained."

What Is Nature's Envelope?

My husband and I have a survey map of
our undeveloped property. It has a heavily
outlined rectangular area labeled "building envelope" to indicate where a house
could be located. Another common construction term is "footprint," which refers
to the outer walls of a building's foundation. Wasowski concurs that the term

Jack-in-the-Pulpit

"building envelope" refers to "the skin of the house inward," and describes "nature's envelope" as "the existing landscape from the skin of the house outward."

We have all witnessed what happens when unspoiled land is turned into home sites. I am constantly dismayed to see builders and developers bulldoze and clear wooded areas with total disregard for the land. A typical construction site looks first like a war zone and then like a barren wasteland. Giant bulldozers clank and groan across the landscape, pushing over trees, scraping off the topsoil, and ripping up and destroying the landscape. Is this necessary? No, it is not, but it is the easiest way for the construction workers to accomplish their task in as short a time as possible. And so the argument, "But we've always done it this way!" seems to justify the end results.

Do You Know Anyone Who Has Utilized Nature's Envelope?

My daughter and her husband recently built a new home in Minnesota. Preservation guidelines in their community conform to the nature's envelope concept. After they purchased the building lot, a forester inventoried existing native trees on their site, tagging desirable specimens of 6 inches or more in diameter at breast height (4½ feet above ground level), and marking damaged or undesirable trees for removal. Orange plastic fencing was placed at the drip lines of specimen trees and around groups of trees, the developer was required to post a $1,000 bond per building lot, and sites were monitored regularly to ensure that guidelines were being followed. No vehicles, heavy equipment, fill dirt, trash, concrete sloshing, dumping, or material storage was allowed within the fenced area. As the construction of their new home progressed, there were no huge piles of stumps, logs, and branches along the side of their property waiting to be carted off to the dump. Only the tagged "trash" trees and the few trees inside the building envelope were removed. For each of the tagged specimen trees removed from inside the building envelope, my daughter and her husband were required to plant two balled and burlapped native trees with a trunk caliper of at least 3 inches in diameter.

Because of these guidelines in this Minneapolis suburb, homes look as if they have been set down gently into the natural landscape, creating a neighborhood with character, rather than one with the "nude, plucked-chicken" look of a typical development.

Our daughter's new home is shaded by towering native Red and White Oaks. Wildflowers bloom profusely in the wooded areas around the house, and my grandchildren take delight in a wide variety of birds, butterflies, and other wildlife in this natural habitat. A beautiful doe and her fawn pause to sniff the evening air before venturing out into the open, and a huge Pileated Woodpecker beats a rat-tat-tat-tat on an old dead tree at the edge of the woods. A sleek Fisher scampers up and down that old snag daily, a rollicking pair of masked raccoons chase each other along the woodland trails, and a handsome red fox walks unconcernedly through the back yard. A nesting pair of wood ducks raised their ducklings within sight of the deck. All these wonders of nature would be gone if traditional building techniques had been followed and the surrounding trees felled to make way for construction.

Businesses as well as homeowners can employ the nature's envelope technique, which is gaining in popularity. Many new businesses incorporate large windows to bring the outside in for their employees. A friend from southern Indiana told me that she looks out onto a woods as she sits in the dentist's chair. It makes the experience much less stressful. Fortunate students at a new high school located near the outskirts of Indianapolis look out floor- to-ceiling windows at a wooded wonderland complete with wildflowers, birds, butterflies, opossums, raccoons, and an occasional deer.

The concept of building within nature's envelope has been successfully used in many other parts of the country. According to Wasowski, architect, landscape architect, and urban planner Gage Davis pioneered this concept in 1981 at Desert Highlands, an 850-acre residential community in North Scottsdale, Arizona, just outside of Phoenix. Davis directed that each lot be divided into three zones. The first is called the private area and includes the footprint of the house plus the driveway. The second is a transitional area or buffer zone of 5 to 10 feet to accommodate construction workers and their materials. The third zone—the natural area—is fenced off and remains "off limits" during the entire construction process. In order for this concept to be successful, all of the ground rules need to be determined before the first construction vehicle ever enters the property, and adhered to until the last one leaves and you move in.

Why Must the Fenced Enclosure Be So Small?

When trucks are driven over an area, severe soil compaction occurs which is literally impossible to renovate. Even parking a truck under a tree for a short time can cause irreparable damage.

Dumping dirt over the feeder roots of the trees will smother a tree, causing early death. You should never add more than 6 to 8 inches of soil over the soil surrounding a tree, even when you are amending the soil to plant a garden there.

Washing out concrete and throwing around building debris compromises the soil and causes problems with existing vegetation as well as with anything you want to plant.

Even if your building lot is not filled with native trees and shrubs and was previously an agricultural field or a vacant lot, this method is still recommended to save any desirable existing trees and shrubs, to avoid soil compaction, and to save the topsoil.

But What if I Want a Lawn?

Most homeowners seem to want at least a small typical turf-grass lawn. Using the nature's envelope concept will make that task easier, too. Instead of the typical rock-hard, barren soil around the new home, the surrounding soil can be fertile, native, and uncompacted, ready to accept seeds, trees, shrubs, and flowers.

Building within nature's envelope can help maintain a natural-looking landscape, preserve and protect indigenous vegetation, and save time, money, and frustration. But in order to make this concept work, it is essential to discuss the plan with architects, contractors, and building crews, so that all understand and agree to the necessary ground rules in a written contract.

If you take steps early enough in the building process, it is possible to protect the integrity of your property. Building lots are expensive, especially those with indigenous trees, shrubs, and wildflowers, which cost a premium to replace. Insist upon the right to protect your investment.

How Can I Protect My Site during Construction?

1. Begin by discussing your plan with the builder and contractor so that all parties agree that the only area the workmen will be permitted to use will be the part inside the fenced area. The part outside the fencing is to remain inviolable. No dirt piled up in that area, no trucks parked there, no concrete washed off there, no driving there—in other words, the area outside the plastic fencing is just as sacred as if it belonged to another homeowner. Construction workers would not feel free to depredate a neighbor's property. They should be just as willing to protect the outer limits of your property, so that when the house is completed, it looks as if it had been set gently down into the landscape.

2. Next, determine where your driveway will be. Mark this area and insist that all construction vehicles use this "road" for all traffic in and out of the construction site, rather than driving willy-nilly all over the area.

3. Enlist the services of a forester or arborist and mark all desirable trees of 4 inches in diameter and above. The girth is measured at breast height, usually 4½ feet above ground level. Use a different mark to designate trees that you want to have removed—trees that are undesirable, damaged, within the tight area where the home and garage will be built, or on your "road."

4. When fencing around trees you want to save, extend the fencing beyond the drip line, or you will lose that tree within a few years. The most important feeder roots of a tree are not next to the trunk, but out to and beyond the drip line, so protect that area from compaction.

5. Fence off the area surrounding the actual building site, using plastic, cyclone, or chain-link fencing materials. Five to ten feet between the building envelope and the fence should provide enough space for workmen to move vehicles and materials and construct your new home.

6. Ask the builder to stockpile and save your topsoil at some pre-arranged location when excavating the foundation for your new home, rather than carting it away. This soil is your native soil and may be filled with native plant seeds for the future. It will save you money on replacement topsoil, and is probably superior to any purchased.

What Can I Do to Make Sure This Really Works?

To make the builder financially responsible for damage incurred during construction, Wasowski recommends attaching actual price tags to existing trees to lend emphasis to the value you place upon them, and explain this step to the individual in charge of the building process. My insurance company representative told me that companies that reimburse homeowners for trees toppled by wind or lightning damage can document the value of a tree of a certain height and caliper. For a tree to reach a height of 40 to 60 feet or higher takes many decades. That same tree can be felled in a matter of minutes.

Unfortunately, some trees are just too large to be relocated, and because of their placement on the lot will have to fall under the woodsman's ax, but whenever possible, consider moving trees that are growing within space where the house will eventually stand, or on the specified driveway that would otherwise have to be cut down. Contract with a local landscaping firm to plant and grow these trees for you until they can be safely transplanted back into the new landscape, and offer to give them any specimens which you cannot use. If there is ample time after the specimens are marked and before they need to be removed, the landscaper may be able to root-prune desirable trees or shrubs.

Landscapers routinely dig and transplant large trees with a machine called a tree spade. Transplanting large specimens takes considerable care, but can be successful with diligent watering for the next two to three years. The rewards are a larger, more mature indigenous tree, rather than the typical small "token sapling" plunked unceremoniously in the middle of the front yard. With careful planning and cooperation, your new home can have that established look—as if it has always been there.

How Will This Concept Help Our Environment?

My sister who lives in Tacoma, Washington, writing about the January 1997 flooding in the Pacific Northwest, told of a friend who was stranded in his house for five days: "The only access road to his development is closed because of a new 'lake' over the road so deep that a car that was trying to go through it is still stuck in the middle with water halfway up its windows." Other new "lakes" completely covered several blocks of main roads and highways, causing road closures and detours; and she added, "Now mud slides are bringing houses down onto the Interstate."

In addition to the aesthetic reasons for protecting indigenous vegetation during new construction, there are also environmental reasons. Undeveloped natural areas help soak up rain; perhaps this relatively recent flooding in the Pacific Northwest may be attributed to increased development. As development expands across our land, and more potential homeowners and businesses seek larger land parcels away from urban sprawl, responsible behavior toward the environment becomes critical on the part of each individual. As Aldo Leopold stated, "The real substance of conservation lies not in the physical projects of the government but in the mental processes of its citizens."

4.

Turn over a New Leaf

Creating a Framework with Native Trees

As I work on this book at the computer in my home office, I can see a huge Sugar Maple outside the window. In the autumn, this magnificent tree resembles a cloud of burnished gold, gleaming brightly in the autumn sunlight. It lights up glowering, leaden-gray skies, or glistens in the rain, and is a source of constant joy to me as I write, regardless of the weather. There are multitudes of native trees with magnificent fall color, but probably none so well known or as easily recognized as the Sugar Maple *(Acer saccharum)*, a tree that turns a wooded landscape into a rich, golden delight.

In many parts of the Lower Midwest, native beech-maple climax forests greeted pioneers as they arrived to settle the land. According to Webster's Dictionary, a "climax" is a series of events occurring progressively so that the most forceful is last. A climax forest is composed of those self-perpetuating, dominant species that will eventually reappear through

Gray Dogwood

natural succession if an area is left alone for many years and allowed to return to nature on its own. German immigrant Jacob Schramm knew that the soil was excellent where Sugar Maple, walnut, Red Elm, and beech trees abounded. When he arrived in Indianapolis in November of 1836, he noted, "These trees were growing there in quantity, so I bought the land without delay."

From Sugar and Black maples comes sap for maple syrup and maple sugar, both staples of the frontier diet. Oliver Johnson wrote that in 1830 his county was known as Sugar Flats because of all the large Sugar Maples. He reported, "Lots of them showed the scars where the Indians had tapped them in the springtime for sugar."

Tapping Sugar Maples is still popular. In late spring before the buds begin to swell, when the days are warm and nights are still frosty, drive a tap into the trunk and hang a bucket or heavy plastic collection bag beneath the tap. It takes 45 to 50 gallons of raw sap boiled down to make 1 gallon of syrup and 3 or 4 gallons of syrup to make 1 pound of sugar. I have been told that all that moisture can loosen your wallpaper! It may be better to follow the example of early settlers and hang a kettle over the fire outdoors on a nice early spring day if you want to make maple syrup.

Why Should I Choose Native Trees?

The ability to withstand minimum temperature extremes is the basis for the USDA plant hardiness map, and is an important factor in plant selection. Trees that are not rated hardy within your zone may fail to flower or may even succumb when temperatures drop too low. Exotic Japanese Maples have a soft, fine texture and are dependable performers in Japan, but in certain areas of the United States these lovely little trees may need special protection in order to survive. Magnolia trees produce a spectacular floral display in warm climates, but when planted north of their range, the beautiful blossoms can suffer from a late frost and turn into ugly brown rags.

Trees create the framework for your garden, complement your home, whatever its age, and in general "set the stage," so as we discuss the use of native plants in the landscape, let's start from the top down and begin with trees.

Native trees have adapted to local climatic swings, temperature extremes, and existing soil conditions. Think of your state tree. One reason for its selection was probably that this particular tree performs well in your area, accepts local cultural conditions, and becomes a handsome specimen at maturity. Indiana and Tennessee have chosen the towering, straight-trunked Tulip Tree. Nearly everyone knows that Ohio is the Buckeye State. Wisconsin selected the Sugar Maple; Michigan, the White Pine; and Missouri, the beautiful Flowering Dogwood. Kentucky shares its name with its state tree, the Kentucky Coffee Tree. The mighty oak is the state tree of Iowa and Illinois. These magnificent natives are among the top-selling trees in the nursery trade because they are recognized as dependable performers that will thrive in the landscapes of the Lower Midwest.

How Do Trees Get Their Names?

Before you make your list of possible trees to plant, pause and have a little fun. As you know, botanical names often identify a particular characteristic of a plant. We depend upon these botanical names to acquire the exact specimen we want, because there are often many common names for the same species. Botanical names are unique for each species and often provide accurate descriptions or clues about a particular species; they can help you understand much about any given plant.

Common names are also informative. The impression of a tree is often reflected in common names like Quaking Aspen, Stinking Buckeye, Pagoda Dogwood, Shining Willow, Ironwood, Musclewood, Smoke Tree, or Swell-butt Ash (which grows in swampy areas and develops a base somewhat swollen above the water level). Sometimes we find habitat-descriptive names such as Swamp Oak, Water Beech, and River Birch.

Our most famous Lower Midwestern resident, Abraham Lincoln, may have derived his last name from the Linden tree. When Romans inhabited Great Britain in the first century A.D., they called their camp on the east side of the British Isles, "Linden Colona" after a grove of Linden trees present in the area. This name was anglicized to Lincoln Colony or camp, and through the centuries was shortened to Lincoln. President Lincoln's ancestors came from this general area.

Poverty Birch is another name for Gray Birch, which is known for aggressively overtaking abandoned fields or burned-over forest areas. Past and present uses for a tree can be determined by reading names like Canoe Birch or Post Oak.

Color names are common: White Ash, Red Maple, Black Oak, Yellow Poplar, Purple Plum, Green Hawthorn, Blue Beech, Brown Ash, Silver Maple, Gray Pine, and even Striped Maple.

Names like Yellowbark Oak, Winged Elm, Shagbark Hickory, Cork Elm, Paper Birch, and Speckled Alder describe the bark. Additional examples of names that describe various components of a tree include: (leaves) Small-toothed Aspen, Large-leafed Holly, Parsley Hawthorn, Bigleaf Magnolia; (flowers) Redbud, Yellow-flowered Magnolia, Yellowbud Hickory; (fruit or seed) Cucumber Tree, Downy Cottonwood, Black Walnut, Wild Red Cherry, Buckeye, Staghorn Sumac, Butternut or Oil Nut, Waxy-fruited Thorn; (sap) Sweet Gum, Black Gum, Honey Locust, Sugar Maple.

As you make your selections, learn both the common and botanical names for each of your trees and try to understand how the names were chosen. Obviously, this knowledge will not determine which tree you choose, how to plant it, or how it will grow, but it may make owning that tree more interesting, increase your awareness of its particular characteristics, and help you to identify it when you see it in another location.

How Do I Begin My Landscape Design?

Picture your house with its floor, walls, and roof. Your garden should be planned in much the same fashion, with low-growing plants such as wildflowers and native perennials covering the floor or "ground level," shrubs, vines, and small trees creating the walls or "understory," and taller trees as the canopy, roof, or "overstory." Each garden, like each home, needs all three components in order to be successful in its design.

A ranch-style gable roof with its central ridge is probably the most practical house roof, but it is certainly not the most interesting. You can plant matching identical trees in your landscape, but it may be more interesting with a little variation. On the other hand, just as a roof with no matching or complementary components would be a hodgepodge, you need to remember *unity* as a principle of design as you choose your trees and begin planning your landscaping.

Planting in odd multiples creates visual interest—1–3–5–7. Even with a plant as large as a tree, there may be times when you want more than one of each specimen. In nature you often see a grove of identical trees, in contrast to that single magnificent oak standing as a sentinel in the center of an open area. So study your landscape to determine what kind of effect you wish to create, how best to complement your home, and how to incorporate good seasonal interest with your choices, grouping some trees and using others as specimens.

How Do I Decide Which Tree to Choose?

In design, form follows function. Before choosing a tree, determine what function you want it to perform. Will it soften an architectural feature of the house? Is its chief function to give privacy, or will it serve as a windbreak? Is a tree needed to shade the deck or patio, or to help cool the house in summer? Is it to be part of a garden; to attract wildlife; to provide fruit or nuts? Does it need to be small, or can it grow as tall as it wants? Are there utility wires nearby? Sidewalks or driveways?

Does the space dictate a wide-spreading tree or a columnar variety? Do you need a single tree, a multiple-stemmed specimen, or a group of trees? As the tree grows and matures, will its shade interfere with a flower or vegetable garden? Or will it be valuable as it shelters shade-loving plantings? Decide whether you want dense, light, or dappled shade. Small leaves common to species like willow, locust, or aspen lend a light, airy look, while maple leaves cast a heavy shade beneath the tree canopy.

Many trees are planted for shade, but sometimes their primary function is to screen off unsightly views or to give some privacy. In 1972, when we lived in Iowa City, Gretchen Harshbarger, a well-known local landscape architect and garden editor, suggested that we plant a group of three River Birch very close to the front of the deck that faced the street. The small heart-shaped leaves provided privacy and dappled shade, and the peeling bark gave textural interest to the front of the house.

She also suggested that we plant two fast-growing trees to shade our raised deck, and to shield the view of the deck from the street. She recommended a 'Marshall Seedless' Green Ash *(Fraxinus pennsylvanica)*. The first ash tree was dormant and bare-root, and was planted in early March. The other arrived later, in a large pot, and had leafed out. Initially the potted tree seemed to grow better, but in a few years the bare-root tree overtook and surpassed it.

Gretchen helped us with another visual problem. Our neighbor had a large fenced area where he kept many hunting dogs. The kennel was always full of dogs and puppies of varying sizes. The ground inside the fence was barren and strewn with their gnawed dogbones. Because the dining room of our split-level home was almost at a second-story level, we saw this eyesore out the large windows when we sat at the table. Gretchen recommended a property-line zigzag planting of White Pine *(Pinus strobus)* to provide a visual screen. She told us that, once established, these evergreens could grow three feet a year to create a solid screen. We purchased five White Pines, 5–6 feet tall, in the spring and planted them 6–8 feet apart on-center. In October, a local nursery had 18-inch White Pines on sale for a dollar apiece, and we added four of these tiny trees on either side of the initial zigzag. After fifteen years, all of the trees have matured to about the same height and create a beautiful living privacy fence. Not even the neighbor's house is visible from the dining room windows.

Many evergreens, such as arborvitae and hemlock, can be grown as tall specimen trees, pruned as a hedge, or planted closely to form a living wall for winter interest and protection from prevailing winter winds. These plants provide food, cover, and nesting sites to encourage wildlife on your property.

Trees are a long-term investment, and may take twenty years to reach maturity, so careful selection is important to fit the right plant to the right site. A Tulip Tree needs an open space. Small understory trees like Redbud, Dogwood, and Serviceberry prefer peeking out from the edge of a forest, and don't do as well when planted as a specimen tree in the center of the lawn. Even though a Red Maple is native to North America, it may not flourish if it is not indigenous to your particular part of the country. Remember the word "provenance" when you purchase a tree. Trees grown from local or regionally collected seed grow more reliably than trees grown from seed collected outside of the region.

Many trees are not fussy, while others insist on specific site conditions. Before you decide where the tree will be planted, check to see if the location gets full sun or is shaded part of the day. Note how moist or dry the site is. Is the soil composition primarily clay, sandy, or loam? Is it acidic, alkaline, or neutral? Will the tree be in an open area, next to a building or fence, or grouped with other plantings? Is the site on the north, south, east, or west side of the property?

Whether you choose a small, delicate tree or one destined to be a forest giant, careful planning can help you choose the right tree for the right site. In years to come, imagine your pleasure on a quiet summer afternoon as you sit and relax in a garden shaded by beautiful trees, and listen to the happy trill of the wren as she sings her warbling song, or the "pretty, pretty, pretty" call of the bright red cardinal as he flits about, gathering food for his nestlings.

Where Can I Get Native Trees?

The easiest way to acquire native trees is to purchase them from your local garden center or nursery. Unlike woodland and prairie wildflowers, many native trees and shrubs are well known, have been available in the nursery trade for years, and can be purchased balled-and-burlapped, potted, or bare-root when dormant. Look for a well-branched specimen and choose a balled-and-burlapped tree if your budget can afford it, or plant dormant bare-root stock. Bare-root specimens are cheaper, lighter, and easier to handle than a balled-and-burlapped specimen, or even a tree in a large pot, and will usually catch up in a few years. Bare-root native trees are available from many mail-order nurseries as well. Trees potted in large containers can be planted any time, and potting causes no problem for many trees, particularly if they are small.

Forestry departments often offer bundles of 25–100 seedlings of native trees and shrubs for a reasonable price. Consult the listing at the back of this book for a source near you if the area you propose to develop is larger than the grounds surrounding a typical home. These 1- to 2-year-old seedlings are small, unpruned whips, rather than landscape specimen trees, and are intended for wildlife plantings, windbreaks, and natural areas.

You can also start trees from seed or from cuttings, and if a site is being developed, it may be possible to rescue small native trees from the bulldozer. However, if you choose this means, be sure to get permission before you dig, choose smaller, rather than larger, and try to dig when the tree is dormant if possible. Never dig from the wild unless the area is being developed.

It may be that the tree you choose to rescue has a large taproot or some specific requirement that makes it notoriously difficult to transplant. Try to identify some of these hurdles before you pick a particular specimen. For example, transplanting trees with a large taproot may succeed if the tree is dug when it is very small. Some trees send out multiple suckers near their base. These may not survive transplanting, but a true seedling of the same tree may transplant easily, so do some research on the tree you propose to dig to learn what precautions are necessary for success.

Can You Give Some Advice on Planting the Tree?

The old cliché "Don't put a ten-dollar plant in a ten-cent hole" is particularly important to remember when you plant a tree. The width of the planting hole should be at least twice as wide as the soil ball of the tree. A tree must not be planted deeper than it grew in nature, or in the pot, so don't dig your hole to China!

Small trees up to 30 feet tall at maturity can safely be planted close to your house, your sidewalks, or close to power and telephone lines and can be planted as specimens or grouped. Medium-sized trees grow 50–60 feet tall at maturity, and large trees can reach 60–80 feet or more. Plant medium-sized trees at least 30 feet, and large trees at least 50 feet, away from your house, sidewalks, or power lines to prevent heaving concrete, tree roots in your sewer pipes, or interference with utility lines. These distances can also be used as guidelines for space between plantings to give each tree adequate room to develop properly.

"Plants grow! This is obvious but always comes as an outrageous surprise to the gardener, as I well know," wrote *Washington Post* garden columnist Henry Mitchell in regard to the correct spacing of new plants. He wryly concluded, "On the other hand, I do not see much sense in planting stuff at the proper distance for a fine effect fifty years from now. Such plantings will come to perfect maturity just in time for some jerk to bulldoze the place to sell french fries on."

What about Watering, Fertilizing, Mulching?

Set the tree in the planting hole, and before you replace the soil around the roots, fill the hole with water and allow it to drain completely. I usually add one tablespoon per gallon of vitamin B–1 to the water. This liquid lessens transplant shock. With the addition of a couple of pieces of "tree candy"—slow release fertilizer tablets—the tree should be off to a good start. Do not add any more fertilizer until the roots are established. Replace the soil, tamping it lightly around the roots and soil ball. Add soil until it comes to the mark on the trunk that indicates its original planting depth, and slope the soil away from the trunk to the surrounding area for proper drainage. Mulch the ground under the tree, but be sure to pull the mulch away from the trunk, or the moisture can encourage pests and disease. Dig a small depressed furrow around the dripline of the tree, or build up a narrow ridge of mulch at least 2 feet from the trunk to prevent moisture from running off when watering. Choose a particular day of the week, and slowly pour one 5-gallon bucket of water around each newly planted tree on this day every week for the entire first growing season to ensure survival of your newly planted tree.

Does It Need Any First-Year Protection?

When trees are young, the trunk can be wrapped with tree wrap to prevent sun scald or animal damage. Remove this in the spring of the second growing season. If rabbits, deer, or beavers are troublesome, it may be necessary to protect the bark with a tightly woven wire cage installed 6–8 inches from the trunk. If the tree is tall and prone to lean, secure it to a stake using cloth ties or wire, sheathed with pieces of old garden hose or bicycle innertubing. Remove the staking after the first growing season.

How Shall I Prune My New Tree?

Shape your new tree as it grows, pruning any crossing, damaged, or unsightly branches, and removing the lower branches. Do not paint tree wounds with black tree paint. Untreated wounds heal better. Cut each branch back to the "collar" rather than flush with the tree trunk.

A fourth-grade teacher once asked her class, "If you carved your initials on that small beech tree, how high would your initials be when you came back after you were grown up?" The correct answer is: "At the same height you initially carved them." The lower branches of a tree will never grow any higher; if they are too low for the tree at maturity, prune them while they are still small.

What Should I Look for in a Native Tree?

Look for native trees that can lend interest to several seasons, providing color, fruit, flowers, or fragrance. Clouds of white blossoms on a spring-blooming Wild Plum *(Prunus americana)* will make you pause to drink in the heavenly fragrance. Not only does this pretty little tree have incredible white flowers, it will treat you to small edible plums as well. Thomas Jefferson grew this tree at Monticello and enjoyed its tart fruit.

The delicate lavender-rose, pealike flowers of Redbud *(Cercis canadensis)* bloom in natural wooded areas with delicate white Serviceberry *(Amelanchier canadensis)* to grace early spring landscapes. Flowering Dogwood *(Cornus florida)* is often found blooming with Redbud and native crabapples along the edge of the woods, or tucked in an opening. These small understory trees provide puffs of pink and white in the spring landscape. In the autumn, the leaves of the Serviceberry change to orange or dull red. Dogwood leaves turn a rich red, in contrast to the golden yellow of Redbud and Wild Plum. Their fruits attract birds and wildlife. In winter, their unique skeletons and interesting bark go on show.

In autumn, a haze of bright yellow leaves grace Yellowwood *(Cladrastis kentukea)* and Sassafras *(Sassafras albidum)* trees. Wahoo *(Euonymus atropurpureus)*, which can be a small tree or a shrub, has unusual rosy to bright red leaves. Its fuchsia fruit capsules hold shiny, bright red seeds that persist into the winter. Small hawthorn trees also hold their bright fruit into the winter, attracting birds and wildlife to the yard. Even the bark of the trunks can be design elements in the landscape. The rough, peeling bark of River Birch or Shagbark Hickory has a different textural quality than the smooth, gray bark of the American Beech, or the blue-gray bark of Musclewood. A white-peeling Birch or the ebony-black bark of a Wild Plum can provide contrast and enhance the walls of a building.

What Are Some Dependable Large Shade Trees?

Native trees that eventually mature at 60–100 feet with a trunk diameter of up to 6 feet include oak, maple, ash, elm, Kentucky Coffee Tree, Cottonwood, American Linden, and Tulip Tree.

The Tulip Tree has interesting tulip-like yellow flowers edged with orange. The leaves, with four pointed lobes, turn bright golden yellow in the fall. Its trunk grows tall and straight, and in the wild the first branches emerge many feet above the ground, making it a valuable timber tree. Trees grown in the open exhibit beautiful symmetrical growth; hardy and fast-growing, they prefer moist, well-drained, loamy soil. George Washington reportedly planted a Tulip Tree at his home in 1785 that was named Mount Vernon's official Bicentennial Tree in 1976.

The American Beech *(Fagus grandifolia)* becomes a huge, impressive specimen easily recognized by the smooth, steel-gray bark that tempts a teenager with a pocket knife. The long slender buds are easily identified, and leaves turn golden yellow in fall. Beechnuts are sought after by many species of wildlife, including bears and Wild Turkeys, and settlers in early America turned swine out into beech forests for this "mast." Beech trees will tolerate shady locations, but must have rich, moist, well-drained soil.

Kentucky Coffee Tree *(Gymnocladus dioica)*, is similar in growth habit to the more familiar Honey Locust, but has shorter, broader seedpods. Its name arises from early settlers' use of roasted seeds for a poor coffee substitute. The Kentucky Coffee Tree is dioecious, and since the raw seeds are poisonous, you may want to choose a male tree, although the flowers are more prominent on the female trees. The compound leaves, which can grow up to 3 feet long, provide a light, dappled shade, and turn a clear yellow in the fall. This tree is easily started from scarified seed, but should be planted in an area that is not closely manicured because it sheds leaflets and seedpods throughout the growing season.

White Ash *(Fraxinus americana)* is not as commonly used in the landscape as Green Ash, but is a very impressive shade tree. The underside of the leaves is lighter than the top, and provides a bright, shimmering shade. The leaves turn golden-orange in the fall, and are a favorite larval food for the Tiger Swallowtail butterfly. The grayish bark has zigzag furrows for easy identification, and the sapwood of the White Ash has produced many baseball bats. This tree will easily germinate from seed, is easy to transplant, is very fast growing, and prefers moist, well-drained soil. The cultivar 'Autumn Purple' has particularly beautiful deep red fall foliage.

American Linden or Basswood *(Tilia americana)* demonstrates the advantages of using native species, since the European species is more susceptible to borer and insect damage. Fragrant greenish-yellow blossoms are an important nectar source for bees in early summer, and develop into "monkey-nuts." The heart-shaped leaves of the Basswood become yellow in the fall. This tree is difficult to grow from seed, and requires rich, deep soil that holds moisture.

There are over 100 species of oak trees. Magnificent at all times, the White Oak *(Quercus alba)* is best grown in an open space where there is plenty of room for its wide spreading branches. It is a slow-growing tree and can be difficult to transplant, so purchase it from a reputable nursery rather than attempting to dig a wild seedling. If you decide to start this mighty oak from an acorn, choose the spot where you want it to grow and tuck the acorn under the soil lying on its side. The leaves of the White Oak turn a variety of crimson shades in the fall. This tree prefers a sandy loam and does not appreciate being too wet.

Bur Oaks *(Quercus macrocarpa)* were the trees of the pioneer "oak openings" and can easily be identified by the fringe at the base of the acorns. The common name Mossy-cup Oak comes from this unusual trait. The interesting leaves are almost like two separate leaves joined with a long, narrow section in the center. This elegant tree does not have a distinctive fall coloration, but makes up for it in summer with beautiful leaves that are very dark green on top, shiny light green on the underside, and fairly sparkle in the sunlight. The Bur Oak is often found in the wild as a small shrub-like tree, but can grow as tall as 150 feet, with a 6- to 7-foot-diameter trunk. Bur Oaks need rich, well-drained soil and full sun.

The leaves of the Chestnut Oak *(Quercus prinus)* are shiny, dark yellow-green in summer, and turn yellow in the fall, which makes this oak very attractive for ornamental planting. It has distinctive bark. It is more readily transplanted than most of the oaks, will tolerate acidity, and grows rapidly. Plant Chestnut Oaks in well-drained soil. Species like the Shingle Oak *(Q. imbricaria)* or Willow Oak *(Q. phellos)* have narrower leaves and require moist planting sites. Pin Oak *(Q. palustris)* needs moist, acidic soil, while the Chinquapin Oak *(Q. muehlenbergii)* and Bur Oak prefer alkaline soil.

One of my favorite oaks is the Scarlet Oak *(Quercus coccinea)*. It has exquisite, brilliant red foliage in the fall. This tree has very small acorns, is relatively easy to start from seed, and is the official tree of Washington, D.C. It grows fairly rapidly, but does not become nearly as large as the Red Oak at maturity. Scarlet Oak can be a bit asymmetrical when young, so careful pruning may be necessary to encourage a nice shape. This oak is not as susceptible to the Oak Wilt that is decimating the Northern Red Oak *(Q. rubra)* in the more northern states of the Midwest, but if Oak Wilt is prevalent in your area, you should probably choose a shade tree from another genus.

What Medium-Sized Trees Are Good Choices?

Medium-sized trees can be excellent for shade as well. These are trees that are usually 30–60 feet tall at maturity, with a trunk diameter from 2 to 4 feet. Particularly nice native selections include Hackberry, American Yellowwood, Sassafras, and Mulberry.

I have always liked Red Mulberry *(Morus rubra)*. This handsome shade tree has a beautiful form and large rounded leaves. It attracts many wildlife species, including over 30 species of songbirds, which relish its tasty berries. Since birds reportedly prefer mulberries to cherries, you may be able to enjoy more of your cherry crop by planting a Red Mulberry tree nearby. I can also attest that these berries can be combined with rhubarb or wild blackberries to make a delicious pie! However, many dislike Red Mulberry trees because bird droppings stain outdoor furniture, driveways, and clothes hung on the line to dry, so it is probably best to plant this species in a naturalized area.

If it is spectacular fall foliage you want, Sassafras is among the top performers. It has a variety of interesting leaf shapes that can be oval or mitten-like with one or two thumb-like projections. These leaves turn a multitude of colors in the fall, ranging from golden-yellow to orange to brilliant red. In the spring, puffs of yellow flowers cover the tree to produce the late-summer dark blue fruits sought by many songbirds. Plant this aromatic tree in full sun.

Sassafras trees send out suckers that do not transplant well. To ensure success, dig a true seedling rather than a sucker. They are easily grown from seed. Sassafras roots were some of the first medicinal exports from early Massachusetts. Parts of the tree were used to flavor cough medicines and root beer, and used as a root beer–flavored tea, until recently, when it was deemed to possess mild carcinogenic properties. The mature bark of the Sassafras is a dark reddish-brown with deep vertical furrows. It generally grows 35–50 feet, although specimens of 100 feet have been recorded.

Hackberry is described in Chapter 10, Yellowwood at the end of this chapter.

What Are Some Dependable Small Trees?

Smoke Tree *(Cotinus obovatus)* is a striking tree in the landscape with smoke-like flower puffs in late spring. These flower clusters produce fruit that is highly sought after by many birds. Some references list Smoke Tree as medium-sized. It matures at about 35 feet. It can be grown as either a single or a multiple-stemmed specimen, needs sun and well-drained soil, and is easy to transplant. In the fall, the 4-inch-long leaves turn a brilliant fiery orange. This unusual, remarkably hardy tree will definitely be a conversation-piece in the garden.

Hornbeam *(Carpinus caroliniana)* is also known as Ironwood, Musclewood, and Blue Beech because the smooth bluish-gray bark of young trees is reminiscent of the bark of the beech tree. This slim, small tree rarely reaches 30 feet in height and is spectacular in the fall with yellow, brilliant orange-red, or deep crimson leaves. The curious nut-like fruits can be planted and will germinate the following season. It can be successfully transplanted as long as you dig wide enough to get all of the tree's relatively shallow roots. The interesting trunk and branches resemble sinuous, smooth muscles. Early settlers called this "the horne-bound tree" because the wood was so exceedingly hard. It is still used for tools requiring sturdy handles. This small tree is another interesting specimen tree and provides a step back in history.

Fringe Tree *(Chionanthus virginicus)* boasts pure white, airy flowers in late spring. The long leaves look thick and waxy, and turn yellow in fall, but like the Buckeye, also drop early. This small tree is dioecious—the dark blue fruit, enjoyed by many species of wildlife, is borne only on the female trees. Fringe Tree needs to be well drained and will grow in sandy soil or silty clay. It can also be grown as a large shrub with multiple stems.

How About "Interesting" Trees?

American Holly *(Ilex opaca)* is difficult to transplant from the wild and slow growing, but once established makes a beautiful specimen tree. We have male and female holly trees in our front entry, and the dark, shiny leaves accent the bright red fruits on the female. I tease friends by noting that the male is tall and slim, while the female is short and plump. These trees like moist, well-drained, acidic soil. Our soil is alkaline, and the hollies were suffering when we first moved into this house. I refused to follow a landscaping firm's suggestion to "cut them down and replace them with something else." Each year in May, June, and July, I dissolve 5 tablespoons of Miracid in a 5-gallon bucketful of water and pour the mixture within the dripline to improve the soil pH. This treatment evidently acidifies the soil sufficiently, as the hollies are beautiful.

American Hop Hornbeam *(Ostrya virginiana)*, another tree called Ironwood, is a medium-sized understory tree with exquisite leaves. The textured leaves are almost translucent, with a delicate tracery of veins, and become a clear yellow in the fall. The fruits are hop-like, the trunk is thickly furrowed with narrow vertical grooves, and the exfoliating bark gives winter interest. The proverbially strong wood is used in the manufacture of tools where great strength is required. As Hop Hornbeam has a deep taproot, it can be difficult to transplant, but once established it rapidly grows into a beautiful, wide-spreading tree, and is an interesting specimen in the landscape.

We have three magnificent Ohio Buckeye trees *(Aesculus glabra)* in our front woods. These leaf out early in the spring, but I couldn't understand what caused them to defoliate early in the fall. I suspected disease or lack of moisture or nutrients until I learned that buckeyes normally go dormant early. Since they will drop their leaves even earlier if they become too dry, this species needs to be kept well mulched and watered during drought. Because the nuts are poisonous to cattle and other livestock, it has been cut down in many agricultural areas and is no longer so prevalent in Ohio. Squirrels love to gather and bury these nuts, so there are many seedlings in our wooded area that can be transplanted easily. When the husk is partially opened, the light scar against the dark nut resembles the eye of a deer—a buck-eye. Ohio Buckeye trees mature at 35–40 feet.

Red Buckeye (*A. pavia*) has spectacular, rich crimson flowers in early spring. Summer leaves are dark and lustrous, but since this species also goes into early dormancy, it is best planted with other trees rather than as a specimen. Smaller than Ohio Buckeye, Red Buckeye grows 15–18 feet tall.

Yellow Buckeye (*A. octandra*), also known as Sweet or Large Buckeye, is hardy to Zone 6. It is the largest of the native buckeyes, maturing at 60–75 feet. This disease-resistant tree is an impressive specimen in the landscape, and has striking yellow fall foliage. Wildlife love its sweet fruit.

Buckeyes in general are good trees to plant for wildlife. They attract a variety of butterflies and birds, and are a favorite of hummingbirds.

Franklin Tree (*Franklinia alatamaha*) rarely gets taller than 15 feet, although it can reach as high as 30 feet. In mid to late summer it is covered with 3-inch gold-centered, fragrant white flowers. It has fiery orange-red fall foliage, and interesting gray bark. It is hardy in Zone 6 and marginally hardy in Zone 5. It requires acid, humus-rich, well-drained soil. This small tree was originally native in Georgia, where it was first discovered by John Bartram on the banks of the Altamaha River in 1765. It is now found only in cultivation.

Pawpaw (*Asimina triloba*) is known as the Indiana Banana and is discussed in chapter 10.

Are Nut Trees Desirable?

The large nuts of the Black Walnut (*Juglans nigra*) have two coverings. A soft, greenish-yellow outer covering or hull turns black and needs to be removed before you can crack the dark walnut shell and retrieve the delicious nutmeat inside. Intense staining occurs when you work with these nuts, but the treat inside is worth it! At Christmas time, my grandmother used two quarts of shelled Black Walnuts to make a bushel-basketful of huge, soft German cookies called Lebkuchen.

Black Walnut trees are allelopathic, emitting a toxic chemical called juglone that prohibits many plants, especially tomatoes, from surviving under the canopy. These are magnificent trees that "grow to the sky." The wood is prized for furniture and cabinetry.

Butternut (*J. cinerea*) is also known as White Walnut and Oilnut. My grandfather spent hours in the woods every fall collecting butternuts. I can still picture him with his pliers, sitting by the old cast-iron wood stove, cracking the small tan-shelled nuts for the tempting coffeecakes my grandmother baked. A Butternut tree is wide-spreading, and has compound leaves. As it can be messy, this is a tree to tuck into the woods rather than to use as a specimen. Plant a nut and a little Butternut tree will sprout. Its soft, close-grained wood is used to make furniture. In 1830, Oliver Johnson wrote, "A good cathartic for grownups was made by bilin down the sap from white walnut trees." Native Americans made sugar and syrup from the sap of Butternut and Black Walnut trees. Butternut trees are reputedly having disease problems in parts of Indiana, so research before you plant.

The Pecan (*Carya illinoinensis*), a native of the Mississippi Valley, is related to the Hickory. These handsome trees have been prized as shade trees in the South. The native species bear smaller versions of the familiar thin-shelled, brown nuts available in supermarkets across our land. Pecan and hickory trees both have compound leaves. Grafted trees are recommended.

Of the native hickory species, the most attractive may be Bitternut Hickory (*Carya cordiformis*). This graceful, wide-spreading tree has yellow foliage in the fall and a large, smooth, tapered trunk. Unfortunately, the nuts are bitter and inedible. Shagbark Hickory (*C. ovata*) has shaggy peeling bark. It is too messy to plant in the yard, but lovely in the woods. Its tasty nuts are collected in the fall by people and wildlife, especially squirrels. James Russell Lowell wrote of a squirrel that "on the shingly shagbark's bough now saws, now lists with downward eye and ear, then drops his nut." Mockernut Hickory (*C. tomentosa*) gets its common name from the small nutmeats. It has deeply furrowed bark that provides good winter interest. Pignut Hickory (*C. glabra*) is an attractive, ornamental tree with smooth, dark-gray bark, but its small nuts are not tasty (except perhaps to pigs, since its former botanical name was *C. porcina*). The first three hickories are medium to large trees, maturing at 50–80 feet; the Pignut grows to 60 feet.

Six Suggested Trees

1. Red Maple *(Acer rubrum)*

Red Maple lives up to its name in all seasons. Small, attractive red flowers bloom early in the spring before any of the other maples break their winter dormancy. These flower clusters hang from reddish twigs, and emerging leaves have a hint of red. The reddish, winged seedpods, called samaras, mature in late spring. Even after summer arrives, the leaves still maintain interesting red-tinted veins and leaf stalks. Red Maple has beautiful fall color, interesting smooth, gray bark and reddish twigs in winter. It attracts several species of songbirds, as well as small mammals.

Choose the underused Red Maple as a fast-growing shade tree rather than the often recommended Silver Maple *(Acer saccharinum)*. It is more disease and insect resistant, and its flexible, limber branches withstand wind and ice storms. It grows 40–60 feet tall. Provenance is important; purchase one grown in your area. For example, a cultivar named 'Northwood' has been developed from a stand of Red Maples near Excelsior, Minnesota, since cultivars from warmer climates were not winter hardy there. To be sure the fall color is red rather than yellow, purchase one of the named cultivars. 'Red Sunset' has an abundance of red flowers in the spring and particularly brilliant red fall foliage; 'October Glory' holds its stunning red foliage late into the fall. A narrow columnar form has been bred into the cultivars 'Bowhall' and 'Armstrong'.

PLANTING REQUIREMENTS: Also known as Swamp Maple and Soft Maple, this adaptable tree will tolerate shade and flooded conditions, and will survive in well-drained or in poorly drained soil. It prefers rich, loamy soil but will also grow in hard clay, or on sandy, upland sites. It does not like drought or highly alkaline soils and may develop manganese-deficiency chlorosis if the pH is too high.

PROPAGATION: Red Maple is easy to transplant and is readily available in the nursery trade. I got a "whip" from the National Arbor Day Foundation, and 12 years later that tiny rooted branch is a beautiful, well-shaped tree about 25 feet tall. Seeds germinate reliably and should be planted as soon as they are ripe.

PLANTLORE: The Latin word *Acer* means hard or sharp; in addition to furniture, Romans used European maple for pikes and lances.

2. Black Gum *(Nyssa sylvatica)*

Brilliant scarlet red leaves of Black Gum or Tupelo trees are radiant in the autumn landscape. This is one of the most spectacular fall foliage trees. The horizontal branching, which seems to radiate from a common center, resists wind and ice damage, and lends a layered effect to this picturesque tree, whose only drawbacks are that it is difficult to transplant and is a very slow grower. It usually grows 30–40 feet tall, but can reach heights of over 60 feet.

PLANTING REQUIREMENTS: Once established, Black Gum will withstand climate extremes, including drought and flooding; it is adaptable to many different soil types, and grows naturally along riverbanks and on floodplains. Provenance is important. Male and female flowers are on separate trees, and both are needed for fruit.

The small hanging clusters of 2–3 dark blue fruits are devoured by small mammals and many birds, including Ruffed Grouse and Wild Turkey.

PROPAGATION: Although the roots are shallow, this tree is very difficult to transplant from the wild or as a field-grown tree. Have the nursery dig the specimen with a tree spade, purchase small container-grown trees, or plant cold-stratified seed where the seedling is to remain.

PLANTLORE: Tupelo is from a Creek Indian word meaning swamp tree. *Nyssa* refers to a Greek water nymph. All tupelos or gums prefer swamps, and *sylvatica* designates this tree as "of the woodlands." Its hard wood was used for ox yokes, chopping bowls, flooring, rollers in glass factories, hatters' blocks, gunstocks and pistol grips, and musical instruments. Drainage culverts were made of hollow Black Gum logs in the 1800s.

3. American Yellowwood *(Cladrastis kentukea,* formerly *C. lutea)*

Yellowwood is a relatively rare native tree, found growing wild in only a few of the Lower Midwest states, but it is hardy to Zone 3, thrives in most home landscapes, and is extremely desirable for ornamental planting. Insect and disease resistant and tolerant of temperature extremes and pollution, it is a good choice for urban environments. This medium-sized tree matures at 30–35 feet, has an upright vase-shaped crown, and is beautiful in all four seasons. Yellowwood is relatively slow growing and needs to be about ten years old before it will begin profuse flowering. 'Rosea' is a pink-flowered cultivar.

PLANTING REQUIRE-MENTS: Yellowwood is easily transplanted in the spring. It prefers a sunny, well-drained site, but it is tolerant of shade and even drought once established. It should be pruned to a central leader. Prune Yellowwood in late autumn because it is a copious "bleeder" when actively growing.

PROPAGATION: Soak the dark brown seeds in 120° water for 24 to 36 hours until they are swollen, and plant immediately. Or purchase a specimen tree from a nursery using the botanical name. It is commonly listed as Virgilia in the nursery trade.

PLANTLORE: Early settlers made a yellow dye from the heartwood. This practice gave the tree both its common and former scientific names. *Lutea* means yellow. *Cladrastis*, the Greek word for fragile branch, refers to the brittle twigs. Yellowwood was occasionally used to make gunstocks.

4. River Birch *(Betula nigra)*

Generally grown as a multiple-trunked specimen, this fast-growing, disease-resistant birch has exfoliating reddish-tan bark and small lustrous green leaves that turn yellow in fall. It grows 30 to 50 feet tall and is a nice landscape accent, particularly when several are planted in a group.

PLANTING REQUIREMENTS: River Birch prefers a sunny, moist, acidic site and can develop chlorosis if the pH is too high. It tolerates flooded or dry conditions but does not like shade.

PROPAGATION: Seeds mature in the following late spring or early summer and can be planted immediately. Softwood cuttings root fairly quickly, and these little "whips" can be planted in a bundle for multiple stems. River Birch is readily available in the nursery trade and transplants easily.

5. Green Hawthorn *(Crataegus viridis)* 'Winter King'

Spectacular red fall foliage, handsome red berries that hang on all winter, and interesting exfoliating silvery-gray bark make this a tree for all seasons. Migrating Cedar Waxwings will flock to your yard to feast on the pendulous red fruit. In the spring, this small tree has masses of pretty white blossoms and glossy green leaves. It grows 25–30 feet tall, and is one of my favorite small landscaping trees. The hawthorn is a valuable tree for wildlife. It attracts a variety of birds, including Pine Grosbeaks and Purple Finches.

PLANTING REQUIREMENTS:
Hawthorns will tolerate nearly any soil or moisture conditions but need a sunny location to ensure good flowering and fruiting. They perform beautifully as a massed hedge, or as part of a mixed shrub border or biohedge, providing shelter, nesting sites, and safety for songbirds and small mammals, as well as interest and beauty all year. Most native hawthorns have wicked thorns; choose a thornless cultivar if you are using this as a specimen tree. 'Washington Hawthorn' may be a better choice for Kentucky and Tennessee because it tends to be more heat tolerant than 'Winter King'.

PROPAGATION: Hawthorns are relatively slow growing, transplant easily, and are readily available in the nursery trade. Plant fresh seed immediately or cold-stratify for at least four months. Some of the Hawthorns have seeds which are extremely thick and may need an acid bath in order to germinate.

6. Pagoda Dogwood *(Cornus alternifolia)*

Horizontal branching gives a layered Oriental pagoda–like effect and makes the Pagoda Dogwood interesting with or without leaves. It can be grown as a large shrub or a small tree. It grows 12–25 feet tall. Delicate white spring flowers are followed by alternate whorled leaves and small dark purple fruits on colorful red stalks.

PLANTING REQUIREMENTS:
Plant in humus-rich, moist, acid soil in partial shade.

PROPAGATION: Choose a small container-grown tree. These tend to recover from transplanting faster than larger trees. Plant fresh seed in the fall or cold-stratify for at least four months.

Tip cuttings are generally quite successful and form roots readily.

PLANTLORE: Early twentieth century landscape architect Jens Jensen planted the Pagoda Dogwood to signify the far-reaching expanse of the prairie. *Cornus* means horn in Latin, referring to the hardness of the wood. The wood of Pagoda Dogwood, also known as Blue Dogwood, Alternate-leafed Dogwood, and Green Osier, is not used commercially.

Prickles and twigs and bloom and bunchiness and berries and bird nests and stout stems and slender stalks laced like seams where systems meet; cowlicks where mice run from glade to garden; sutures where brambles meet the grass. Where our land's anatomy is stitched.

—*Sara Stein, 1998*

5.
Plant a Biohedge

Using Native Shrubs

In *The Natural Habitat Garden,* Ken Druse describes a biohedge as a combination of shrubs and trees of varying sizes and shapes to be planted as an alternative to the traditional monoculture hedge. Picture a hedge with the early spring yellow flowers of Spicebush *(Lindera benzoin),* followed by puffs of delicate white Serviceberry *(Amelanchier canadensis)* flowers. For a summer display, add a taller, coarsely textured Buttonbush *(Cephalanthus occidentalis)* near a shorter Virginia Sweetspire *(Itea virginica)* with long, white flower spikes. New Jersey Tea's *(Ceanothus americanus)* pure white flowers in late fall will be accented by the dark blue berries, tucked in among the red foliage of Serviceberry. Spicebush leaves turn bright yellow and make a spectacular fall picture if planted near a brilliant red Virginia Sweetspire. Include some evergreens such as Hemlock *(Tsuga canadensis)* or Arborvitae *(Thuja occidentalis)* for contrast and winter interest and you have created a

Buttonbush

biohedge—a four-season natural area to furnish color, habitat, and food for wildlife as well as beauty and privacy, that is more apt to stay healthy than a hedge composed of, say, a row of forsythias. This type of mixed border will also supply a multitude of habitat offerings to encourage little four-footed or winged neighbors to take up residence in your yard. Birds, butterflies, and wildlife need to be able to find protected places for shelter, nesting, food, and safety from predators, and can satisfy these needs within your biohedge.

To use hedges to build walls for your outdoor rooms or to create a privacy screen, plant your shrubs in a zigzag pattern. This gives a fuller, more unified appearance to your hedge or screen since the shrubs will grow together as a unit, rather than looking like a row of shrubs marching single file. A mixture of closely planted shrubs and trees can provide privacy just as well as a typical six-foot cedar privacy fence. Besides, I would rather prune occasionally than paint or stain that fence, or replace it when it starts to fall down! More on biohedges later.

Any good realtor will stress the importance of "curb appeal" in selling a house. Like the walls of your home, the "middle story" of your landscape is probably noticed first; so in terms of curb appeal, shrubs may actually be the most important part of your home landscape. They can provide individuality, accent your home, serve as a privacy screen and a boundary between your property and a neighbor's, help prevent erosion on a steep slope, or act as a backdrop for a garden. They can be found in all shapes and sizes, with large leaves or small, evergreen or deciduous. Many shrubs have a variety of seasonal interest; some have flowers or fruit. In a prairie or meadow garden, this "middle story" may be shrubs or some of the native grasses.

In our analogy of house and garden, we compared the "overstory" trees to the roof, the "ground floor" flowers to the foundation and floor, and shrubs to the "middle story" or walls of a house. Many gardeners concentrate on choosing trees and flowering plants or ground covers but forget about the shrubs. Think of forested areas where the deer population has become too large. Everything is eaten from "browse height" down, including the flowers. When you see this, you realize something is missing. Another analogy might be to consider a well-dressed gentleman, complete with hat, suitcoat, tie, fancy shoes, and executive socks, but without his trousers. Without the "middle story," our landscape is incomplete.

Using Shrubs in the Landscape

As you plan your landscaping, consider the effect you are attempting to create in the various parts of the yard. Your goal will be different in the front yard—the public area—than in the more private back yard. One of the best ways to determine what types of landscaping design you like or dislike is to be observant as you walk through your own neighborhood or drive through surrounding areas. Observe how a variety of shrubs and trees can bring seasonal interest. Do the plantings in the front yard effectively complement the house? What do they tell the casual passerby about the residents within? Like it or not, landscaping makes a statement. Is this statement positive or negative?

Shrubs help to give character to your yard. They improve wildlife habitat, providing food and shelter and encouraging birds and other wildlife to frequent your yard. Well-chosen shrubs give color and interest, and contribute to the element of surprise as you follow a path through a woodland or meadow. They provide a calm, green backdrop for colorful flowers or interesting grass inflorescences.

Plants keep right on growing even when you are sleeping, and if you plant them too close together when they are small, particularly in the front area, you will have a jungle to contend with in a few years. It is better to purchase fewer shrubs and fill in the spaces with ground cover and blooming plants, giving each shrub room to grow and mature to its proper size. Homeowners often say, "I want my landscaping to look full right away, so I will just remove every other one when they get bigger." A few years later, they will probably find that because of the crowded conditions imposed, the individual shrubs have not had adequate room to develop, and may be lopsided, diseased, or spindly. Save yourself time, money, and energy by planning and planting wisely from the beginning.

Learn what the mature size of the shrub will be. In general, a shrub 8 feet tall will also have an 8-foot spread. Leave enough room between shrubs, as well as next to your foundation, for the shrub to develop properly. Remember that no rain falls under the overhang of your roof, so plant the shrubs beyond the dripline of the roof. You can mulch the area under the overhang to provide clean, easy access to the back side of your shrubs for pruning, fertilizing or watering chores. It is also a good place to hide the hose!

Why Should I Choose Native Shrubs?

The woods in many of the southern states and in the Pacific Northwest are a blaze of color in early spring when the azaleas and rhododendrons bloom. These beauties can bloom and survive out of their zone, especially in protected areas, but are more apt to thrive in areas where they are native, providing dependable flowering with a minimum of care. Long-term survival rates are higher with plants that are indigenous to your particular region.

Study the characteristics of shrubs that you might consider incorporating into your landscape. Wander through a nearby arboretum or botanical garden to determine how a shrub looks at maturity, as you study shrubs native to your area. Visit the bookstore or your local library and learn all you can about native shrubs before you make your final selection, because they will be a vital part of your landscape for many years to come. Choosing the right native shrub for the right place will save you time, money, and energy.

Planting Shrubs

Many native shrubs are easily obtained from local or mail order nurseries. If your purchases are balled and burlapped, remove the burlap before replacing the soil in the planting hole. When a homeowner purchases a balled-and-burlapped shrub or tree, he is often advised to leave the burlap in place, and plant the shrub or tree "as is."

Three large yews grew in front of our house when we first moved in. The original owner had installed them about twenty years earlier. The yews had overgrown the planting area, had to be severely pruned annually to keep them "in bounds," and were no longer attractive in the front yard. However, they were alive and healthy, so we decided to try to move them to an open area in the back yard where they would provide winter interest. We found that it was no problem to lift these balled-and-burlapped specimens and replant them, because, even after twenty years, the burlap was still intact and neatly tied to the base of the trunk!

Check the roots of potted shrubs. Clip or pull them away from the potting soil before planting so that the roots will grow properly. Don't be afraid to "get rough" as you pull the roots out of the twisting, circular pattern. Many potbound shrubs die in the first few years because the roots have not been properly positioned in the initial planting.

Dig a hole 2½ to 3 times as wide as the root ball but no deeper than it has grown in the pot or in the ground. Amend the soil with sphagnum peat moss and sand, set the shrub in the planting hole, and fill with water. When all the water has drained out, replace the amended soil, tamp lightly, and water again. Mulch well, keeping the mulch away from the stem and sloping it away from the plant. Make a small furrow around the base of the mulch to keep the water from running off in rivulets.

First-Season Maintenance

Prune crossed, diseased, or broken branches. Otherwise the only maintenance during the first season is to water at least once a week or more often if the weather is hot and dry to keep the soil from totally drying out. Be careful not to water so much or so often that you drown the plant. Overwatering and underwatering are equally destructive. Both are often indicated by yellowing leaves, and either will eventually kill the plant.

To Prune Or Not to Prune . . .

Every neighborhood has its share of balls, boxes, and giant hands guarding the landscape. Shrubs each have their own unique, natural shape, and if given the proper space and environment in which to grow, will need very little pruning. The natural shape of any shrub is more pleasing than one that has to be clipped and heavily pruned to force it to fit into a space that is too small. Determine the height and width of the area before purchasing a shrub. Redstem Dogwood grows to be 8 feet high and 8 feet wide at maturity and can become as tall as 14 feet. If you choose a young specimen of this shrub to plant under your windows or beside your front door, you will be constantly pruning and clipping. Instead, plant this interesting bush where it has room to grow, and choose a smaller shrub like

Virginia Sweetspire or Shrubby Cinquefoil *(Potentilla fruticosa)* to plant in the small spot. Your landscaping will look better as a result.

You can make a shrub bushier by pinching out the terminal growth of each branch. If you feel the need to shorten a shrub, cut each branch back to a node for a more natural look, rather than pruning with a hedge clippers. Otherwise, you will get a "witches' broom" effect. Remove old, woody branches at ground level. You can remove up to ⅓ of the shrub in this manner each year without damaging its natural shape.

How Do I Plant a Biohedge?

Zigzag your plantings and repeat species, using each bush or small tree 3 times or more within the biohedge, if possible. You can plant these shrubs more closely than ones you would use in front of your house as specimens, because you want a dense, tightly knit effect. Choose shrubs with similar cultural requirements and amend the soil if necessary to provide proper soil and moisture conditions. Most of the native viburnums are excellent choices for a biohedge. Each has unique characteristics. Consider incorporting a variety of these adaptable shrubs into your biohedge.

Viburnums are among our more popular landscape shrubs. They prefer humus-rich, well-drained soil, and full sun. Many can tolerate shady conditions, but will not bloom or fruit as profusely as those in a sunnier location. There is a wide variety of native and nonnative viburnums to choose from at most nurseries. If you choose a species that is native to your area, you should not experience the winter-kill that occurred a few years ago in central Indiana when temperatures dipped to –27° F. That year many homeowners lost Korean Spicebush *(Viburnum carlesii)*, while the native American Highbush Cranberry *(V. trilobum)* was not affected.

Black Haw's *(V. prunifolium)* glossy, dark green leaves, similar to those of plum trees, become plum-red in the fall, two characteristics that influenced the choice for its botanical name. This graceful, multi-stemmed viburnum can be grown as a shrub or small tree. It grows 12 to 14 feet tall and about three-fourths as wide, and is a size adaptable for smaller properties. White, 3-inch flat-topped flowers bloom in the spring. Colonists and Native Americans enjoyed the edible, sweet, bluish-black fruits, which are also sought by birds and wildlife. This species is a better selection for a mixed shrub border than Nannyberry, because of its resistance to mildew.

Nannyberry *(V. lentago)* is a little larger shrub, maturing at 16 to 18 feet. Its dark green leaves turn wine-red in fall. It does well in a naturalized setting, but good air circulation is necessary to prevent mildew, a common problem of this species. 3- to 4-inch white flower clusters bloom in May. The berries are attractive to wildlife and are rose-colored, maturing to black. Early Americans called this shrub Sheepberry, Cowberry, Nanny Plum, and Wild Raisin.

The creamy 5-inch white flowerheads of Rusty Blackhaw *(V. rufidulum)* look almost fuzzy when they cover this large shrub in late spring. It is generally only 15 to 20 feet tall, but can become 30 feet tall, towering above other viburnums. It tolerates shade and dry soil, has handsome, shiny green leaves with "rusty hairs" underneath, and produces dark blue fruit. In the fall, its deep reddish-purple leaves glow at the edge of the woods. Incorporate this shrub into a biohedge, group several together, or plant it as a privacy screen.

Mapleleaf Viburnum *(V. acerifolium)* has pretty maple-like leaves that change to several shades of red in the fall. Small clusters of shiny black fruit follow the early summer-blooming white flowers, and persist into the winter to tempt wildlife and overwintering birds. It suckers heavily to form colonies, and like most viburnums, is shade-tolerant. This underused, little 5- to 6-foot shrub will also grow in dry sites.

Other native viburnums include Withe-rod *(V. cassinoides)*, also known as Appalachian Tea, Swamp Haw, Wild Raisin, or Teaberry. It grows about 12 feet tall and has white flowers and blue-black fruit. Deam's *Flora of Indiana* lists Arrowwood *(V. dentatum)* as a species that is native east of Indiana. Hobble Bush *(V. alnifolium)* is also an eastern native.

Willows can be used in a mixed hedge or planted alone. A Pussy Willow *(Salix discolor)* branch is the florist's "touch of spring" to tuck in with bouquets of daffodils and tulips. These root easily in water, or in a mixture of sand and perlite. The gray catkins are actually the flowers. (Weeping Willow *[S. babylonica]* is not native to North America).

Willow has a long history of medical uses and contains a substance in its bark that was referred to as "Salicine" in early medical books. It was used as a substitute for quinine, especially in intermittent fevers. Doses were administered three to four times daily; "from eighteen to thirty grains being generally sufficient to break up a case of fever and ague."

Flower arrangers often add an aspirin (acetylsalicylic acid, the artificial equivalent of willow) to a vase of cut flowers to make them last longer. Many gardeners swear by "willow soup." They gather willow twigs and small branches less than ¼ inch in diameter, and steep these in water (like "sun tea") until the water turns amber-colored. Droopy plants, wilted transplants, and stubborn cuttings of trees and shrubs appear to respond to this concoction. One "believer" advocates using it as a foliar spray on rhododendrons and azaleas to prolong the bloom, and swears it works better than Miracid.

Huge clusters of off-white flowers bloom profusely on Elderberry (*Sambucus canadensis*) in midsummer. Commonly found in ditches and at the edges of roads, these 6- to 12-foot shrubs naturalize nicely in the sunny transition area near a woodland. Since they tend to have a wild, unkempt appearance, they are not generally planted in more civilized locations. In late summer, purple-black elderberries can be gathered to make delicious jelly or beautifully colored wine. 'Variegata' is a variegated cultivar that is smaller and more compact than the species.

Winged Sumac (*Rhus copallina*) is also known as Fragrant, Dwarf, Shining, Mountain, or Wing-rib Sumac. Greenish flowers appear in early summer. This heavily suckering shrub can become 20 feet tall, and will grow in harsh conditions where many other shrubs would fail. Interesting flower panicles appear in late summer. Its fall color is spectacular. A cultivar, 'Creel's Quintet', has burgundy fall color and only grows 5 to 8 feet tall. Sumac is a source of tannin.

Small, gray-green, pinnate leaflets and bright yellow flowers bloom for an extended period of time on Shrubby Cinquefoil (*Potentilla fruticosa*). There are many cultivars of this popular landscaping shrub, including 'Mandshurica', which is less than 18 inches tall. If there is a nearby arboreteum, visit it to see which cultivar you prefer for your landscaping needs.

Sand Cherry (*Prunus pumila*) is another popular landscaping shrub, with dark reddish-purple leaves. It is fast-growing and quickly becomes 6 to 8 feet tall. It has an upright growth habit, small white flowers, and dark blue-black fruits in the fall. This colorful shrub can be used to soften stark architectural features on a house, to form a privacy barrier, or be incorporated into a biohedge.

Bladdernut *(Staphylea trifolia)* is a unique 15-foot-tall shrub with nodding bell-like clusters of white flowers. In the fall, its strange, fat, bladder-like seed capsules will be quite a conversation-piece.

Purple-flowering Raspberry *(Rubus odoratus)*, also called Thimble Berry, has lovely hot-pink or rose-purple flowers. It flowers over a long period, sometimes blooming for two months. The plant grows in full to partial shade, making it a desirable addition to a woodland edge. It prefers moist soil. This 3- to 6-foot shrub has large, green maple-like leaves and inedible but attractive red fruits in late fall. Deam refers to it as unarmed since it has no thorns, bristles, or prickles. It suckers heavily, forming colonies. It becomes too rampant if it is planted in a sunny area.

Shrub roses have become popular with rose growers because of their easy care. Our native Virginia Rose *(Rosa virginiana)* has lovely deep rose, flat, open flowers, glossy green, disease-free foliage, and shiny, bright red fruits that the birds love.

Wild Hydrangea *(Hydrangea arborescens)* is also called Smooth Hydrangea. A cultivar named 'Grandiflora' produces larger flowers; those of 'Annabelle' are even more impressive. Wild Hydrangea can grow to 6 feet tall and equally as wide. Plant this pretty shrub in full sun, if possible, to increase the numbers of large, round, white flowers. Wild Hydrangea can be found in the shade in the wild, but will not bloom as profusely as those plants found in a sunnier spot. Keep it happy in humus-rich, well-drained acidic soil with plenty of moisture to promote and maintain a compact growth habit.

Few blooming shrubs that are hardy in the Lower Midwest elicit more admiration than Mountain Laurel *(Kalmia latifolia)*. This is a shrub that deer won't bother, because they seem to know that it is poisonous. It must be planted in acidic, humus-rich, well-drained soil. It will not survive in alkaline or clay soil, nor in unprotected areas where temperatures dip too low in the winter. Its evergreen leaves "disappear" under the mass of pink and white blooms in late spring. It tolerates full sun to full shade, although it blooms more profusely in more sunlight. This beautiful shrub is relatively disease-free. Its genus name, *Kalmia*, is for Pehr Kalm, a student of Carl Linneaus, who was responsible for collecting botanical specimens in the northeast in the eighteenth century.

More biohedge suggestions can be found in chapter 12.

* * *

Six Suggested Shrubs

1. Winterberry Holly *(Ilex verticillata)*

Bright scarlet-red berries cover this deciduous holly in the winter for an impressive picture against the snow or near a light colored building or wall. Mass Winterberry Holly, plant as a hedge, use as a specimen, or incorporate into a mixed planting. The stiff, glossy holly leaves persist late in fall, when they may become yellow or bronzy-purple. Winterberry Holly is generally about 6 feet tall, but can grow as tall as 10 feet. 'Winter Red' is an excellent cultivar with longer lasting berries.

PLANTING REQUIREMENTS: Plant in moist, humus-rich, well-drained, acid soil in a sunny location. Winterberry grows naturally in swamps and wet places. Include one male for pollination. 'Southern Gentleman' and 'Jim Dandy' are examples of male cultivars.

Note: Possum Haw *(I. decidua)* tolerates drier, alkaline soils and windy locations, but can become quite unkempt and overgrown, so Inkberry *(I. glabra)* may be a better choice in this type of planting environment. However, Inkberry has black rather than red berries.

PROPAGATION: Winterberry is relatively inexpensive, so it is probably best to purchase started plants from the nursery. If you like to experiment, terminal branch cuttings root easily or you can try planting stratified seed, but be advised that hollies are very slow growing.

2. Silverbell *(Halesia tetraptera; H. carolina)*

Delicate, extremely beautiful, small white bell-like flowers appear in early spring on this unusual multi-stemmed understory shrub or small tree, followed by interesting four-winged fruits in the fall. Silverbell matures between 20 and 30 feet tall and should be used more often in landscape plantings since its subtle beauty never fails to elicit admiration.

PLANTING REQUIREMENTS: Group multi-stemmed plants in

moist, well-drained, acid soil in a protected location. It will be happy growing with rhododendrons and azaleas and looks handsome when sited in front of a grouping of Hemlocks. High pH will cause chlorosis.

Note: This tree will probably not prosper in areas where temperatures fall too low in the winter, or where the soil tends to be alkaline. Deam reports its appearance in southern Indiana and southern Illinois, and it is hardy in zones 5–8.

PROPAGATION: Plant ripe seed directly in the ground in the fall or cold-stratify for 5–6 months. Seeds may take up to two years to germinate. Cuttings are easy and reliable, or purchase nursery stock. It transplants well.

PLANTLORE: Silverbell was one of Thomas Jefferson's favorite small trees on the grounds at Monticello. In *Landscaping with Native Trees*, Jim Wilson and Guy Sternberg describe a large grove of Silverbell trees at the Abraham Lincoln Memorial Garden in Springfield, Illinois. These trees were part of a famous lakeside design executed in the 1930s by well-known naturalist and landscape architect Jens Jensen.

3. Virginia Sweetspire *(Itea virginica)*

Fragrant 2-to-6-inch-long racemes of white flowers droop from the ends of arching branches, creating an attractive midsummer picture. This underused shrub has glowing glossy green leaves in summer and spectacular red foliage in the fall. It is beautiful when planted in a mass at the middle of a border and grows 2 to 5 feet tall and nearly twice as wide.

PLANTING REQUIREMENTS: Sweetspire prefers sun or light shade and moist, well-drained, fertile soil, although it will tolerate nearly any soil conditions. It is easy to grow, suckers heavily, will readily create a mass planting, and is an excellent choice for a shrub border.

PROPAGATION: This plant roots very easily from firm softwood or hardwood cuttings. You can also dig and transplant a rooted sucker. Plant ripened seed immediately and keep the planting medium moist. Sweetspire is readily available in the nursery trade.

4. American Highbush Cranberry *(Viburnum trilobum)*

Cranberry-like fruits enhance this handsome 8- to 12-foot bush. Spectacular red autumn foliage makes this an excellent choice for a hedge, massed as a border or planted as a large specimen. Large, showy 4-inch flat clusters of white spring blossoms cover the bush in late spring. The dwarf form, 'Compactum', is about half the size of the species.

PLANTING REQUIREMENTS: American Highbush Cranberry will coexist with large trees since it is tolerant of root competition. Once established, it will also tolerate a drier site. Plant these woodland natives in rich, organic, well-drained soil in partial shade or sun where you can enjoy the seasonal changes from your window.

PROPAGATION: Collect ripe seed and store at room temperature for three months, cold stratify in the refrigerator for an additional three months, and plant. Cuttings taken early in spring root readily, or you can pin attached branches to the soil beneath the shrub and cover with soil. These will root and can be removed from the mother-plant in fall and transplanted. Viburnums are available from most nurseries.

PLANTLORE: The berries provided a source of Vitamin C to early settlers and were stewed with sugar to make a cranberry-like sauce.

5. Witch Hazel *(Hamamelis virginiana; H. vernalis)*

Small, narrow twisted petals of yellow or orangey-red cover two of our native Witch Hazels *(H. virginiana* and *H. vernalis)* to give late fall and winter interest. These interesting shrubs blossom when temperatures plummet. The fragrant yellow flowers of Eastern Witch Hazel *(H. virginiana)* blend with the golden fall leaves, while *H. vernalis* waits until midwinter or very early spring to grace the stark landscape with small, profuse, bright orangey-red flowers.

Ozark or Spring Witch Hazel *(H. vernalis)* is the smaller of the two natives, generally maturing at under 10 feet, while *H. virginiana* can grow as tall as 25 feet.

PLANTING REQUIREMENTS: Plant in well-drained acid or neutral organic soil with morning sun or dappled shade. Witch Hazels do not perform well in alkaline soil or intense sun. These plants make an attractive mass, a striking specimen plant, or an impressive addition to a mixed shrub border. They are particularly effective when backlit by the sun. Plant *H. vernalis* where you can enjoy viewing it from inside your warm, cozy house, and give it an underplanting of spring-flowering crocus and daffodils for a spring "pick-me-up."

PROPAGATION: Collect seeds and store at room temperature for three months, then in the refrigerator for an additional three months, and plant. Young branches cut early in spring will root easily in sand or a soilless potting mixture, or you can purchase started plants from the nursery.

6. Red Chokeberry *(Aronia arbutifolia)*

Red Chokeberry provides interest in all seasons and is particularly effective when planted as a mass. Incorporate into a mixed shrub border, or plant as a hedge or a specimen. Small clusters of white flowers bloom in spring. Handsome dark green summer leaves turn brilliant red in autumn and enhance the ripening clusters of berries. These bright red berries remain throughout the winter. Black Chokeberry *(A. melanocarpa)* has black berries and wine-red fall foliage. Both species are generally 5 to 10 feet tall. The berries are not sought after by wildlife, but are beautiful in the landscape. 'Brilliantissima', with spectacular fall foliage, is one of the best cultivars .

PLANTING REQUIREMENTS: These plants prefer a humus-rich, well-drained neutral to acid soil in full sun or partial shade. The fall color is more reliable with more sun.

PROPAGATION: Plant ripe seed in the fall or cold-stratify three months. Take cuttings in June or July or purchase started plants.

6.

Go Vertical

Using Vines

Kentucky Wisteria

We've always lived in wooded areas, where we look out at nature, rather than at the neighbor's gas grill. When our youngest daughter and her husband were looking for their first house, they found the cost of homes in natural areas beyond their budget. Their new two-story home, with a small back yard, is surrounded by others just like it. Neighbors share a 6-foot privacy fence, but Kristen felt she was "on display" when she read or relaxed on the sunny patio. Several small trees along the fence held out promise for the future, but what could be done for shade and privacy right now?

Twelve-foot-long 4 x 4-inch posts were installed on each corner of the patio, with 3 feet sunk into the ground and encased in concrete. 2 x 2 boards fastened to the top of the posts created the framework to attach additional 2 x 2 boards for the open roof, and lightweight cedar lattice pieces created an upright wall at one end. The soil beneath the lattice was amended 18 inches deep with peat and sand to make a good garden loam, and then Kristen planted fast-growing Trumpet Creeper vines 1 to 2 feet apart, mulched, and attached them with plastic-covered wire to the lattice. The first season, interplanted annual vines of Scarlet Runner Beans and blue Morning Glories filled the area quickly. Metal screw-eyes in the roof frame received hanging baskets and a wren house. A homemade windowbox under the kitchen window held a mass of colorful annuals and trailing vines.

Now the Trumpet Creeper has grown up over the lattice, covering the top of the structure, giving privacy, dappled shade, and a feeling of spaciousness and elegance to their back yard. Hummingbirds dart back and forth gathering nectar from the tubular red-orange flowers, chickadees and wrens have taken turns nesting in the little bird house hung at one side of the patio, and butterflies flit through the yard. Kristen is delighted with this simple solution: "When I look out the family room windows, that wonderful wall of cool green leaves and beautiful flowers makes me almost feel like I am in the woods!"

A wide variety of native vines grow wild throughout North America. In the 1820s, Oliver Johnson told of masses of wild grapevines clinging to the trees, "some of them as much as eight or ten inches through and wound around a half dozen trees or so." In mid-October 1852, as Fredrika Bremer sailed on the Mississippi River between Wisconsin and Iowa, she saw islands full of wild vines festooned among leafless trees, and observed, "The wild vines are yet green." She titled Cincinnati, Ohio, "the vine-district of North America," and wrote, "The vine which grows luxuriantly wild throughout the whole of North America, has been cultivated on the heights which border the Ohio River."

Just as they do in the wild, vines and climbing plants help to "complete" a garden. They have been used for centuries to cool and shade private areas and have a longstanding tradition as special accents. If you close your eyes, you can envision purple wisteria draped over the corner of an old Victorian porch, English Ivy covering the walls and arches of Gothic university buildings, bright red roses scrambling over a white trellis, or even Kristen's fragrant, cool patio. Most gardeners can relate to the feelings of serenity and mystery that leafy vines can give, and the coolness experienced as one walks under a grape arbor. As Jane Austen wrote, "Here's harmony, here's repose."

How Can a Vine Enhance My Garden?

Trees and shrubs are the foundation for the landscape—the infrastructure or "bones." Vines are the finishing touch to a beautiful garden. They cover unsightly structures and soften hard edges. Rising determinedly up the side of a fence, climbing on a trellis, or scrambling up a tree, vines give unmatched vertical interest.

In small suburban yards, vines can provide privacy and welcome shade. Since most vines like to have their roots shaded as they reach for the sun and have relatively small root systems, the landscaping area around and in front of vines can be planted with shrubs, perennials, or annuals. Even an unsightly tool shed can become an asset to your garden design when covered by a vine.

Some vines have beautiful flowers, others colorful fall foliage. When our grandson was four, he and his dad built a tepee of tall wooden staves and planted pole beans. Eric loved to sit inside his secret spot that summer, running his little toy cars around in the dirt and reading his books. Virginia Creeper could make a more permanent tepee that would turn blazing red in the fall.

A vine can attract wildlife to nibble the berries, drink nectar from its flowers, or nest in its leafy shade. Crossvine will effectively camouflage a chain-link fence. If the fence is visible from a window, so much the better; the brightly colored orange or red bell-like trumpet flowers of this evergreen vine will attract hummingbirds—a much nicer picture to look at than the chain-link fence!

Shorter, twining vines can be planted in containers and trained to climb a lattice on a patio, or allowed to trail down over a fence or wall. Vines are effective in hanging baskets, and can also be used horizontally as ground covers.

Contrasting vines can be combined for special effects. Strong woody vines generally prefer being combined with a more delicate twining vine, rather than another woody one. Virgin's Bower (*Clematis virginiana*) is a native clematis with clusters of small white flowers, and its mopheaded fruits, called "Old Man's Beard," give late fall and winter interest. Try accenting the white flowers and fuzzy fruits of native clematis with evergreen Crossvine. Or consider planting seeds of an annual flowering vine in early spring and let the annual intertwine with the perennial vine.

Yellow Trillium, Wild Blue Phlox, False Rue
Anemone, and Great White Trillium glisten in the
rain in the author's woodland garden.

Brilliant red berries of an American Holly tree
sparkle against the snow and attract a variety of
winter birds to the author's front entryway.

Ferns, Virginia Bluebells, and a host of spring ephemerals arise from their winter's slumber.

Elisabeth Ball (1897–1983), of the Ball Glass family, was an early advocate of gardening with wildflowers. Native plants like Twinleaf, white Wild Phlox, Wild Hyacinth, Wild Geranium, and Ostrich Ferns have spread throughout her naturalized gardens at Oakhurst Mansion in Muncie, Indiana.

Private residence with colorful prairie flowers. Native plants make few demands, which makes them popular with gardeners and landscapers.

Delicate lavender-pink blossoms of a Redbud tree herald spring at Fort Harrison State Park in Indianapolis.

Goldenrod lights up the earth under stark Black
Oaks as autumn comes to northern Indiana

Even alleyways can be beautified with prairie flowers, as this colorful spot shielding the owner's dog run attests.

Summer puffs of feathery flowers cover a small Smoke Tree planted near a pond at Cheekwood Mansion in Nashville, Tennessee.

Yellowwood's graceful shape and handsome leaves are only a small part of its charm. It is truly a tree for all seasons with wisteria-like white racemes of spring flowers, interesting bark, and brilliant yellow fall color.

The leaves of a magnificent Tulip Tree are silhouetted against the Lincoln Birthplace Memorial, near Hodgenville, Kentucky (top left). The state tree of Indiana and Tennessee, Tulip Tree is a golden delight in autumn, and its flowers never fail to elicit wonder (photo by Emily Daniels). A beautifully formed young specimen at a Nashville, Tennessee, residence (bottom right).

Many a jar of jelly or bottle of wine has been concocted from the black berries that follow the showy white flowers of common Elderberry. This shrub is a good choice for naturalizing at the edge of a wooded site.

Although still young, this 'Annabelle', a recommended cultivar of Smooth Hydrangea, puts on a spectacular show in early summer.

Buttonbush gets its common name from the large, spherical "buttons" that cover this unique moisture-loving shrub in late summer.

Brilliant scarlet-red berries of Winterberry Holly are stunning against a snowy landscape, or near a light-colored building (photo by Lee Casebere).

Cranberry-like fruits give the American Cranberry Bush, also called American High-bush Cranberry, two of its common names. Its three-lobed leaves turn brilliant red in the fall.

Sand Cherry is a popular landscaping shrub that lends vertical interest. Here, its burgundy leaves make a good backdrop for Black-eyed Susans.

Maypops, our native passionflower vine.

Hummingbirds drink nectar from the tubular flowers of the fast-growing Trumpet Creeper vine.

Dutchman's Pipe is not native to the Lower Midwest, but it grows well here and is readily available in the nursery trade.

A popular vine for the front porches and arbors of early settlers, Trumpet Honeysuckle is attractive, fast-growing, dependable, and attracts hummingbirds and butterflies.

Bearberry, also called Kinnikinnick, was used as a tobacco substitute by Native Americans. This unusual ground cover needs acid soil.

Our native pachysandra, Allegheny Spurge, with its scalloped deep green or mottled leaves, makes a handsome ground cover, and its flowers have more pizzazz than the common Japanese pachysandra.

Green and Gold is a cheerful little plant that is tolerant of a wide range of environmental conditions

Virginia Creeper is generally observed climbing trees, but here this versatile vine doubles as a ground cover under native White Pine and Eastern Hemlock trees. Its leaves turn fiery red in the fall.

Wild Ginger quickly colonizes a woodland site to create an ever-increasing mass of heart-shaped leaves.

Tiny lavender and gold flowers of Crested Iris are tucked within narrow, strappy leaves. This delicate wildflower can be used as a small accent, a ground cover, or an edging along a path.

Tightly coiled Ostrich Fern fronds signal the rebirth of spring.

Goldie's Fern makes a strong statement in the garden of J. Paul Moore, Nashville, Tennessee. It is one of the largest clump-forming ferns.

Delicate Maidenhair Ferns contrast with a coarsely textured, horseshoe-like leaf of Green Dragon and its tri-leaved cousin, Jack-in-the-Pulpit.

Gray-headed Coneflower is readily identified by dark cone-shaped disc flower heads that become gray as the season progresses.

Purple Coneflower, a popular seed source for goldfinches and chickadees, is also a favorite of nectar-seeking butterflies and bees.

At the edge of a prairie planting, narrow onion-like leaves clasp the base of the flower stalk of low-growing Nodding Onion, whose delicate flowers resemble an upside-down pink umbrella.

(opposite) A brilliant blue sky shows off the unique globe-shaped gray flowers of Rattlesnake Master, a plant often mentioned in pioneer diaries. Fibers from its yucca-like leaves were used by Native Americans to line moccasins.

Airy, upright, white candelabra spires of Culver's Root contrast with the small, bright red blossoms of Royal Catchfly.

The uniquely shaped flowers of Michigan Lily were a common sight as settlers crossed the prairie.

Compass Plant towers above other prairie plants and earned its common name from the tendency of the leaves to orient themselves north and south.

Gayfeather or Liatris, also known as Blazing Star, grows with Switch-grass and Black-eyed Susan in the newly installed butterfly garden at the Indianapolis Zoo.

What Are the Advantages of Native Vines?

Many nonnative vines are considered tender or half-hardy, and to survive temperature extremes in the winter they need burlap, straw, leaves, dirt, or even styrofoam sheets or glass window panes for protection. They also may have specific cultural requirements not needed by natives. Native vines thumb their tendrils at low temperatures and variable soil conditions. They have adapted to their region, and grow without cultivation in the wild, where they happily clamber up trees or along fencerows, surviving regardless of weather extremes.

Asian wisteria, English Ivy, and roses are not native to the Lower Midwest, and need special attention to stay healthy. Most climbing roses have been grafted and must be removed from the trellis, laid on the ground, and covered with burlap and soil in northern climates to protect the graft. Even in Zones 5–6, the graft needs the minimum protection of a winter collar fashioned from four layers of newspapers filled with leaves. Roses need to be fed and watered regularly, and sprayed with a fungicide every 7–10 days, as well as a miticide in the spring and an insecticide when harmful insects attack. Few flowers can compare with the beauty of a rose, but roses do need extra care.

Wisteria is often used in gardens. The species most commonly sold in garden centers are the lovely natives of Japan *(Wisteria floribunda)* and China *(W. sinensis)* that can winter-kill in exposed areas if winter temperatures plummet. Kentucky Wisteria *(W. macrostachya)* is a native with beautiful flowers and woody stems. Climbing over an arbor, it creates a serene, mysterious area under its leaves. The long drooping racemes of purple flowers are similar to those of the Asian Wisteria.

Even ivy can succumb if environmental conditions are less than optimum. A neighbor had an extensive ground cover of English Ivy. Nearly the entire planting winter-killed the year that winter temperatures dipped to –27° F. Some good native substitutes for ivy are two sturdy relatives of Wild Ginger named Woolly Dutchman's Pipe and Dutchman's Pipe. The large, glossy heart-shaped leaves of these two are dark green and overlap like roof shingles. Established woody vines can be cut to the ground in the spring and will quickly regrow.

Passionflower is a beautiful, exotic-looking flower, and there are several nonnative species from South America, but these tender exotics need to be grown in a greenhouse or brought indoors for the winter in the Lower Midwest. Maypops, one of two native passionflowers, has 2-inch white flowers with a striking fringe of purple filaments. Yellow Passionflower, the other native, grows in moist or dry woods, especially near streams. The greenish-yellow flowers are smaller than those of Maypops, generally less than 1 inch across. Both of these native species have interesting leaves, and neither requires any special attention to survive in Zone 6, although they may need some protection in Zone 5 if winter temperatures dip too low.

Are There Any "Bad" Native Vines?

"Leaflets of three, let them be; berries white, take ye flight" is the old adage for Poison Ivy *(Rhus radicans)*. Anyone planning to hike in the woods, rescue or transplant wildflowers, or weed wooded areas should become familiar with this vine. This member of the Sumac Family is poisonous in any season, and even burning it can cause severe allergic reactions. Early in the spring, Poison Ivy leaves may be red and greasy-looking, but as the season progresses the leaves get larger and turn medium-green. The leaves look very similar to Virginia Creeper, except that Poison Ivy has three leaflets and white berries, while Virginia Creeper has five leaflets and blue-black grape-like berries. I like to describe the two outer leaflets of Poison Ivy to my grandchildren as "mittens," since they often have a coarse tooth on the side which looks like a thumb. The center leaflet may be smooth, or may have a broad tooth on each side. There is a similarity in the shape of Poison Ivy leaves and the leaves of the Poinsettia. Birds love the berries of Poison Ivy, so even "bad" natives have some good qualities.

Conditions in their native environments generally control vines with aggressive tendencies. In contrast, introduced aliens may have no natural checks where they are not indigenous. Two native Japanese species, originally hailed as miracle vines, have become monsters in this country. Kudzu *(Pueraria lobata)* covers and strangles everything it meets, and Japanese Honeysuckle *(Lonicera japonica)*, also known as Hall's Honeysuckle, suffocates and destroys indigenous vegetation as it covers thousands of acres in states of the South and the Lower Midwest. Native vines, even if they are aggressive, can be controlled by pruning, and none exhibit the extreme invasive characteristics of Kudzu or Japanese Honeysuckle.

How Do You Site a Vine?

In the Lower Midwest, temperatures can turn balmy early in the spring, only to swing wildly back to freezing. Plants in Zones 5–6 are particularly susceptible to early frost damage, so that early spring flowering vines will perform better if they are not located on an east-facing wall or fence. On walls and fences facing north, south, or west, the frosted flowers and leaves have a chance to thaw before the sun hits them, and are often unharmed by an early frost, but if early morning sunshine strikes a flower before the frost melts, the flower is generally ruined. Gently sprinkling the frosted flowers and foliage with water before the sun hits them can help to minimize frost damage. (This can also save frosted hosta leaves!)

Tips for Siting Vines

1. If a vine prefers shade, plant it beneath a taller-growing tree, or on the north or northwest side of the house or fence.
2. Plant the roots of a vine at the base of a tree or next to the trunk, where they will not have to compete with the feeder roots of the tree, located primarily out near the dripline. The other option is to locate the roots of an understory plant or vine out beyond the outer edge of the tree's canopy. To shade the roots and keep them cool, plant vines on the north side of a tree or shrub.
3. It is better to plant a vine in the center of a fence, a few feet away from the upright post, to help distribute the weight as the vine grows.
4. If the vine is planted to cover a building, keep its roots away from the corner so that the wind exposure isn't too severe.
5. If the roof has an overhang, plant the roots just outside the overhang so they can receive adequate moisture from rainfall.

How Do Vines Climb?

Twining vines may have thin, fine tendrils, like wisteria, or coiling spring-like tendrils, like grapes, that grab and attach to a wire or fine branch. Clematis threads its stems around a support. Virginia Creeper and Poison Ivy hold securely onto any rough or uneven surface with finger-like roots along their stems. Some vines, like roses, lean and climb with back-facing thorns.

Most vines have their own means of attaching to a fence, a wall, or a tree, but to help them get started, tie some of the stems to the support. Vines that create "stick-tights" can be helped at the beginning with chewed gum to hold the stem to the wall or fence.

Vines with tendrils will happily climb wire mesh, such as chicken wire, or homemade mesh made with galvanized or green plastic coated wire. Attach the mesh to the wall with screw eyes, or with wall nails installed in the mortar between bricks. Some gardeners even attach plastic hooks with super glue to hold the mesh. Before the vine is planted, figure out how the entire mesh wall can be detached and laid on the ground while repairs or painting are accomplished.

Lightweight, smaller vines will climb a wooden or metal trellis if you loosely secure the stem to the trellis with twine, twist-ties, or plastic covered wire. An 18- to 24-inch mesh cylinder can be installed around the base of a tree trunk, and usually a vine will grab the trunk and continue to climb as it becomes established.

Woody vines are heavier and require more support than vines that climb with tendrils. Build a sturdy trellis or provide strong support for these hefty vines.

What Are Vines' Planting Requirements?

Vines have small root systems compared to their above-ground growth. Most vines prefer cool feet, loamy soil, good drainage, mulch, and good air circulation to stay healthy.

1. Dig a hole 18 to 24 inches deep and twice as wide as the root ball. Fill the hole with water and let it drain. If this takes more than five or six hours, sand needs to be added to the bottom of the hole to help with drainage.

2. Amend the excavated soil with equal amounts of humus, compost, and sand. This is particularly important if the vine is to be planted next to a foundation, which probably has the worst soil on your property, composed of rubble and subsoil.

3. Place a gallon bucketful of moistened sphagnum peat moss or good

compost mixed with soil in a mound at the bottom of the planting hole.

4. Spread the roots of the vine over the mound, cover with the amended soil, mulch, and water thoroughly.

Six Suggested Vines

1. Virginia Creeper *(Parthenocissus quinquefolia)*

Bright scarlet-red leaves light up the woods when this beautiful vine takes center stage in autumn. Sweet nectar in the small greenish-white flowers attracts hummingbirds, butterflies, and bees. The early summer–blooming flowers are followed by inedible grape-like clusters of blue-black berries that ripen in the fall. Virginia Creeper provides food and cover for over 35 species of wildlife. It is effective as a climbing vine or as a ground cover.

Five leaflets instead of three distinguish this woody vine from Poison Ivy (which also turns red in autumn but has white berries). The scientific species name *quinquefolia* is from the Latin. *Quinque* means five and *folia* means leaves. Other common names include Woodbine and Five-leaf Ivy.

Small discs at the ends of tendrils enable Virginia Creeper to climb nearly any type of natural or building material. Evolutionist Charles Darwin reputedly tested the holding tenacity of Virginia Creeper and determined that one small disc could support two pounds!

PLANTING REQUIREMENTS: Plant in shade or partial sun. This vine will tolerate nearly any type of soil and moisture conditions as long as the soil is well drained, but does best in humus-rich woodland soil, where it generally grows in the wild.

PROPAGATION: Remove the flesh of the berry and plant ripe seed immediately in fall, or stratify for two months for spring planting. Or lay a portion of the stem on the ground and cover a node with soil, and small rootlets will form. This section can be cut away from the mother plant and transplanted. In his comprehensive book *The Reference Manual of Woody Plant Propagation*, Michael Dirr recommends using a section of the vine with no tendrils because buds do not form on nodes with tendrils.

PLANTLORE: Chippewa Indians cut the stalk in short lengths and boiled and peeled it. Frances Densmore noted in *How Indians Use Wild Plants*, "Between the outer bark and the wood there was a sweetish substance which was eaten somewhat after the manner of eating corn from the cob. The water in which the woodbine had been boiled was then boiled down to a syrup. If sugar were lacking, wild rice was boiled in this syrup to season it."

2. Woolly Dutchman's Pipe *(Aristolochia tomentosa)*

Huge, overlapping heart-shaped leaves shingle buildings or trees where this woody vine grows. "I have seen the dead trunks of large trees shingled with it to a great height—83 feet long and 10 inches in circumference," wrote Charles Deam, who reported in 1921 that he also had it planted "as a porch trellis." The leaves can be as long as 10 inches and equally as wide. This deciduous vine is a member of the Birthwort Family, as is Wild Ginger, and the insignificant brownish-red flowers are similar.

Dutchman's Pipe *(Aristolochia macrophylla* formerly *A. durior)*, the species more commonly found in the nursery trade, grows well in the Lower Midwest but is native farther east. Woolly Dutchman's Pipe is our native pipevine. It is also sometimes called Woolly Dutchman or Woolly Pipevine. The flowers of both species resemble a curved Dutchman's pipe, and both species are similar in growth habit, but *A. tomentosa* has downy leaves.

Pipevine Swallowtail larvae depend upon the Aristolochias for survival. This butterfly's food sources, which also include Virginia Snakeroot (*A. serpentaria*), Wild Ginger (*Asarum canadense*), and Knotweed (*Polygonum* spp.), cause it to have a nasty taste that is unpalatable to birds.

PLANTING REQUIREMENTS: Plant in moist, humus-rich soil in light shade or sun. It can be used to cover a building, to climb on a heavy trellis, or to provide privacy on a porch. These hefty vines need extremely sturdy support.

PROPAGATION: Both spread vigorously by suckers, can be divided, and grow from a sturdy rootstock with fibrous rootlets. Sow ripened seed immediately or cold-stratify for three months.

3. Trumpet Creeper (*Campsis radicans*)

Trumpet Creeper is also known as Hummingbird Vine because the nectar from the orange-red tubular flowers is so attractive to the tiny birds. Ruby-throated hummingbirds sip nectar from Trumpet Creeper flowers in Audubon's well-known painting. The striking 3-inch-long flowers bloom all summer. This aggressive woody vine can climb over 30 feet by aerial roots. The scientific name *radicans* means "rooting" and indicates this tendency. The dark green opposite compound leaves have 7–10 serrated-edged leaflets. Some people have an allergic reaction similar to Poison Ivy when they come into contact with this vine.

PLANTING REQUIREMENTS: Plant in full sun to part shade in humus-rich, moist soil in an area where it cannot escape into the wild. Charles Deam called it Hell-vine, and wrote, "My advice is to exterminate it wherever found and never permit the vine to mature seed." However, it can be very effective if it is planted in an area where it can be controlled and contained. Pick off ripe seed capsules before they open to control the spread. Provide sturdy support. For a variety of color, choose the cultivar 'Flava' with yellow flowers, or red-flowered 'Crimson Trumpet'.

PROPAGATION: Winged seeds develop in 4- to 6-inch long seedpods. Plant ripe seed immediately or space individual plants 2 feet apart. This vine roots easily from softwood or root cuttings.

4. American Bittersweet (*Celastrus scandens*)

Scandens means "climbing" and aptly describes Bittersweet. This woody vine twists and twirls like a grapevine around branches of trees. It clambers over hedges, fences, and rocks as it grows to lengths of 30 feet or more. It has an extremely long, creeping, bright orange root about the diameter of a middle finger. Small clusters of fragrant, insignificant greenish-white flowers bloom in early summer at the tips of the branches.

The alternate oval leaves of American Bittersweet are pointed at the tips and have serrated edges. They turn golden yellow in fall just as the bright orange berries ripen. These berries split open after the first frost, curving backwards to reveal the bright red seed-bearing berry within. They persist throughout the winter for birds and small mammals to feed on. Bittersweet is familar to floral arrangers, who use it in fall bouquets. (Asiatic Bittersweet *[C. orbiculatus]* is an aggressive, invasive exotic. Its flower clusters are axillary rather than terminal, growing in the axil of its round, blunt leaves.)

PLANTING REQUIREMENTS: Transplant young seedlings 2 to 3 feet apart. Bittersweet prefers moist, humus-rich, well-drained soil but will tolerate dry, average soil. Plant in partial shade or sun. The plants are dioecious so it is necessary to plant several in order to assure pollination.

PROPAGATION: Remove the flesh from the bright red berry and plant the ripe shiny brown seeds in sand or sawdust. Seedlings can be transplanted after the third set of leaves emerges. Seeds can also be stratified for 2 to 3 months and planted in spring. This vine can be propagated by softwood cuttings in late summer, by root cuttings, or by layering.

PLANTLORE: The bark of the root was said to be a "powerful and useful medicine." It was administered to induce sweating and was used as a diuretic. Simmering one measure of bark for several hours with two measures of lard produced an ointment that was strained and used to reduce swelling, hemorrhoids, and tumors.

5. Maypops *(Passiflora incarnata)*

In early summer, fascinating tropical-looking flowers cover the native passionflower vine commonly known as Maypops. The center of each solitary 2-inch white flower is a striking crown-like fringe of white or lavender filaments edged with purple. Butterflies constantly flit about, gathering nectar from these beautiful flowers.

Birds, animals, and humans enjoy the sweet 2-inch-long yellow berries as they ripen. Maypops has finely serrated leaves with three to five deeply cut lobes. This plant spreads by underground runners. It is hardy to –10° F. and may survive lower temperatures with adequate winter protection.

Passiflora lutea is the yellow-flowered native. Its flowers grow in pairs and are much smaller and less showy than those of *P. incarnata*. Its lobed leaves are reminiscent of maple leaves. Growing requirements are similar, although Yellow Passionflower is more shade tolerant. The fruit is a small, edible blue-black berry.

PLANTING REQUIREMENTS: Plant in full sun or very light shade in moist, humus-rich, well-drained soil. Passionflower will tolerate clay soil, but needs consistent, even moisture. Fertilize and prune or pinch back the tips once established to encourage bushiness and to keep the plant vigorous.

It can be trained like clematis on wire cages, trellises, or tree trunks, or allowed to climb where it wants. It can be also used as an effective ground cover.

PROPAGATION: Remove the flesh from the fruit by rubbing it in a sieve under running water. Plant the cleaned ripened brownish seed immediately or stratify in moist sphagnum moss in the refrigerator. Germination may take up to two years. Thin the vine and root these cuttings in early summer or divide established plants.

PLANTLORE: Early Roman Catholic priests in Brazil chose the

name because they believed the flower was a symbol of Christ's passion. The beautiful center (corona) represents the crown of thorns. The leaves represent the hands of the persecutors, and the tendrils the whips and the ropes used to bind Jesus. The stigma was thought to resemble nails, and the anthers represented the wounds.

6. Crossvine *(Bignonia capreolata)*

Bright orange-red tubular flowers resemble slightly flared ringing bells and cover the vine in late spring. Hummingbirds, butterflies, and bees hover over the flowers, gathering the sweet nectar. Opposite smooth-edged leaves are oblong and lance-shaped. The glossy green leaves are handsome in the summer sunlight as Crossvine climbs trees, trellises, fences, or chicken-wire cages around posts. It climbs by tendrils and can reach heights of 60 feet. A lovely cultivar named 'Tangerine Beauty' with light apricot flowers is available in the nursery trade.

PLANTING REQUIREMENTS: Plant in rich, fertile soil with plenty of moisture in full sun.

PROPAGATION: Freshly ripened seed can be planted immediately or cold stratified for 2–3 months. Propagate by stem or root cuttings or divide established plants.

PLANTLORE: A cross found when the stem is cut gives this plant its common name.

Indigenous plants shine where grass is difficult to grow and maintain.   —*Fine Gardening, 1995*

7.

Go

Horizontal

Using Ground Covers

Novice gardeners often make the mistake of assuming that all they need to do to establish a beautiful garden is to spend a little money. It is important to prepare the soil thoroughly whenever you begin a new garden, but it is especially crucial with a ground cover planting that you hope to plant once and then expect to run, multiply, and fill in on its own. Unless you are planting in a natural woodland, or have amended the soil with leaves, mulch, and compost over the years, your existing soil is probably poor subsoil with only a thin layer of topsoil, and soil preparation is imperative for plant survival whether the ground cover is native or alien.

Eight years ago, neighbors employed a new landscaping firm to install nonnative myrtle *(Vinca minor)* in an island bed at the front of their forty-year-old home. Workers removed the debris, raked and roughened the existing soil, and plunked the little seedlings into the dirt. Even though the owner ran his over-

Virginia Creeper

head sprinkler at first, most of the new plants died before the next season in this hostile environment. Since then, this particular island bed has been planted four or five times by different firms, who unfortunately all used the same general method. The island bed is still barren dirt with only a few sparse, uneven sections of ground cover.

At the same time, another neighbor planted myrtle along the property line, but first rototilled humus, sphagnum peat moss, and a little sand into his existing soil. He also watered with an overhead sprinkler at the outset. Eight years later, his ground cover is lush and full.

A ground cover can be defined as any plant that spreads to completely cover the ground in a planting area. Generally, ground covers are low-growing plants, not exceeding 15 inches in height, but some ferns, grasses, flowering plants, and shrubs make serviceable ground covers if they have aggressive growth habits. Ground covers usually spread by rhizomes, runners, or stolons. A variety of upright, prostrate, trailing, medium or low-growing native plants can be used as ground covers to reduce maintenance, cover a problem area, bind the soil, or just give a different "look" at ground level. Sun-loving plants prefer a south, east, or west exposure. North-facing hillsides should be planted with shade-tolerant plants.

Strawberry-like ground covers include Common Cinquefoil *(Potentilla simplex)* and Barren Strawberry *(Waldsteinia fragarioides)*. Wild Strawberry *(Fragaria virginiana)* bears small, sweet, edible strawberries. These all grow in well-drained, average garden soil in sun or partial shade. Wine Cups or Poppy Mallow *(Callirhoe involucrata)* is a spreading plant with vivid magenta flowers. It prefers a prairie or meadow environment in full sun. Cultivated forms of Creeping Phlox *(Phlox stolonifera)*, well known to gardeners, prefer moist, humus-rich soil in sun or partial shade. Phlox is native in some of the eastern states of the Lower Midwest, and grows well within a wide range in Zones 5–6. For sunny, dry slopes, try the clump-forming Moss Phlox *(Phlox subulata)*, which will blanket a rock garden or hillside with long-lasting pink flowers.

Pussytoes *(Antennaria plantaginifolia)* forms a rosette of gray-green leaves and can be planted at the edge of the woods. The small fuzzy flowers never fail to delight small children, who invariably cry, "Oh, they feel just like the paws of a kitty."

What Is the Best Ground Cover for My Yard?

Try to determine the purpose of a ground cover planting. Is it to make an area look uniform and green and simply cover the dirt? Is it to encourage wildlife? Is it for the flowers or fruit at varying times of the year? Do you want color in the fall? Think about your needs and choose accordingly.

Ground covers can serve as small accents, to fill in under trees or shrubs, or be used alone as erosion control on hillsides and stream banks. Dwarf Crested Iris *(Iris cristata)* is a tiny lavender iris that will spread to cover a small area with strappy iris-like leaves in high open shade. It blends well with woodland wildflowers.

Star-like lavender-blue flowers cover Sand or Cleft Phlox *(Phlox bifida)* in summer. It is a good accent ground cover in sandy, well-drained soil.

At the base of a biohedge, or in a hot, dry environment, consider Fragrant Sumac *(Rhus aromatica)*. It prefers sun, but will tolerate shade. Small yellow flowers appear in spring, followed by clusters of hairy red berries that persist throughout the winter. The brilliant red fall foliage is outstanding. This small shrubby plant suckers heavily, and branches root by just lying on the ground. Taller than traditional ground covers—2 to 6 feet—it will entice wildlife to take up residence in your yard. 'Gro-Low' is a new cultivar that reaches a height of only 2 feet.

Prairie Cordgrass *(Spartina pectinata)*, or the variegated form, *S. p.* 'Aureo-marginata', Switchgrass *(Panicum virgatum)*, Sweetgrass *(Hierochloe odorata)*, and Big Bluestem *(Andropogon gerardii)* are prairie grasses that will bind the soil tightly in almost any type of planting environment. Small sedges like *Carex pennsylvanica* make excellent ground covers under trees, especially oaks, and will happily blanket a site.

We generally think of vines as vertical, upright features, but many of them can also double as ground covers to serve as a horizontal design element. In autumn, bright red Virginia Creeper, laden with dark blue berries, creates a spectacular vertical picture as it climbs up the trunk of a burnished gold Sugar Maple, but twines horizontally equally as well, covering the ground to provide a cooling, green mass until fall, when its brilliant red leaves shimmer on the forest floor.

Can I Plant More Than One Ground Cover?

Before you decide to mix and match, study the growth habits of the plants to determine if such a design is practical. Some ground covers are so aggressive that they will overrun nearly any other planting and frustrate your attempts. Rhizomatous natives such as Canada Anemone and Prairie Cordgrass are effective erosion controllers and will efficiently blanket an area, but don't plan to incorporate these species into a small landscape, because they need room to run. There are several less invasive ground covers that are relatively slow growing and will cooperate with other woodland plants to fill a space and be of interest at different seasons of the year.

Acid-lovers such as Partridge Berry, Trailing Arbutus (*Epigaea repens*), Bunchberry (*Cornus canadensis*), and Wintergreen (*Gaultheria procumbens*) are all relatively slow growing and noninvasive. Each has pretty little white or pink flowers in the spring, colorful berries, and handsome leaves. They all require a shady site in humus-rich, moist, well-drained soil.

Another interesting ground cover for acid soil is called Goldthread (*Coptis groenlandica*). This tiny plant has shiny evergreen, three-parted leaves, and small white flowers that bloom in late spring. It spreads by fine golden thread-like rhizomes.

What Maintenance Is Required?

Remove any weeds or tree seedlings that invade the ground cover planting. Ground covers need to be kept evenly moist, but not wet, throughout the growing season to stimulate vigorous growth. Most ground covers will thrive in good garden loam with adequate drainage. Try to apply 1 inch of water per week . If there is insufficient rainfall, give the area a good, deep soaking with the hose, and allow the soil to dry a little before watering again. If the soil is kept too damp, plants are more susceptible to fungal infections and can rot off at ground level.

Should I Fertilize My Ground Cover?

I used to broadcast 12–12–12 granular fertilizer over my nonnative Myrtle (*Vinca minor*) in the spring, but found that this practice encouraged the fungal disease called Black Stem Rot. I believe that the decomposing leaves provide enough nutrients for native ground covers and that fertilizing is generally unnecessary.

One exception may be when you are attempting to establish a new planting. Keep the soil evenly moist and well mulched as the plants are getting established. Using a sprayer or watering can, sprinkle the foliage with a liquid fertilizer such as Rapid-Gro or Miracle-Gro once a week from the middle of May until the middle of July to stimulate faster growth and help the plants to increase and cover an area more quickly.

What about Raking Leaves?

Wait until all the leaves have fallen and have had a chance to settle, and then lightly rake off just enough leaves to keep them from smothering the plants. The others will snuggle down among the ground cover plants and help protect them, amend and rejuvenate the soil, and serve as a natural mulch to conserve moisture and keep weed seeds from germinating. Since most ground covers multiply by stolons or rhizomes, leaves do not seem to hinder their spread.

What if the pH of My Soil Is Wrong for a Plant I Want?

It is possible to amend the soil with soil sulphur, sphagnum peat moss, sawdust, or composted oak leaves to lower the pH and make the soil more acidic. To raise the pH and produce a more alkaline soil, add lime, wood ashes, or bonemeal. Organic matter, manure, and compost tend to neutralize the pH, raising it in acid soils and lowering it in alkaline soils. It is easier to change the pH of sandy soil than either loam or clay soils because of the clay particles. However, before you decide to change the pH, decide how important it is to have a particular plant in your garden. "Messing with Mother Nature" is not for the faint-hearted. It takes not only time and diligence to get it right, but also constant perseverance to keep it right. And is it worth it?

There is an unusual ground cover in the Clubmoss Family which is a close relative of ferns that I once tried to grow in my woods when a friend gave me a "start" from her extensive colony. It did not survive, and I presume the soil pH was the culprit. The common names, Ground Cedar and Running Cedar *(Lycopodium digitatum)*, describe this low-growing cedar lookalike, which seldom gets taller than 10 inches. The spores were once used as flash powder for photography. Since it spreads by 3- to 6-foot rhizomes, this plant is very difficult to transplant. If the site has an acidic soil pH and available moisture similar to the original area, transplanting is more likely to be successful. It thrives with Wintergreen and Partridge Berry, as well as with moisture-loving ferns such as Royal or Cinnamon.

In a shady nook in my garden a small clump of Wintergreen is alive and well, but it is not increasing. I grow it as a specimen plant, water it occasionally with Miracid, and enjoy watching it perform throughout the season, but it will never be a true ground cover in this alkaline clay soil without a continuous, major effort year after year. "Don't fight the site," and your gardening tasks will be easier and more enjoyable.

Six Suggested Ground Covers

1. Green and Gold *(Chrysogonum virginianum)*

Delightful flowers bloom above fuzzy green leaves on this compact little plant, also known as Golden Star. Five golden ray flowers surround a tiny bouquet of minute brown-centered golden stars. Two deep ridges curve through each petal. New 1½-inch flowers continue to reappear for many weeks. This plant blooms prolifically and continuously in the spring, and periodically for the remainder of the season. The small oval leaves are opposite.

It is low growing, seldom topping a foot in height. It makes a neat semi-evergreen clump requiring little or no maintenance except for occasional dividing, and self-sows readily.

Several cultivars are available, including petite 'Pierre', only 6 inches tall. 'Mark Viette' has larger flowers, and 'Springbrook' has shiny leaves.

PLANTING REQUIREMENTS: Green and Gold will accept a wide variety of environmental conditions. It will thrive in full sun or partial shade, but needs at least half a day of sun to bloom well. Plant in moist, average, well-drained garden soil. It does not need additional fertilizer or water except in serious drought. Mass this cheerful little ground cover along a path, near the base of a tree or rock, or plant a specimen near the front door to greet you each day.

PROPAGATION: Divide established clumps in early spring or fall by gently "rocking" the crowns apart, or cutting with a sharp knife. The brittle rhizome should be kept moist when dividing and transplanting.

The ripened seeds are dark brown nutlets. Plant these immediately, or stratify 2–3 months. Sand or pea gravel at the base of the plant will provide an excellent growing medium to encourage self-sown seedlings. Tip cuttings, older stems attached to a piece of the rootstock, or root cuttings will also root in sand and perlite.

2. Wild Ginger (*Asarum canadense*)

In early spring, tiny wrinkled leaves peek from the soil, then unfold and expand into the familiar large, heart-shaped leaves of Wild Ginger as spring temperatures rise. A 1-inch purple-brown flower, shaped like a small bell with three flared pointed lobes, grows at ground level in the crotch of two hairy leaf stalks. Wild Ginger grows 4 to 9 inches tall and is an excellent ground cover for a wooded area. Its shallow roots coexist with fibrous rooted trees like maple or beech. This attractive dark green plant colonizes readily, carpeting the forest floor. It is a larval food source for the Pipevine Swallowtail Butterfly.

PLANTING REQUIREMENTS: Wild Ginger needs a moist, shady environment with good drainage. It prefers the typical organic-rich loam of its native woodland but will grow in any good garden soil that has been amended with humus. Plant 10–12 inches apart in early spring.

Thin, yellowish, jointed rhizomatous stems creep horizontally just beneath the surface of the soil. Small branched roots delve deeper into the soil to anchor the plant. Cover the rhizome with $1/2$ to $3/4$ inches of soil and mulch. Wild Ginger is deciduous. It needs consistent moisture and will wilt or even resort to early dormancy if conditions become too dry.

PROPAGATION: Divide early in spring or when dormant in fall. Wild Ginger can be increased by rhizome cuttings after the flowers bloom. Cut a small piece with a pair of leaves attached and root in moist sand and perlite.

Wild Ginger will self-sow in moist soil. Look for ripe seed about a month after the plant flowers. Sow the fresh ripe seed after removing the pulp from the fruit. Don't let the seed dry out. Keep the potting medium consistently moist or germination will be poor.

PLANTLORE: The rhizomes have a gingery smell and a slightly bitter taste. Settlers boiled these rhizomes with sugar as a substitute for the spice from the West Indies. They also used Wild Ginger as a stimulant and to induce sweating.

3. Canada Anemone (*Anemone canadensis*)

Glistening white flowers with bright yellow centers brighten up a drab hillside and bloom from late spring to midsummer. Canada Anemone is also known as Windflower. Its seeds are dispersed by wind, and because the flower is on a long stalk it trembles in the wind. Canada Anemone is usually 12–20 inches tall. The leaves are deeply divided into 5 to 7 sections. It is one of the first flowers to bloom on the prairie, and a large colony creates a beautiful picture.

Canada Anemone can make a sunny area sparkle with color and does an excellent job as a tall ground cover, but be wary of using this plant in a normal garden situation or combined with other plants, because it is so extremely aggressive that some gardeners call it the "Canada enemy." It is a great plant for the right site. Just don't plan on controlling it!

PLANTING REQUIREMENTS: Canada Anemone prefers a moist environment. Plant 6–12 inches apart in average, well-drained soil with good water retention, or amend the soil with compost. It grows from a thin but rambunctious rhizome that spreads aggressively. Choose an area where it is free to roam, or containerize the plant in a large bottomless flowerpot and remove the seed "burrs" before they ripen.

PROPAGATION: Easily propagated by division of rhizomes, or by seed. Seedlings generally bloom the third year.

PLANTLORE: According to Greek mythology, Venus mourned the death of her beloved Adonis. As she wept, where each tear fell, an anemone sprang up and trembled in the wind.

4. Allegheny Spurge *(Pachysandra procumbens)*

Did you know that there is a native pachysandra that is much more interesting than the overused Japanese Pachysandra *(Pachysandra terminalis)*? Allegheny Spurge *(P. procumbens)* is slightly taller and stands 6–12 inches high. Its unique scalloped leaves are gray-green and become mottled with age. It has fragrant pinkish-white flowers that look like spiky bottlebrushes. This plant grows from a thin, white creeping rhizome with prominent eyes for next year's growth. It is deciduous in the Lower Midwest, evergreen farther south. It is somewhat slower growing than Japanese Pachysandra, so more started plants may be necessary to cover an area as quickly, but it is readily propagated by division, or by softwood stem cuttings in the spring. It grows more vigorously with additional water during dry spells.

PLANTING REQUIREMENTS: Space plants 8–10 inches apart and plant in humus-rich, fertile loam in partial or full shade (it dislikes sun). Cover the rhizomes with about an inch of soil. Mulch well.

PROPAGATION: Divide established clumps in spring before new growth emerges, or in the fall. Stem cuttings in moist sand and perlite are also successful. This year I tried the method suggested by Colston Burrell in *A Gardener's Encyclopedia of Wild Flowers:* "Hold a stem at ground level and yank it firmly upward. You will get a bit of the old stem as well as some new roots. Treat the stem as a cutting until it is well rooted." Try it. It works!

The leaves of the cultivar 'Forest Green' are plain green with no mottling. Burrell reports that this cultivar is easier to propagate than the species.

5. Foam Flower *(Tiarella cordifolia)*

The delicate white flower spikes of Foam Flower look almost ethereal in a woodland garden. Tiny, airy, star-shaped flowers with bright yellow stamens appear in late spring. These long-lived beauties bloom on a 6- to 10-inch stalk above dainty maple-like leaves. Foam Flower colonizes quickly, forming dense mats, and performs well as a ground cover or as an edging along a woodland path. Mass this little charmer at the base of trees or plant as a specimen. Another native species, *Tiarella wherryi*, forms clumps rather than running and is easily divided. There are several cultivars of Foam Flower available, including the handsome 'Running Tapestry', with dark maroon veins in the leaves.

PLANTING REQUIREMENTS: Plant in moist soil that is high in organic matter. Foam Flower demands consistent moisture; mulch well and water during periods of drought.

PROPAGATION: Lift mature clumps in early spring or fall and gently separate the crowns. Dividing a plant every three years can yield 6–8 divisions. Plant 12 inches apart in moist, humus-rich soil in partial or full shade.

Foam Flower grows from a crown with fibrous roots that sends out strawberry-like runners in spring. These runners develop roots and spread quickly to form colonies of dense mats. The "babies" can be separated and transplanted as soon as they have new leaves.

Tan capsules hold the minute shiny black seeds that ripen about four weeks after the flowers finish blooming. Plant freshly ripened seed immediately. Sow in a seed flat or pot or sprinkle near the mother plant in spring. Well-rooted specimens are available in most local nurseries.

6. Partridge Berry *(Mitchella repens)*

Plant catalogs describe Partridge Berry as "classy," "aristocratic," and "elegant." It is all of the above and more. This small slow-growing evergreen vine has tiny fragrant white flowers that grow in pairs, shiny oval leaves with interesting white center veins, and bright scarlet-red berries that persist into early winter. It creeps along the ground, forming broad matted clumps. Plant it in acidic soil under a Pin Oak tree, at the base of a rock, or by a fallen log. It fills blank spaces in woodland areas inhabited by spring ephemerals, and makes a nice ground cover under evergreens.

PLANTING REQUIREMENTS: Plant in partial to full shade. Space plants 8–12 inches apart in acid soil that is rich in humus and consistently moist. Partridge Berry will not thrive in alkaline soil.

PROPAGATION: Roots will develop along any nodes that lie on the ground, and these sections can be removed and transplanted. Clean the flesh from freshly ripened seeds and plant outdoors in autumn. Divide established plants in spring or root long stem cuttings in sand and perlite in early summer.

PLANTLORE: Pregnant Native American women drank a decoction brewed from the berries for two or three weeks prior to delivery and during labor. In the early 1850s, a treatise entitled *Botanical Physician* claimed this practice "rendered that generally dreaded event remarkably safe and easy with them."

Fossil remains in rocks and coal record their past
and indicate their vastness and grandeur.
—*F. Gordon Foster, 1984*

8.

Plant Feathery

Fronds

Using Ferns

Leatherwood Fern

Rattlesnake Fern *(Botrychium virginianum)*
fascinates my eight-year-old grandson.
After the thick naked single stem coils up
out of the ground, coarse ferny foliage
opens at the top. Jonathan enjoys reading
about dinosaurs and loves to speculate
about which dinosaurs might have nibbled
this prehistoric-looking plant. He is also
intrigued by the common name. He spots
these unusual ferns in the woods behind
his house and has successfully transplanted
several closer to the paths so that he can
study them. He has learned that this
unique fern needs good ventilation or it
may rot off at soil level.

Ferns bring a quiet, cool beauty to any
shady garden or woodland. Some ferns
have elegant, graceful fronds and can be
used as regal specimens near a large rock
or along a path. Others can quickly cover
a hillside, creating a soft feathery texture.
Before you select a fern for a particular
location, determine what function it is to
fulfill and choose accordingly. Ferns make
exquisite focal points, provide a background in varying shades of green for
shorter plants, contrast with coarse-

foliaged plants, and can even be used as a ground cover. Most ferns are not aggressive, but the key is whether the plant forms a crown or spreads by underground rhizomes.

What Kind of Culture Do Ferns Require?

Consistent, adequate moisture is probably the single most important growing requirement for ferns. If they get too dry, they will become ragged-looking and topple over. If drought continues too long, they will actually go dormant. Ferns prefer a shady environment, although some can tolerate full sun if there is enough moisture. The leaves will be a deeper green in a shady location.

Find out in what kind of environment a particular fern normally grows, and try to duplicate those conditions as closely as possible. For most ferns, the planting bed should be thoroughly prepared with compost and sphagnum peat moss to create a humus-rich soil that will retain moisture.

Let the leaves remain on the fernbed rather than trying to be a "neat-freak." Raking is particularly harmful for fern patches, especially in the spring when the new little crosiers are emerging. Crosiers are the small buds found at ground level that uncoil into fiddleheads, and these can be severely damaged by raking, so in the fall it is better to crumble the dried leaves over the fern bed and remove the excess leaves by hand. The crumbled leaves will provide nutrients for the ferns. Additional fertilizing is unnecessary, and can actually be harmful.

Once your ferns are planted in a shady, well-prepared bed, aside from watering during dry spells they need little care. Just enjoy their airy gracefulness as they create a cool haven in the shade.

When Can Ferns Be Moved?

I have the most success moving and dividing ferns in early fall. They go into their winter slumber and awaken in spring as if nothing had happened. Early spring seems to be the second best time to move them. However, there will likely be times when an unexpected opportunity to rescue ferns and other native plants from a construction site occurs. When the bulldozers are in full gear, you cannot wait for the best transplanting season. There will also be times when you simply feel you need to rearrange a garden, or relocate the occasional fern that has escaped to a path. Ferns can survive even if you move them in the summer as long as the soil is well prepared, but you must be diligent about providing adequate and consistent moisture.

How Can I Transport Rescued Ferns without Ruining Them?

Use plastic zipper-lock bags for small ferns, with a little water in the bottom to keep the roots moist. In his scholarly book *Ferns to Know and Grow*, F. Gordon Foster recommends protecting medium and large ferns by placing the entire plant, leaves and rhizomes, in several thicknesses of newspaper and rolling it all into a cylinder. Place several cylinders in a box or basket, sprinkle lightly with water, and transport in the coolest place in the car. He reports, "Using this method, I have carried ferns over 300 miles in July without a wilted or broken leaf."

What Ferns Are Good Specimen Plants?

Shield ferns are handsome in a woodland area, near a large boulder, or massed near a shady pond. Charles Deam refers to Marginal Shield Fern (*Dryopteris marginalis*) as Leather Woodfern. In some catalogs it is listed as Leatherwood Fern. It forms an evergreen clump that gets larger with age but does not spread. I have a group of three planted at the base of a large tree in full shade.

Intermediate Shield Fern (*Dryopteris intermedia*) is a dependable, sturdy fern for a moist woodland area or shady perennial garden. Spinulose Shield Fern (*D. spinulosa*) grows from a crown-forming rhizome. The leaves of the two latter ferns are harvested commercially in New England and purchased by florists across the United States. Deam calls *D. spinulosa* "one of our commonest and most attractive ferns."

The genus *Osmunda* includes Cinnamon Fern, Interrupted Fern, and Royal Fern. Royal Fern (*Osmunda regalis*) doesn't resemble most ferns. Its small oblong leaves look more like locust tree leaflets than like a typical fern. It grows as a clump, getting wider and wider with age. This coarse-leafed plant is handsome planted in drifts. Royal Fern will tolerate a variety of light conditions, although it prefers high open shade. It can become a 4- to 6-foot tropical-looking giant in acidic, very wet soil, but in my woodland garden it remains 2 to 3 feet tall and hasn't moved from its original planting site. Royal Fern is also known as Flowering Fern because the tips of the fertile fronds are reminiscent of clusters of flowers.

The crosiers of Cinnamon Fern and Interrupted Fern are similar and often difficult to distinguish before they unfurl into fiddleheads. Interrupted Fern *(Osmunda claytoniana)* gets its common name from the "interruptions" created when the fertile leaves *(pinnae)* develop in the middle of the frond and shrivel as the spores mature. Both of these ferns are handsome in a woodland area, interspersed with wildflowers, or planted as a backdrop for shade-loving annuals and perennials.

What Ferns Can Be Used as a Ground Cover?

I have a large patch of Ostrich Ferns in the center of the wooded area in my front yard. When these feathery ferns are planted about 3 feet apart, each fern forms a handsome clump. Ostrich Ferns spread aggressively, but are easily controlled. Whenever my fern patch gets too crowded, I share the extras with some friends who have a deep, damp ravine running along the edge of their property. Soil conditions in the ravine must be perfect for these ferns, because they have filled the area, creating an ethereal, tropical-looking wonderland below.

If the site is dry and partly shaded, Hayscented Fern *(Dennstaedtia punctilobula)* will cover the entire area. It has a soft, fine texture, and a hillside covered with this fern will glow with a soft golden-brown light in the fall. Plant it in large naturalized drifts, but don't underestimate its ability to exclude other species. Hayscented Fern takes its name from its scent and prefers a little shade, but will tolerate full sun if the site has some moisture. Ferns that spread by underground rhizomes, like Ostrich or Hayscented, are easy to divide. Simply lift out the new fern and cut through the "umbilical cord," separating the baby from the mother, and plant it in its new location.

Sensitive Fern *(Onoclea sensibilis)*, a fern that will quickly fill in a moist planting area, acquired its common name because its sensitivity to low temperatures will send it into dormancy. This unusual fern has broad, flat, cut leaves that look more like the leaves of a flowering plant than a fern. I have a small planting of it and have never had any problems with insect damage, but sometimes chewing insects can make it look ragged and unsightly. Consider locating this coarsely textured fern farther off in your landscape where leaf damage will be less noticeable. Sensitive Fern spreads aggressively by rhizomes, so plant this interesting fellow where it has room to spread rather than in a small, contained area. I enjoy collecting the dried fertile fronds, which look like "beads on a stick," to add to my dried fall floral arrangements.

New York Fern *(Thelypteris noveboracensis)* is another vigorous, aggressive ground cover. This medium-sized fern does its job of covering the ground all too well, and excludes most other species once established. Either give this beautiful fern an unrestrained area to spread at will, or plant it near a barrier, like the driveway!

Are There Any Small Ferns?

Two tiny spleenworts are perfect in a rock garden or tucked into a pocket of moist woodland soil in the crevice of a limestone wall. Ebony Spleenwort *(Asplenium platyneuron)* is like a miniature Christmas Fern. Maidenhair Spleenwort *(A. trichomanes)* resembles a tiny fan-shaped Maidenhair Fern with rounded leaves and fine, wiry, dark-colored stems. In nature, both spleenworts grow on limestone edges in damp, shady environments in humus-rich, well-drained soil.

Walking Fern *(Camptosorus rhizophyllus)* does just that. Its long tapering leaf tips reach out to touch soil and form a new plant, so that it literally "walks" along a limestone wall or cliff. It is effective in a rock garden. This small fern likes well-drained, neutral soil and will rot if conditions are too wet. With a name like *Camptosorus*, my grandson is certain that this is a prehistoric fern.

*   *   *

1. Christmas Fern *(Polystichum acrostichoides)*

Stiff leathery dark green fern fronds stand as sentinels throughout the season, only lying down to rest in late winter. Then, before most other buds open in early spring, the tightly coiled new crosiers of Christmas Fern begin to stir beneath their blanket of fallen leaves. They rise unsteadily and curve backward at first, but soon stand at attention.

This handsome evergreen fern is very easy to grow. It is usually 12–30 inches tall and equally as wide. It is an effective focal point at the base of a tree or large rock. Mass it as a ground cover on a shaded hillside or plant it near a woodland stream.

PLANTING REQUIREMENTS: Plant 12–18 inches apart in well-drained, humus-rich, neutral to acid soil in partial to full shade. Christmas Fern requires consistent moisture in sunnier sites but can tolerate dry soil in full shade.

PROPAGATION: Divide mature clumps when dormant in early spring or late fall. Dig the entire clump and gently separate the crowns, using a sharp knife only when necessary. Christmas Fern will tolerate transplanting any time as long as the soil is kept moist. It is readily available in the nursery trade.

2. Maidenhair Fern *(Adiantum pedatum)*

Maidenhair Fern is dainty and delicate, and brings a subtle beauty to a woodland garden. As the soil begins to warm in early spring, the dark-colored crosiers silently and mysteriously uncurl, sending up extremely thin, fragile-looking black stems, known as stipes in the fern world. A delicate fan of silky light green leaflets is held horizontally on the thin stipe. This deciduous fern is generally 18–30 inches tall. As the season progresses, the fronds turn a beautiful dark blue-green and create an airy mass above the ground. Its slowly creeping rhizome resembles fine black wire twisted and tangled together.

PLANTING REQUIREMENTS: Plant in loose, fertile, well-drained soil amended generously with compost to create a rich woodland loam. Maidenhair fern needs consistent moisture. It thrives in partial to full shade. Display this beautiful plant as a drift along a woodland path. A large specimen can be spectacular next to a boulder, or plant a group of these lovely ferns with wildflowers.

PROPAGATION: Divide mature overcrowded clumps. Lift the entire clump and cut the fine brittle rhizome into sections, leaving several fronds and eyes on each section.

3. Goldie's Fern *(Dryopteris goldiana)*

Some gardeners love huge plants—"the bigger the better." Goldie's Fern is a sturdy, rugged fern that will please these gardeners. Also known as Giant Wood Fern, it makes a bold statement wherever it is planted. The shaggy-looking crosiers are covered with brown and white scales. It grows 3–4 feet tall and 15–24 inches wide in a stiff upright form. This massive fern makes a strong vertical accent and is impressive as a specimen near a huge boulder. Goldie's Fern has handsome

black stipes similar to those of Maidenhair Fern, but these become pale green near the top of the frond. Plant in groups of three, combine with contrasting wildflowers, or use as a background planting. Goldie's Fern gives added color in autumn when it turns pale yellow. In appearance and growing requirements it somewhat resembles Evergreen Southern Shield Fern (*D. ludoviciana*), which grows in Zones 6–10.

PLANTING REQUIREMENTS: This deciduous fern can be difficult to transplant. It requires consistently moist humus-rich soil in shade to partial shade. Plant 3–5 feet apart and mulch well. Provide extra moisture during drought to keep it from going dormant too early.

PROPAGATION: Divide when dormant in late spring or early fall, or purchase plants. Each fern grows from a hefty rhizome and a raised crown.

4. Lady Fern (*Athyrium filix-femina*)

Soft texture, deeply cut green fronds, and dark brown scaly crosiers clearly identify the Lady Fern. It continues to send up new fronds throughout most of the summer. This beautiful arching fern spreads by a slowly creeping rhizome, is easy to grow, and is not invasive. It grows 18–36 inches tall and looks at home in a woodland garden. It is especially effective at the edge of a pond or along a small stream.

PLANTING REQUIREMENTS: Consistent moisture is probably the most important planting requirement. Plant in partial to full shade in moist or wet well-drained soil. Mulch well.

Lady Ferns can become tattered and tired looking if the soil dries out and may even go dormant. Since new crosiers appear all summer long, just cut off the raggedy fronds, but then try to be more diligent about providing extra moisture during drought. Or better yet, amend the soil more thoroughly with leaf humus, sphagnum peat, and rich compost to help it retain moisture on its own.

PROPAGATION: Divide large clumps when dormant in early spring or fall, or purchase specimens from a nursery.

5. Ostrich Fern *(Matteuccia struthiopteris)*

Beautiful drifts of feathery green plumage characterize a colony of Ostrich Ferns. They provide a cool accent in a woodland garden and quickly cover large areas in a shady, moist environment. Choose a spot where this lovely fern has freedom to roam, because that is its nature. Wild-edibles aficionados tell me that young fiddleheads are a tasty vegetable, similar to asparagus.

Ostrich Ferns grow 3–5 feet tall and can become as tall as 6 feet with good growing conditions. The fronds are deeply tapered at the base and wider at the top. This fern has separate fertile and sterile fronds, and the crosiers appear later than those of many other ferns. The upright fertile fronds turn dark brown in late fall and provide good winter interest. Flower arrangers often collect the stiff, cinnamon-colored fertile fronds late in the season to tuck into fall bouquets.The creeping rhizome sends out aggressive runners, and a new crown can pop up anywhere in the planting area.

PLANTING REQUIREMENTS: Plant in very moist, humus-rich soil in partial to full shade. These ferns can tolerate full sun if the soil is consistently wet. They are excellent indicators of moisture in the soil. They become ugly and unkempt, the stems break and fall to the ground, and the fern may go dormant if conditions are too dry. However, this native can remain lush and beautiful until autumn if soil and moisture conditions are properly maintained.

PROPAGATION: Lift and transplant crowns that have spread beyond the colony in early spring or late fall. Divide large established clumps in fall.

6. Cinnamon Fern *(Osmunda cinnamomea)*

The tightly coiled crosiers of Cinnamon Fern are covered with light woolly hairs in early spring and unfurl quickly as the earth warms. Often the fertile fronds emerge first. These cinnamon-colored plumes give this fern its common name. Then the graceful, arching sterile fronds unfurl. These are normally 3–4 feet tall and appear in various shades of green. This tall, vase-shaped fern can reach a height of 5 feet in an extremely moist environment. The fronds turn golden-brown in autumn.

Ostrich Fern is often mistaken for Cinnamon Fern because of its upright persistent dark-brown fertile fronds. However, after the chestnut colored plumes of Cinnamon Fern mature and release the spores, they collapse to the ground. These withered fronds remain during the growing season and help identify this fern.

PLANTING REQUIREMENTS: Cinnamon Fern requires wet, acid, loamy soil that is rich in humus and organic material. It does not tolerate drought. Drifts or colonies of Cinnamon Fern grow well on a stream bank or near a small pond. It thrives in very wet areas. Use this tall, stately fern as a backdrop for blooming woodland plants like Wild Geranium or Celandine Poppy. These long-lived plants are slow to become established. They are not invasive and actually spread quite slowly. Space 3–5 feet apart to give them plenty of room to "show off."

PROPAGATION: Heavy rhizomes form clumps that become very large. Cut the thick rhizome with a sharp knife to divide established plants late in the fall after they go dormant.

9.
Dig
into History

Creating Prairies and Meadows

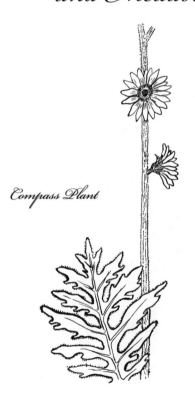

Compass Plant

The word prairie is derived from the French, and signifies meadow. In America it means grass-land naturally free from timber.

—*Patrick Shirreff, farmer, 1835*

Before the settlers arrived, the Great North American Prairie provided game, forage, a home, and food for the native American Indians, as well as a habitat for a wide variety of plant and animal species. Pioneers compared these prairies, which stretched from western Indiana across the Great Plains to the edge of the Rocky Mountains, to the sea. In 1839, Captain Frederick Marryat wrote, "Look round in every quarter of the compass, and there you are as if on the ocean—not a landmark, not a vestige of any thing human but yourself." Early travelers wrote of grass so tall and so vast that a man on horseback, unable to see above it, would lose his way; but if he could ride toward a tall yellow flower rising above the grass, he could look at its leaves, which pointed north and south, and regain his sense of direction. And so our native Compass Plant got its common name.

Early settlers of the Lower Midwest wrote glowingly of beautiful flowering meadows, and of prairies filled with a riot of color. Near Story City, Iowa, Norwegian immigrant Peder Gustav Tjernagel recorded, "That spring the wind flowers came very early, those wonderful little elf-like beings of the wild prairies, just about as delicate as nothing at all." Fredrika Bremer traveled across Illinois in mid-September of 1853, and sent glowing reports to her sister in Sweden of glorious days with bright blue skies, "the sun of purest gold," and calm air that was full of vitality. "Prairies! A sight which I shall never forget—far, far out into the infinite, as far as the eye could discern, an ocean-like extent, the waves of which were sunflowers, asters, and gentians."

Since the arrival of the settlers, the sod of the prairies has been broken, and, instead of a historic prairie, we have farms, subdivisions, roads, towns, and cities. A survey in Tippecanoe County, Indiana, in 1828 recorded over 300,000 acres of prairie. Today only one acre of that original prairie is preserved—in the Granville Cemetery, in what was known as the Wea Plains. One of the few remaining prairie remnants in Iowa is located in the Rochester Cemetery near West Branch.

The popularity of prairie and meadow gardens has increased in recent years as people become more aware of the advantages of this type of landscaping. After an article on this subject appeared in an issue of *Outdoor Indiana*, I received a flood of inquiries in my capacity as president of the Indiana Native Plant and Wildflower Society (INPAWS), most of which said in effect, "Please send me everything you know about planting a prairie/meadow." I sent out many responses to this general question, about which entire books have been written. "How-to" directions for meadow and prairie gardening are found in gardening magazines, newspaper articles, native plant catalogs, current books, and on the Internet.

As Captain Marryat traveled through the Illinois prairie in 1839, he wrote in his diary, "Instead of sky and water, it is one vast field, bounded only by the horizon, its surface gently undulating like the waves of the ocean; and as the wind (which always blows fresh on the prairies) bows down the heads of the high grass, it gives you the idea of a running swell." He described a multicolored landscape with a profusion of succulent strawberries, and colorful new flowers appearing every three or four weeks, "which die away and are succeeded by others equally beautiful." It is no wonder that modern gardeners yearn to recreate these beautiful word pictures, even if only in a small way.

Are There Different Kinds of Prairies?

The tall-grass prairie originated at the western edge of Indiana and covered the land to Fort Dodge, Kansas. This type of prairie is characterized by rich, moist soil, and plants that grow over waist-high. Roots of tall-grass plants could reach depths of over 20 feet into the earth.

The short-grass prairie in the western part of the Great Plains continued beyond Fort Dodge and was composed of shorter grasses and forbs. The ground was drier and less fertile than the soil of the tall-grass prairie. Roots of short-grass prairie plants seldom delved deeper than 3 feet.

Hill prairies are found on bluffs, ridges, hills, and steep slopes. Plants on hill prairies can tolerate dry, infertile, and often inhospitable conditions. Savannas are dotted with trees, primarily oak species, and boast a prolific ground covering of wildflowers. In addition, there are dry, moist (mesic), or wet prairies, as well as moist and wet meadows.

I Have Heard of a Sand Prairie. What Is It?

My friend has a large kennel for his two hunting dogs located next to the alley behind his home. He has beautified and screened this seemingly hostile area with a variety of brightly colored prairie flowers that flourish in the gravel next to the fence with no maintenance except an annual burning. Bright yellow Partridge Pea *(Cassia fasciculata)* self-sows readily along the edge below Gray-headed and Purple Coneflower, Butterfly Weed, and Foxglove Beardtongue. Lupine *(Lupinus perennis)* has lovely blue flowers and inflated seedpods that persist throughout the growing season. Rough Blazing Star *(Liatris aspera)* and Wild Bergamot *(Monarda fistulosa)* bloom gaily in the heat of the summer. In the fall, Stiff Goldenrod *(Solidago rigida)* and Smooth Aster *(Aster laevis)*, with sky-blue flowers, are a handsome contrast to Side Oats Grama *(Bouteloua curtipendula)*, with its unique bright reddish-orange stamens. What an improvement over the rest of the alley's combination of weeds and trash cans!

A similar planting environment, found naturally in northern parts of the Midwest, is called a sand prairie. These are scattered sections of the country where there are large natural sand deposits. Because sandy soil drains so rapidly, nutrients are quickly leached out. These unique prairies can be wet or dry.

A small sand prairie is relatively easy to establish and maintain in a sunny area. After removing existing vegetation from the proposed planting site, cover it with 12–18 inches of sand and gravel mix. Plants that grow on this type of "soil" generally do not get as tall as when planted in the existing soils of the Lower Midwest. Select shorter species that do not have extensive root systems, because deeply rooted plants may become confused when they grow through the sand and hit the existing subsoil!

Little Bluestem, Pasque Flower, Prairie Smoke *(Geum triflorum)*, Blue-eyed Grass *(Sisyrinchium albidum)*, Coneflowers *(Echinacea spp.)*, Lead Plant *(Amorpha canescens)*, Black-eyed Susan *(Rudbeckia hirta)*, Showy Goldenrod *(Solidago speciosa)*, Lance-leaved Coreopsis, Penstemon species, and a host of other native plants can make your sand prairie colorful from early spring through October. An interesting plant for a sandy spot is Prickly Pear *(Opuntia humifusa)*, a cactus native to the Lower Midwest, with large yellow flowers in the spring and reddish fruits that persist throughout the growing season. Be advised that this cactus can quickly spread and fill a space. It also has fearsome spines, so wear heavy gloves when transplanting.

A sand prairie might be a viable gardening option to use initially on those impossible construction sites left with a thin layer of topsoil over compacted subsoil. Dump about a cubic yard of pit-run sand and gravel mix somewhere at the edge of the property and plant some of the species mentioned above to brighten the area until there is time to amend the soil.

How Does a Prairie Differ from a Meadow?

Even in our early history there was confusion over the two terms. In 1835, Patrick Shirreff observed, "Prairies of a few yards' extent are found in the midst of dense and extensive forests, and rows of trees jutting miles into the open country, without visible agency to account for their preservation," and he questioned how these occurred. Other early diarists refer to these as meadows.

Historically, prairies were much larger than meadows. Both are composed of a mixture of grasses and forbs with showy flowers, but in nature, a prairie typically has a higher percentage of grasses, while a moist meadow may have more forbs. Prairie grasses and forbs are usually taller and more robust than meadow plants, although there are exceptions, and many plants will grow happily in either situation. Both meadows and prairies need full sun; both can be maintained by mowing or burning in the spring.

In this book, meadows and prairies are treated together, since initial site preparation requirements are the same. Soil, moisture, light, maintenance requirements, and plant selections frequently overlap, and either will provide similar benefits in the landscape. Since there are so many similarities and exceptions to the rule, unless the object is to recreate or restore a historical area, the plant selection and garden design are up to the homeowner.

Think about the effect you want to create in your landscape. Are you ready for a full-scale meadow or prairie, or do you just want a representative border of prairie plants? Do you want a sampler garden, or a large mass of one variety? What color combinations do you like? Do you want grasses, and if so, how tall should they be?

Many natives can live for a quarter of a century or more, so study their habits and cultural requirements before you plant. Flowering plants bloom prolifically in full sun, and most do best in the home garden in a mixture of topsoil and humus with some sand or grit for drainage. However, extremely tall species typically found on dry prairie sites prefer soil without much humus, and may develop weak stems and need staking when grown in better soil. Plants that bloom later in the season are generally taller than spring-flowering plants and may also need staking unless you incorporate grasses to help support them. Some species multiply quickly and can crowd out less aggressive plants, and may need to be confined in a bottomless 5-gallon bucket, or be planted as a monoculture. Deeply rooted species are excellent for erosion control, but once established may not transplant easily.

The most important information I can impart is that neither a prairie nor a meadow is established as easily as a typical perennial border filled with potted plants from the nursery. A "Meadow-in-a-Can" will not give you an instant, weed-free, multiflowered meadow, regardless of the claims. Initial site preparation and establishment can easily stretch over three to five years, so this is not a project for the fainthearted or the impatient. As Carl Linnaeus wrote in 1750, "Nature does not proceed by leaps." However, once this unique ecosystem is in place, it will require very little maintenance other than annual mowing or burning.

Consider starting small, and then if and when you decide to "go for the gold," if you are patient, determined, and persistent, you will be rewarded with a living, blooming example of our heritage, and a relaxing place through which to stroll and listen to the song of birds and the hum of bees on a warm summer's day. As Fredrika Bremer wrote in 1853, "What solitude—nothing except heaven and the flower-strewn earth." It is worth the time and effort. Just don't forget the patience!

But What if I Don't Have Much Patience?

If you need faster results, or don't want to work that hard at the beginning, there are alternatives. Design a small sampler prairie or meadow garden, or incorporate native plants into an existing perennial border, just as you would add any other perennial.

A huge Rattlesnake Master can be a focal point near the edge of a sunny path. A July 1998 *Science* magazine report on prehistoric footwear describes articles found in the Arnold Research Cave, located in the Missouri River bluffs of southeastern Callaway County, Missouri. Sandals and slip-ons constituted the major types of shoes found, and four specimens held padding made from Rattlesnake Master fibers. Share the fascinating history of this uniquely flowered yucca-like plant with your friends as they meander on the paths.

Add a specimen clump of grass with unusual seed heads, like Side Oats Grama, whose purple-tinted spikelets wave from one side of the stem and become golden in the fall, or Northern Sea Oats with its flat oat-like inflorescences. Gaily blooming perennials such as Liatris, Coreopsis, and Black-eyed Susan can create a colorful swath to draw the eye to a grouping of Big and Little Bluestem at the opposite end of the border. A flowering cluster resembling an upside-down turkey foot waves from the top of the nearly 6-foot, blue-green stems of Big Bluestem. Little Bluestem stands at attention around the base of the big grass. In the fall, Little Bluestem's narrow, upright bluish leaves turn increasingly more fiery red-orange as fall progresses, to contrast with the reddish-brown color of Big Bluestem. Include some native perennial Hardy Ageratum or Mistflower *(Eupatorium coelestinum)* in your border. Its bright blue-purple flowers seem almost electric against the warm tones of the grasses. Mistflower can be aggressive, but can be contained in a large bottomless pot sunk into the ground.

Pale Purple Coneflower's *(Echinacea pallida)* foliage is similar to our common native perennial, Purple Coneflower, but since the two plants bloom a few weeks apart, a low-maintenance, longer-lasting flowering mass can be created by planting them alternately in a zigzag pattern. For a calm look, incorporate some pastel colored flowering natives such as pink Nodding Onion at the front and white Wild Quinine *(Parthenium integrifolium)* at the back of the bed, or plant bright orange Butterfly Weed in front of the coneflowers for vivid color effect.

In the only sunny spot in our back yard, I put in a small, oval prairie garden. It is less than 10 feet in diameter, and because I wanted to use some of the "moist prairie" species, I amended the clay soil heavily with sphagnum peat moss and compost and keep this tightly planted area well mulched with wood chips. A clump of tall, regal Indian Grass occupies the center of the oval, and clumps of Little Bluestem and Prairie Dropseed grasses are closely interspersed with red Swamp Milkweed *(Asclepias rubra)*, Royal Catchfly *(Silene regia)*, White Turtlehead *(Chelone glabra)*, Black-eyed Susan, Cardinal Flower *(Lobelia cardinalis)*, Purple Coneflower, and white Culver's Root, in addition to a few cultivars and nonnatives like 'Moonbeam' Coreopsis, annual blue lobelia, and tiny bright yellow annual Dahlberg daisies.

Butterflies flit and dance through the flowers; small birds perch unsteadily, pecking out seeds on the waving flower seed heads; bees collect pollen and nectar. In the fall, the golden and russet tones of the grasses complement the nearby golden Sugar Maples, and even in winter, the stiff grass seed stalks and bristly seed heads of the Purple Coneflower, wearing their jaunty caps of snow, look interesting outside my family room window.

My garden club was asked to design an educational garden on either side of a series of timber steps below the children's playground in an Indianapolis park. Native plants, chosen to provide a butterfly habitat, also tell a story of earlier times and include samples of many of the grasses and flowers that would have been present on the prairie. Since Indianapolis was woodland rather than prairie when the settlers arrived, the Trailing Arbutus members also planted woodland wildflowers on the shady hillside beside the north side of the garden.

The original planting site was filled with thin, scruffy grass, and a few weeds that were pulled by hand. The grass was removed with spades, the planting area was covered with a mixture of good topsoil and sphagnum peat moss, and plants were installed immediately. A few were mail-ordered from an out-of-state native plant nursery, club members and friends donated divisions from their own gardens, and the remainder were purchased from a small, local native plant nursery. The Power and Light Company delivered a big load of free wood chips to completely mulch the new garden.

The new plants were watered every other day for the first three weeks, and then watering and weeding chores were done by club volunteers on a weekly basis or as needed. The water source was located a distance from the new garden, so pulling the long hoses proved to be the hardest maintenance task that first year. The first fall, an additional unplanted area of existing grass on both sides of the top of the steps was covered with eight sheets of newspaper and a 6-inch layer of finely shredded hardwood mulch as an experiment to determine the value of removing the sod before planting. This area was not planted until the following spring, at which time the mulch had decomposed into loamy, friable soil. This method was less labor intensive than removing the sod by hand and proved equally acceptable.

The first summer, plant divisions from club members and friends produced the only blossoms, and the mulch was very noticeable. After four years, our garden was well established. Now the plants are labeled, and school children listen wide-eyed to stories about the north-south–facing leaves of the Compass Plant as they picture covered wagons trundling across the state. The director of the park happily relates, "Anytime I want to find butterflies or hummingbirds for a group of school kids, we head to this garden and are never disappointed." Garden club members learned to distinguish between a wildflower and a weed, enjoyed discovering plantlore and history, and appreciate the advantages of using native plants which haven't needed additional watering since the second year. No more dragging long hoses!

What if I Want a Large Meadow or Prairie?

First, consider the site you wish to use. Is it a portion of your lawn? A field currently used for agriculture? An old weed-filled field? A hillside subject to erosion? Unless you are attempting to restore an existing prairie or meadow, it is crucial to kill all vegetation, including the roots, before you begin to plant either seeds or plants. This process can take anywhere from a few weeks to a full year or more, depending upon the existing vegetation in the area. Regardless of which method you choose, you will still have to contend with weeds, especially the first year. Remember to be patient—beautiful flower-filled meadows and prairies are not established in a single growing season.

Lawn Sites

Choosing a site in your existing lawn assures the least labor-intensive site preparation. Probably the two easiest nonchemical methods are to remove the sod about 3 inches deep, or smother the existing grass. To remove the sod in a large area, rent a sod cutter. For smaller areas, mark the outline of the garden with spray paint or the garden hose. Cut the sod through this line, and by sliding a flat shovel under the sod, lift and remove manageable-sized pieces and compost them. Your planting area will be 3 inches lower than the surrounding grass, so determine whether you want to plant dry, medium, or moist soil plants and replace the soil accordingly. A dry prairie needs more sandy, gritty soil, a medium prairie can be amended with equal amounts of topsoil, sand, and humus to create a good garden loam, and a moist prairie or meadow will do better with more humus. Do not cultivate deeper than an additional 2–3 inches to mix the new soil mixture with the base soil, because you will bring up weed seeds.

To smother the lawn grass, mow it as short as possible and "cook" it (called solarizing) under sheets of clear or black plastic. You can also lay down pieces of plywood, or 5–8 sheets of newspaper held down securely under finely shredded mulch or additional soil. This method takes two to three months to kill all of the lawn grass, and up to a year if rhizomatous perennial grasses such as Quack Grass or Johnson Grass exist in the site. Lawn grass can be chemically killed with a nonpersistent glyphosate herbicide such as Round-up, Kleen-up, or Ranger.

Weedy Areas

In an established weed field, plan on at least one entire year to eliminate existing weeds regardless of the method you choose. If the perennial weed population is profuse, the preparation could stretch to 18 months before all existing vegetation is destroyed. You will need to eradicate existing weeds, the toughest of which are the perennial weeds, if you don't want to wage a continuing war. Annual or biennial weeds will eventually be choked out by the stronger native plants, but any weed will compete for light and moisture to the detriment of young seedlings, and for the first year or two will grow much faster and taller than the newly planted native plants. Whether you use nonchemical methods or an herbicide, it is crucial to rid the planting area of all vegetation. Thereafter, there will be no need for chemicals.

Begin by burning or mowing the existing vegetation. If the area you want to burn is close to homes, trees, or other vulnerable areas or is very large, you really need the help of an experienced professional. Contact a native plant nursery, your extension agent, or an organization like the Nature Conservancy before you attempt burning a large plot on your own. After mowing or burning, rake off the debris and securely cover the area with black plastic or some other opaque material, mulch, and wait patiently; or apply herbicide three times (spring, summer, and fall), which is probably the easier choice. Unless you are planning to cultivate the ground to a depth of 3–5 inches every two weeks for the entire growing season, it is better not to cultivate at all. Weed seeds lie underground and germinate readily when brought up to the surface. (Some organic farmers use a small propane flame thrower, such as a Primus Sievert Weed Destroyer, passing the flame over a prepared bed before planting to thermally control weed seeds. They also report that small weeds can be killed by heating them briefly, rather than actually burning them.)

Hillsides

Cultivation is not recommended at all in the preparation of erosion-prone sites. To prevent erosion, it is generally better to kill existing vegetation on a hillside with an herbicide or by smothering it with 6–8 layers of newspaper covered with straw or hay, working from the top of the hillside down. Once the site is prepared, plug in as many wildflower and grass plants as you can afford, and then sow the entire area with a mixture of wildflower, native grass seed, and oats or annual rye grass as a nurse crop until the native plants settle in.

Agricultural Sites

Try to learn what chemicals have been used on the site in the past, and how recently these were applied. For example, Atrazine can still be found in treated soil up to three years after application and is deadly to prairie plants, so you will need to let some agricultural sites lie fallow until the chemicals have broken down. During this time it may be helpful to shallowly plow the area and plant weed-free oat seed as a cover crop to help control weed growth and improve the soil.

Final Preparation

Once you have prepared your site and are ready to plant, Neil Diboll of Prairie Nursery in Westfield, Wisconsin, recommends covering the entire area with 3 inches of sand to prevent any more weed seeds from germinating. You can seed or plant plugs into this prepared bed immediately.

If you elect not to use sand, Diboll recommends thorough watering, unless the weather cooperates with a good rain. One week later, cultivate the soil an inch deep to destroy any newly germinated weed seeds and then plant immediately. Or you can allow the weeds to grow and, when they are 2–3 inches tall, weed them out by hand. If the area is too large for hand weeding, spray the unwanted new vegetation with an herbicide and cultivate 1 inch deep after 10 days, but remember that each time you cultivate, you bring up weed seeds.

Where Can I Get Native Seeds and Plants?

Many native plant nurseries sell both plants and seeds, and some sell seeds only. When you order, try to learn how thoroughly the seeds have been cleaned, if they have been tested for purity and germination, and whether the quoted price is by the bulk pound or if the company offers pure live seed (PLS). Bulk seed generally has more chaff and fill materials and less actual seed, so you get more seed for your money if you specify PLS.

"Improved" seeds for native grasses may yield an overly vigorous grass which was developed as forage for domestic animals, rather than for use in a prairie or meadow. These improved grasses can grow 1–5 feet taller than the native species and their larger size and vigor may make it difficult for wildflowers to compete.

In the Resources section of this book, there is a state-by-state listing of Lower Midwest nurseries that sell native plants, grasses, and seeds. Many of these companies have excellent step-by-step instructions in their catalogs, including amounts of seed to purchase, planting times and procedures, as well as recommended annual, biennial, and perennial native plants for success in your specific region.

Sometimes government agencies will request assistance in collecting native seed. If you volunteer to help, you will learn a lot, and you can usually take some of the collected seed home. Many native plant societies organize seed collections. Join these organizations to learn more about natives. Again, their addresses are in Resources.

You can also collect your own seed from native plants growing in the wild or ask your friends to share. Request permission before you collect seeds from the wild; do not collect seed in state or federally protected areas; don't take seeds from rare or endangered species, or from any species that is not plentiful. Don't be greedy, and be sure to leave enough for natural repopulation. My dentist told me that his child planted a packet of tomato seeds as a part of his science experiment for school, and over 100 tomato seedlings germinated! If you get this many tomato plants from a packet of seeds, you can see why it is unnecessary to collect huge amounts of native plant seed.

Mark plants from which you want to collect seeds with brightly colored yarn. Be even more precise by color-coding the yarn ties to the color of the flowers. To keep seeds from blowing away, or falling out before collection, encase the seed head in a section of panty hose with a twist tie fastened at the top and to the stem, to hold the seeds. Most prairie and meadow native plant seeds are ripe when the seed coat is hard and dark colored.

Clean the seeds, removing chaff, pods, husks, fruit, or fluff, and store in a film canister or a paper envelope in the refrigerator humidrawer until you can plant them. Many native plant seeds require cold-moist or warm-moist stratification, or both, in order to germinate. Some hard seed coats need scarification. Sow native seeds in flats in the fall, overwinter them outside, and let nature do these tasks for you.

Prairie and meadow plants tend to be much easier to propagate from seed than woodland species, and their seeds can generally be started just as you would start the seeds of any common garden perennial. Tend the seedlings carefully through the first growing season and transplant to a permanent location in the fall. If the seeds of these prairie species germinate just as you begin preparing the site, the young plants should be ready to install when the site is weed-free and ready to go.

What about Wildflower Mix Packets?

After all that intensive site preparation, it makes more sense to purchase native plant seeds from a reputable regional native seed company. Seeds gathered from plants grown in your own region come from a similar gene pool and will be more adaptable to local conditions than those grown in some other part of the country. If you are planning to use seeds, use the best seeds you can get for long-term success.

"Meadow-in-a-Can" and "Wildflower Mix" seed packets contain a high percentage of annual flowers, as well as many species native to Texas, the Southwest, and other parts of the world. These may give you good color the first year, but most of them will not persist, so you will be left with a few weedy, aggressive exotic perennials like Queen Anne's Lace and Feverfew. A typical wildflower seed packet generally includes seeds of Yarrow, Alyssum, Calendula, Bachelor Button, Wallflower, Cosmos, Sweet William, Gypsophila, Dame's Rocket, Flax, Catchfly, Mexican Hat, Black-eyed Susan, Evening Primrose, and Coreopsis. Most of these are exotic species or annuals. Only the last three are native plants, and seeds for them, packaged separately, are readily available at garden centers and grocery stores. Aliens such as Hoary Alyssum and Dame's Rocket are members of the Mustard Family, which seed heavily. Yarrow forms dense, impenetrable root masses which preclude other flowers from seeding. Calendula, Cosmos, and Wallflowers are nonnative garden annuals that are pretty the first year, and may or may not reseed. Bachelor Buttons are beautiful aliens that have escaped cultivation and are causing serious problems in native prairies and on agricultural land, where they seed prolifically. Many of the seeds found in these wildflower mixtures are weedy-looking varieties with small, insignificant flowers. Catchfly is probably Sleepy Catchfly *(Silene antirrhina)*, a nondescript native plant with ⅛" flowers. The desirable species of the genus are Royal Catchfly *(S. regia)* and Fire Pink *(S. virginica)*, neither of which is ever found in over-the-counter wildflower seed packets.

Planting Seed

Mix equal amounts of milorganite, dry sand, and vermiculite or perlite with small wildflower and native grass seeds to give more bulk, promote even distribution, and help make sowing easier. If you purchase individual native plant seeds, rather than a seed mixture, or save collected seed by color, it is possible to create drifts and masses in your meadow if you like that effect.

Mervin Wallace of Missouri Wildflowers Nursery says late fall or winter seeding is more effective than spring planting since overwintering provides the necessary firm seed-bed and accomplishes any essential stratification or scarification. Fall seeding can give plants a head start over those sown in the spring, and germination rates are higher. Seeds should be at or near the surface, but no deeper than ¼ to ½ inch deep. For extensive plantings, Wallace recommends using a no-till drill to drop flower seeds on the prepared weed-free surface. A native plant nursery or your local extension agent may be able to locate someone who has this specialized piece of farm machinery to employ for this task. A mulch that will decompose in less than a year, such as prairie hay, warm season grass hay, or oat straw, is preferred, because a long-lasting mulch encourages the survival of exotic species. Do not apply the mulch too heavily.

Spring is the optimum planting time for grasses. Wallace suggests planting grass seed in late spring using the no-till method and drilling the grass seed to a ½-inch depth. For successful germination of flower seeds planted in the spring, refrigerate the seed for at least two months to break dormancy, and then firm the soil after sowing.

He recommends Lance-leaved Coreopsis *(Coreopsis lanceolata)* as a nurse crop to "suppress weeds and bring in a blast of color the second year." Several nurseries recommend combining native plant seeds with an annual nurse crop such as oats or annual rye grass before sowing to help hold up the young seedlings and to cut down on weed growth, since only one plant can occupy one space at one time! Oats or annual rye grass will die at the end of the growing season, enriching the soil with mulch and nutrients. A nurse crop is also a good indicator of areas which need reseeding.

What Do I Do after Planting?

Water in the morning every other day for the first 4 to 6 weeks, sprinkling just long enough to keep the surface moist. If you do not use a nurse crop, once the vegetation is 6–8 inches high, mow every 3 to 4 weeks, using a string weed whacker or setting your mower as high as possible to weaken any persistent, aggressive weeds and prevent weed seed formation. Do not allow the weeds to grow taller than 12 inches. The native plant seedlings will be very small, so mowing during the first growing season should not harm them as long as you do not cut off any vegetation lower than 6 inches. Make sure the new seedlings get sufficient moisture during the first growing season, since drying out means sudden death.

Once your planting has germinated, it is generally not recommended that you pull weeds until the second year for fear of dislodging the wildflower seedlings. If you do decide to hand weed, be sure you can tell the weeds from the flowers! A sure-fire identification trick, suggested in the Prairie Moon Nursery catalog, is to cover a section with cloth, plastic, or a piece of plywood before you seed the area, and when you have finished seeding, uncover and mark the section. Since this section was never planted, everything that comes up in it is a weed (something you didn't plant). Alternatively, you can plant properly conditioned wildflower or grass seeds in a flat filled with moistened, sterile planting medium to help you familiarize yourself with what you have seeded on a grander scale. Transplant these young plants into your garden, meadow, or prairie in the fall.

Perennial prairie and meadow plants, like any other garden perennial, spend the first year producing a strong root system. Typically they will not have much growth above the ground at all the first year. This is normal; these plants have evolved to withstand dry soil, heat and drought, and need the huge root growth in order to survive and flourish. In the second year there will be a moderate amount of growth above ground and some of the plants may even bloom, but not until the third year will these natives put on a good show. Include Gray-headed Coneflower, also called Yellow Coneflower, to serve as an indicator plant; it is one of the first to grow large enough to bloom and will likely give your prairie color in the second year. However, be patient and remember that most prairie plants need at least three years to settle in and really bloom well.

Using Plants

If you can afford it and your area is not too vast, it will become established more quickly and dependably if you choose started plants. When it is time to set your new plants in their permanent location, give each one at least a square foot of space in which to develop and mature. Dig a hole twice the width of the root ball, and set the new plant on a mound at the bottom of the hole. Plant it at the same depth at which it was growing. Fill the hole with water, drain, and then replace the soil, tamping lightly. Water again, mulch to retain moisture and inhibit weed growth, and keep the new transplants moist, but not soggy, for at least 4 to 6 weeks. Protect them from the sun or try to plant when the weatherman says it will be cloudy or rainy for a while. I have had better luck with plants installed in the fall, but if you start your plants indoors under lights or order plants in the spring, your spring planting can be successful if you practice proper maintenance. Even though native plants do not usually need supplemental watering once they are established, they do need your tender loving care at first.

How Can I Use Grasses?

Grasses of all sizes, shapes, and colors have become popular as landscaping accents in recent years. Nearly every new development or commercial headquarters sports clumps of grasses that give visual interest even in the winter. Grasses, sometimes referred to as the "hair of Mother Earth," are typically deep rooted, low maintenance, and easy to grow. A majority of those currently used for landscaping are aliens, such as Maiden Grass *(Miscanthus sinensis* 'Gracillimus'), Fountain Grass *(Pennisetum alopecuroides)*, and Feather Reed Grass *(Calamagrostis acutiflora* 'Stricta'). Undeniably, these are beautiful. They grow rapidly, and most are well behaved. However, when aliens escape to the wild, the natural checks that control aggressive native species are lacking, so they can cause environmental problems. Chinese Silver Grass *(Miscanthus sinensis)* is currently spreading in several eastern states, and a few escaped aliens, such as Canary Reed Grass *(Phalaris arundinacea)* cause serious problems in wetlands, clogging waterways, disrupting habitat, and changing the ecosystem.

Native grasses have been admired since the first settlers arrived. They wave and bend in the wind just as gracefully as alien grasses, have beautiful coloration and interesting flower stalks (generally called inflorescences), and are adapted to the region. They respond well to management by fire or early spring mowing, and grow in dependable, predictable patterns. Their roots are 2 to 3 times as long as the growth above ground, and reach deep into the earth, building and binding the soil. Native grasses survive heat, drought, wind, and other extremes of nature, and any aggressive tendencies are controlled within their native environment through natural checks and balances.

Some meadow gardeners want all flowers and no grasses. As a gardener, you have the option of using native plants in any combination. However, grasses tend to fill in spaces, shade the ground, and help to keep out weeds in meadows and prairies. They reduce staking tasks by serving as a natural support for extremely tall prairie plants like Compass Plant or Cup Plant. They create a soft, cool green, rippling background to set off small and medium meadow or prairie flowers with color, texture, rhythm, and even sound, as they sough and sigh in the wind. These graceful natives will also provide food and shelter for wildlife and give fall and winter color.

The primary reason that I think native grasses are so special is because of the role they have played in our nation's history. Let me urge you to consider adding a tiny shred of this history to your yard by planting at least one clump of native grass, and to learn as much as possible about the species you choose. Because of these sod-building grasses, the major component of the Great Prairie, America is blessed with some of the richest, blackest soil in the world. Nutrient-laden, rich, black topsoil extended over 20 feet deep in some areas of the tall-grass prairie, which stretched across western Indiana, Illinois, Iowa, and west across the Great Plains. Early settlers earned the name "sod-busters" as they broke up the tightly laced soil. It took two men, guiding 6 to 8 yoke of oxen pulling a strong plow, to break through the maze of grass roots before the farmer could plow his new field in order to plant seeds for crops. These men could attest to the tremendous root systems present in native grasses.

Where erosion has not been excessive, it is still possible to determine whether a newly plowed farm field was originally woodland or prairie by observing the color of the soil. Deep, rich prairie soil is black throughout, while woodland soil will have shadings of tan, brown, black, and gray. Look for these telltale signs on the ridges of a newly plowed field the next time you are traveling through an agricultural area in the Lower Midwest.

What Maintenance Is Necessary for Prairies and Meadows?

The prairies of the Great Plains were perpetuated by regular fires that swept over them, burning trees and other woody plants and conserving the grasses and forbs, which could rejuvenate from their roots the next spring. Only scrub oaks withstood the fires, and an unidentified British diarist declared, "their stunted growth and gnarled appearance bespoke the rough raising of prairie trees, exposed to winds, fires, frosts, and snows." Prairies and meadows that are not maintained to keep out shrubs and tree seedlings succumb to natural succession and revert to forests.

Although burning is the "maintenance of choice" for well-trained employees of private, state, and national agencies who manage large prairie areas, let me warn you of possible dangers before you decide to do this yourself. A friend who was about to burn his large meadow called the local fire department to alert them in case the fire went out of control. His prairie quickly became a raging inferno, and the fire department had to come extinguish the blaze.

One calm March morning, I decided to burn my small prairie, located about 20 feet behind my house. The dried prairie grasses burned rapidly and furiously, and quickly set the dried lawn grass on fire as well, so that soon I had an unexpectedly large area in flames. Fortunately there was no wind and I had the garden hose ready, so I was able to put out the fire without incident.

Last spring, I decided to cut the prairie grasses back to 8 inches before lighting the match, and then burn only the stubble. I laid the cut grass-tops nearly 4 feet from the garden, but as the garden burned, sparks suddenly and unexplainably "jumped" over to the cut tops and set them on fire.

These rather frightening experiences taught me to be very respectful of fire. It can rage out of control in an instant. If your prairie is of any size, and you intend to maintain it by fire, it should be located no closer than 40 or 50 feet from any combustible structure. Incorporate fire breaks, read and study proper burning techniques, wear protective clothing, have an ample supply of water and a shovel ready, and obtain any required permits before you venture into the unknown. You may want to volunteer to help at a controlled burn conducted by one of our government agencies in the spring before you decide to burn your own site. Be well informed before you light that little match!

Mowing to a 3- to 4-inch height works almost as well as burning. Either should be done in early spring before new growth is 10–12 inches tall. Mowing should be done annually, while burning can be done once every two to three years after the prairie or meadow is established. In his Prairie Nursery catalog, Neil Diboll recommends rotating annual maintenance by burning or mowing only one-third to one-half of the area each year in order to protect wildlife habitat, prevent any single species from dominating, and encourage more diversity of plant material. Diboll relates, "In fall, the burned section was dominated by prairie grasses, while the unburned part exhibited fewer grasses but more asters and goldenrods."

Shall I Create Paths?

Whether or not you plan to use fire as a maintenance tool, it is wise to incorporate paths and mowed grass strips to serve as fire breaks. In addition, paths give closer access to the plants so that you can actually walk into your meadow or prairie and be enveloped by a variety of sights, smells, and sounds. Paths might twist and wind through the area to create an element of surprise as you walk around the bend. Small flowering plants or clumps of Prairie Dropseed grass can be sited near the path for easy viewing and appreciation. Tuck in some large specimens such as a Compass Plant or Prairie Dock as focal points. A mass of beautiful rosy-pink Queen of the Prairie located near your path can create a stunning picture against the rippling grasses. Plant large clumps of Switchgrass around a tight bend. Children love having their noses tickled as they explore this historical wonderland.

Getting Started

A meadow or prairie garden can be as large or as small as your time and energy allow. As you can see, this type of garden is initially very labor-intensive. However, once you have thoroughly prepared your site, installed your native plants following your landscaping design, given them tender loving care, and then continue to maintain them by means of annual mowing or biennial burning, there is little else to do in a meadow or prairie—except to stroll on your meandering paths and enjoy the rustle of the grasses, the scents of brightly colored flowers, the songs of birds, and the hum of bees on a warm summer's day. Or you may want to just lie down in the midst of the area as Fredrika Bremer did in 1853 to enjoy a little solitude with nothing to distract you "except heaven and the flower-strewn earth."

How about Using Grasses as a Monoculture?

Some homeowners in the western states have experimented with substituting native grasses such as Buffalo Grass *(Buchloe dactyloides)*, Side Oats Grama, or some of the sedges, like *Carex communis* or *C. lacustris* for turf grass with considerable success. These grasses, which can be mowed or allowed to grow to their normal height, take less water than our typical water-guzzling bluegrass lawns, no fertilizer, and little maintenance. Buffalo Grass likes a dry environment, while sedges need moisture to survive. Side Oats Grama would require mowing in a "civilized spot."

Broom Sedge *(Andropogon virginicus)*, which is really a grass, is an effective cover for wildlife and ground nesting birds and, with its reddish-brown winter coloration, makes an old field more attractive than the customary mixed perennial weeds. This relatively aggressive grass is effective in a meadow planting.

Another attractive monoculture planting for a field, along a roadside, or as drifts in a meadow is Purple Love Grass *(Eragrostis spectabilis)*. Mass plantings of it make an entire area appear reddish-purple when the grass blooms in late summer.

How Can Native Grasses Help Prevent Erosion?

Just think of the changes that were effected in our environment after the sod-busters came through, when there were no longer any grasses to bind the soil. During the period of the great dust storms in the 1930s, topsoil simply blew away. Thousands of farmers, like the Joads in Steinbeck's *Grapes of Wrath*, left their depleted, unproductive farms to emigrate westward. My mother-in-law, who grew up near Story City, Iowa, tells of dust storms so fierce during this period that the noon sky was as dark as midnight. The role played by tightly laced grass roots in controlling erosion became painfully evident at that period of our history. It may be a role we should reevaluate. If you have an erosion-prone hillside or streambank on your property, consider planting a colony of native grasses. In addition to their aesthetic attributes, plantings of these deep-rooted native grasses on hillsides, at freeway interchanges, and along streambanks could help to alleviate many present-day erosion problems.

Local officials of a small community, in an attempt to control soil erosion on the banks of a rapid stream near the center of town, plan to cut down the few trees remaining on the streambank and cover the entire site with limestone riprap, although the financial burden to the community will be tremendous. Recent studies indicate that riprap may actually *contribute* to erosion, washing away the soil as water trickles and runs under the layers of broken rock. By planting deep-rooted grasses instead, they could create a beautiful, naturalistic landscape, make a habitat for wildlife, and save the trees. Grasses would be more economical and more effective for erosion control than unsightly riprap.

Prairie Cordgrass *(Spartina pectinata)* is a rhizomatous sod-builder that grows naturally along streambanks as well as in marshes and on wet prairies. Extensive rhizomes weave and knit the soil of the bank, helping to control erosion. This grass was well known on the tall-grass prairie. Its graceful, arching, glossy green leaves turn bright golden yellow in the fall. It loves full sun and will tolerate a variety of soils. It prefers a moist environment, but once established will tolerate drought fairly well. A cultivar named 'Aureomarginata', available in the nursery trade, has yellow variegation in the center of each blade.

Sweetgrass *(Hierochloe odorata)* is another rapid-growing rhizomatous grass. It has a fascinating history of use by Native Americans, who wove its long, graceful blades into ceremonial baskets and used the scented grass as incense and perfume. Sweetgrass thrives in a moist, sunny area and can tolerate some shade.

What Are Sedges?

Even though these grass-like plants are relatively unfamiliar to most gardeners, sedges are widespread. According to Charles Deam, "Much of the fertile soils of our region today would still be barren mudflats were it not for the part played by these sedges in the conversion of the once vast boggy areas into a turf."

Sedges look like grass and are often mistaken for grass. However, it is easy to determine if the plant in question is a grass or a sedge by simply running your thumb and forefinger up and down its flowering stem, called a culm. Sedge flowering stems are sharply triangular, rather than round like grass stems, giving rise to the little saying, "Sedges have edges." The culms of sedges are not jointed, and they are solid, while grass culms are jointed and usually hollow. Historically, sedge culms have been used as roof thatch.

There are over 2,000 species of sedges, most of which belong to the genus Carex. They are commonly found in shady, moist, or wet areas, although many tolerate dry sites. These grass-like plants provide food, shelter, and habitat for wildlife; they are the larval food source for several butterflies, including the Mulberry Wing Skipper, Two-Spotted Skipper, Sedge Skipper, Appalachian Brown, Black Dash, and Mitchell's Satyr. The seeds and rootstocks were a food source for Native Americans, trappers, and settlers.

Sedges can be used as specimen plantings and ground covers, to restore a wetland, or for erosion control. Some are attractive planted as specimen clumps near rocks, around pools, or tucked into rock gardens; others make nice accents in the woodland garden. A single species can be planted alone, or several can be combined by using a mass of each variety. Use them under trees, as part of a meadow, or to cover a large area. Species like Fox Sedge, Crested Sedge, and Lake Sedge are useful in marshy or wet areas, sedge meadows, and wetland restorations. As mentioned earlier, some sedges can even be substituted for our traditional lawn grass.

As is true of most plants, those sedges with creeping or running rhizomatous roots tend to spread more than clumping species. The former are obviously more invasive, so they are not recommended except for erosion control or to cover a large area. Clump-forming varieties stay where you put them, increasing only in girth. Six sedges suggested for home gardens are listed at the end of this chapter.

Shining Bur Sedge *(Carex intumescens)* is found primarily in acidic wet woods, mesic swamps, or moist prairies. It also grows in depressions in beech-maple forests, or in flat or low woods. It is commonly found with Red Maple, Spicebush, Cinnamon Fern, Royal Fern, Partridgeberry, and Red Oak. This unique, clumping sedge grows 1 to 2½ feet tall. Its striking, ball-like seed heads, which can be up to 1 inch wide, have 5–10 inflated spikes radiating out in all directions. Where soil and moisture conditions are correct, a clump of this little sedge makes a nice accent in the garden.

Pennsylvania Sedge *(Carex pennsylvanica)* is a great ground cover under trees. Since it does particularly well under oaks, it has also been dubbed Common Oak Sedge. This stoloniferous, narrow-leafed sedge flowers in early spring. It is usually found in drier, well-drained environments, where it creates extensive colonies.

Fibrous-rooted Sedge *(C. communis)*, often called Common Beech Sedge, has been recommended as a substitute for lawn grass because of its finely textured, light green foliage. It can be used effectively as a ground cover or a massed edging. This adaptable little sedge only grows 4–12 inches high, and will thrive in moderately shaded sites or in full sun, in dry, open wooded sites or in medium-moist (mesic) environments. It is often found growing naturally with Sugar and Red Maples, beeches, and Red Oaks.

Spence Restoration Nursery highly recommends Fox Sedge *(C. vulpinoidea)* as a plant that "should be included in all sedge meadow installations" because of its adaptable nature. It grows well in full sun or partial shade, tolerating wet, moist, and even dry conditions. This tall, broad-leaved, deep-green sedge is found in swampy places, roadside ditches, marshes, swamps, low open woods, and ravines.

Crested Sedge *(C. cristatella)*, another good choice for sedge meadows, likes full sun or partial shade. It grows 2–3 feet tall; erect flower stalks rise above fine, bright green foliage. It is prevalent in low open woods, swamps, marshes, and roadside ditches, meadows and thickets, and on flood plains and banks of streams.

The 3- to 5-foot-tall, bluish-green foliage of Lake Sedge *(C. lacustris)* is attractive when planted as a mass near a pond, a stream, or a lake. Also known as Pond Sedge, this stoloniferous plant effectively controls erosion. In a home garden, it should be contained due to its aggressive nature. Its medium-textured foliage can be handsome near a driveway or pavement, and because of its large size, it can be used as a hedge or border. It has been suggested as a substitute for turf grass in shaded lawns, where traditional turf grass is difficult to grow, but would need to be mowed.

Tussock Sedge *(C. stricta)* looks like a fat little mophead. It is commonly found near creeks, in marshes, and in open swamps, where it forms dense tussocks. It may be the dominant plant in moist sedge meadows, and often grows with Scouring Rush *(Equisetum spp.)*, Spotted Joe-Pye Weed *(Eupatorium maculatum)*, and Boneset *(E. perfoliatum)*. Tussock Sedge grows up to 4 feet tall in full sun or partial shade. It prefers consistently moist, rich soil. It has 1- to 2-inch finely textured, dark green leaves and grows from a horizontal, stout, scaly rhizome. This winter-hardy sedge is a good choice for a water garden, near the water's edge, or as part of a moist meadow. 'Bowles' Golden' is probably the best known cultivar, widely grown for its striking variegated golden foliage.

* * *

Six Suggested Forbs for Short-Grass Prairies/Meadows

1. Pasque Flower *(Anemone patens)*

Pasque Flower heralds the rebirth of spring with its beautiful lavender, blue, or white flowers. Only 4–6 inches tall, this finely cut, ferny plant has hairy stems and leaves to protect it from the cold of early spring. Delicately colored 1-inch sepals surround a large yellow-orange center, which later contains the feathery plume-like, wind-borne seeds. Also called Prairie Smoke or Windflower, it is native to the northern states of the Lower Midwest.

PLANTING REQUIREMENTS: Plant the crown 1 inch deep in well-drained sandy or average garden soil in full sun or high open shade. Leave 12–18 inches between plants. Pasque Flower needs moisture as it blooms, but tolerates drought and will go dormant later in the summer. It is a good choice for a sand prairie.

PROPAGATION: Divide plants in early spring, plant fresh seed immediately, or plant cold, moist stratified seed the following spring and barely cover with soil. The seedlings will bloom the third year. Pasque Flower is easy to transplant, and even tiny pieces of root will produce a new plant. Parts of the fibrous root system become fleshy, and if the top of the plant is damaged new growth will sprout.

PLANTLORE: Pasque Flower was on the official list of the U.S. Pharmacopoeia from 1882 to 1908 and was used as a diuretic, expectorant, and to induce menstruation. Native Americans used it to treat rheumatism.

2. Nodding Onion *(Allium cernuum)*

Nodding umbels of pink, lavender, or white hang from 8- to 24-inch bent flower stalks above strappy onion-like foliage to create a spot of lavender-pink in midsummer. Papery dried seeds rustle in the autumn winds to create another seasonal interest. It is possible to find Wild Onion in a variety of sizes, flower colors, and bloom times. A recent cultivar named 'Shoshone' var. album has pure white flowers above gray foliage. Some cultivars have deep magenta flowers.

PLANTING REQUIREMENTS: The onion-like bulbs do well in any average fertile garden loam with good drainage to prevent rot. Nodding Onion can be grown successfully in nearly any light exposure from full sun to deep shade, but the plants will bloom more profusely with more sunlight. It is effective when massed, planted in a rock garden, scattered through a wildflower area, or planted along the edge of a path.

PROPAGATION: Nodding Onion forms large clumps that should be divided every 2–3 years to maintain adequate bloom. Pull apart the multiple small bulbs in overgrown clumps in early spring or late fall. Plant ripe, fresh seed in fall. Space seedlings 3–5 inches apart and set the top of the bulbs 1 inch deep.

PLANTLORE: Used as food and seasoning by Native Americans and settlers.

3. Spiderwort *(Tradescantia ohiensis)*

Each three-petaled, bright blue flower generally opens in the morning and lives for only part of a day, as I learned when I tried to photograph a hillside of them in mid-afternoon. A cluster of multiple buds on each flower stalk ensures a good display for three weeks or more in late spring. The three petals can also be lavender, bright rose, or white, and some cultivars have variegated petals. Blooms on my magenta cultivar last all day. Spiderwort grows 1–2 feet tall. Plants tend to fall over in more shade and do not bloom as long as those grown in sunnier locations. The fleshy, jointed stalks will root at a node when they are in contact with soil. This versatile plant does well in naturally moist areas, along streambanks, in an open prairie setting, or on a wooded hillside.

PLANTING REQUIREMENTS: Spiderwort thrives in any average, fertile, well-drained garden soil. Bloom will be more profuse in a sunny location, but light to moderate shade is acceptable. The foliage is generally darker green and more attractive in part shade.

PROPAGATION: Plant the freshly ripened seed immediately or root the stem cuttings in sand. In 2–3 weeks new roots will form, and these seedlings can be transplanted. This plant can also be propagated by dividing the underground runners.

Plants should be divided every 2 or 3 years to maintain profuse blooming. After flowering, cut the foliage to the ground to force a second flush of growth and rebloom in the fall. Spiderwort self-sows readily and is easy to transplant.

PLANTLORE: Spiderwort was believed to be an effective treatment for spider bites. It was used as a potherb by Native Americans and settlers. Recent studies have determined that the flower color is affected by radiation, so this plant is currently being used to monitor nuclear activity near selected reactor sites.

4. Shooting Star (*Dodecatheon meadia*)

This beautiful ephemeral is also known as Prairie Pointers, Cranesbill, and Rooster Heads. The common name arises from the swept-back petals that resemble the tail of a shooting star. A rosette of basal leaves hugs the ground, and the 6- to 20-inch flower stalk rises from the center. It branches near the top and holds multiple cyclamen-like flower petals that sweep back from a pointed beak. These flowers range in color from white to varying shades of pink, deep rose, and magenta. Keep the plants well watered during flowering. Shortly after flowering, they will accept drier conditions as they begin to go dormant.

Shooting Stars abound with other wildflowers in a native prairie setting at Rochester Cemetery, near West Branch, Iowa, where one can barely take a step without treading on a plant. Caretakers report little concern with "little old ladies in tennis shoes with trowels," since visitors respect this beautiful pioneer cemetery and leave their "rescue" equipment at home, taking nothing but photographs.

PLANTING REQUIREMENTS: Plant in drifts or colonies 10 to 15 inches apart along a path or at the base of a large tree or rock where the delicate plants can easily be seen and enjoyed as they bloom in mid-spring. Shooting Star prefers moist, well-drained, humus-rich woodland loam that is neutral or slightly acidic. Spread the white fibrous roots of the coarse fragrant rootstock over a mound of soil and cover the crown with ³/₄ to 1 inch of soil. Shooting Star will tolerate full sun or light to medium shade.

PROPAGATION: The fibrous rootstock can be divided in early autumn. This plant can be propagated by seed or root cuttings, but fragile new seedlings need an extra measure of TLC in order to survive. Mulching is recommended.

5. Butterfly Weed *(Asclepias tuberosa)*

Broad, flat clusters of brilliant orange, fiery red, or occasionally bright yellow flowers draw myriads of butterflies to this spectacular prairie plant. It is 18–30 inches tall with alternate, rough, pointed, narrow leaves. The sap of this species is watery rather than milky. It is one of the best butterfly attractants for a sunny garden and is sought out by Diana and Fritillary butterflies. It is an important larval food source for Monarchs.

PLANTING REQUIREMENTS: Butterfly Weed demands full sun and does well in average soil as long as it is well drained. The long, deep taproot helps it tolerate drought and extremely dry soil. It thrives in sand prairies, but will rot in heavy or poorly drained soil. Prairie Nursery in Westfield, Wisconsin, offers a "clay buster" variety for gardens with naturally heavy, moist soil.

Several flowering stems can originate from the brittle carrot-like taproot. Once established, this plant is extremely difficult to move to another location, so plant it where you want it to grow. It is particularly effective when massed at the front or middle of a border and is enhanced by the complementary colors of nearby deep blue or purple flowering plants.

PROPAGATION: Each seed in the spindle-shaped capsule is attached to a silky plume. Propagate Butterfly Weed easily by planting this fresh, ripe seed immediately. Either plant the seed where you want it to grow or transplant it when the seedling is still very small to keep the taproot intact. Seeds will germinate in less than 5 weeks. Be sure to mulch young seedlings the first winter.

Because of the large taproot, mature clumps of Butterfly Weed can neither be moved nor divided successfully. Two-inch root cuttings can be taken from the taproot in late spring or fall, and should be planted vertically in sand.

PLANTLORE: The large white root was the only part of the plant used medicinally. It was reputed to induce sweating to break fevers, reduce flatulence, and alleviate lung problems. Early settlers brewed a tea as a popular remedy for pleurisy, which gave rise to its common name of Pleurisy Root.

6. Purple Coneflower *(Echinacea purpurea)*

Echinacea, from the Greek, means hedgehog or sea urchin, and accurately describes the rusty-orange cone in the center of the Purple Coneflower. The seeds attract small birds like goldfinches and chickadees. Purple daisy-like ray flowers that bloom nearly all summer droop or spread nearly flat from this bristly cone. This 2- to 4-foot tall perennial has rough, dark green leaves with coarsely toothed edges and a dark, thick, fibrous rootstock that seldom needs dividing. 'White Swan' and 'White Lustre' are two white cultivars available in the nursery trade.

PLANTING REQUIREMENTS: Plant in a sunny spot in average, fertile, well-drained garden soil with a neutral pH. This plant is very effective when massed. *E. pallida* has thinner ray petals of pale lavender and blooms earlier than *E. purpurea.*

PROPAGATION: Easily propagated from freshly ripened seed planted immediately or moist-cold-stratified for 3–4 months and planted in early spring. Increase your stock by taking root cuttings in early fall or late spring.

PLANTLORE: Physicians have believed in the curative powers of *Echinacea* for many years. Modern-day herbalists tout this plant as a "boost to the immune system." It has been used as a painkiller, to treat insect and snake bites, for cuts and scrapes, and for sore throats.

*   *   *

Six Suggested Forbs for Tall-Grass Prairies/Meadows

1. Foxglove Beardtongue *(Penstemon digitalis)*

Mass Foxglove Beardtongue, also called White Beardtongue, for a spectacular effect in early spring. The beautiful tubular white flowers are two-lipped and resemble snapdragons. Flower stalks can be as tall as 5 feet. The toothed, shiny leaves form a rosette at the base of the plant, and the plants spread by thin, shallow creeping roots.

There are about 10 species of Penstemon in the eastern United States, with flower colors of lavender, violet, purple, pink, blue, or white. The cultivar 'Husker Red' has reddish-purple leaves and blush pink flowers, but like many cultivars, it is not as hardy as the native plant.

PLANTING REQUIREMENTS: Foxglove Beardtongue likes full sun or light shade, wet areas and dry ones, and good drainage. It does not spread as quickly in heavy clay soil as it does in rich garden loam.

PROPAGATION: Provenance is very important for success with this plant, so try to find plants or seeds grown nearby. It may be reluctant at first, but once established, it self-sows profusely. Pick off the seed capsules before the seeds mature to control the spread if it gets too vigorous. This plant needs to be divided every 4–5 years to remain robust.

PLANTLORE: Early settlers used Penstemon to help with the chills and fever of the "ague," and packed the mashed root into a tooth cavity to ease pain. It is commonly called Beardtongue because of its hairy, modified stamen.

2. Rattlesnake Master *(Eryngium yuccifolium)*

The species name, *yuccifolium*, from the Greek, describes the strap-like, leathery, blue-green leaves that resemble those on a yucca plant. The leaves, which can be 1–3 feet long, have soft spines on the edge. Another common name is Button Snakeroot because of the unique, tightly compact flower heads. Each flower head is covered with tiny, greenish-white five-petaled flowers and pointed bracts. These rough-feeling, ½- to 1-inch globe-like buttons rise 2–5 feet above the leaves. The tiny flowers bloom in early summer, and the dried flower heads are interesting until late in the fall. Young plants will generally flower in their second year.

PLANTING REQUIREMENTS: Plant Rattlesnake Master in rich, moist, well-drained soil in full or partial sun. Once established, this plant is not fussy about moisture conditions.

PROPAGATION: Rattlesnake Master develops a thick rootstock that is difficult to transplant, so plant young, small seedlings where you want them to stay. Sow fresh seed outdoors in the fall, or provide at least 2 months of cold, moist stratification in the refrigerator before planting in spring.

PLANTLORE: The thick root was used by Native Americans and settlers to treat liver and bladder problems. Rattlesnake Master was also used as an emetic, but was of no value to anyone bitten by a rattlesnake. Some believe the plant got its name because of the sensation caused by backing into it.

3. Gayfeather *(Liatris spicata)*

Florists commonly accent floral arrangements with the bright purple spikes of Liatris. Also called Blazing Star, Spiked Gayfeather, and Dense Blazing Star, Liatris is a wonderful butterfly magnet that can grow 6 feet tall in the wild. The narrow, grass-like leaves form dense clumps. In cultivation, it is generally 2–4 feet tall, and blooms between July and September, complementing the multitude of yellow late-summer bloomers. The small, compact flowers open from the top down.

The Iowa Department of Transportation has used *L. pycnostachya* (commonly known as Prairie Blazing Star or Kansas Gayfeather) in roadside plantings.

PLANTING REQUIREMENTS: Space plants about 18 inches apart in full sun, since Liatris languishes in shady spots. This native prefers regular moist, well-drained garden soil and will be shorter in drier soil.

PROPAGATION: Cut apart the tough, woody rootstock crowns in

very early spring before the plant leafs out, or lay the entire flower stalk on the ground in the fall and lightly cover it with soil. The seeds are small ¼-inch dark gray nutlets. Seedlings will appear the following spring.

PLANTLORE: The root was used to make a strong tea to treat kidney problems and back pain, and was known as Backache Root. Early medics also recommended using the root as bitters and mixing it with gin for urinary infections.

4. Compass Plant *(Silphium laciniatum)*

Compass Plant is one of the most fascinating plants of the tall-grass prairie because of its tendency to orient its huge, deeply divided leaves north and south. Large 5- to 6-inch yellow sunflower-like flowers tower 8–10 feet high in the air to attract butterflies and other insects.

PLANTING REQUIREMENTS: Plant 3–4 feet apart in full sun in a location where the interesting leaves can be observed and enjoyed. The taproot can reach over 6 feet into the soil, so don't plan on moving or dividing it once it is mature! Compass Plant will tolerate dry or moist soil as long as it is well drained.

PROPAGATION: This plant will self-sow readily, but the seeds need cold, moist stratification to germinate. Plant seeds immediately after they ripen in the fall or store in the refrigerator 4–6 weeks for spring planting.

PLANTLORE: *Silphium* is from the ancient Greek, meaning resinous. Early Americans enjoyed the resinous sap as chewing gum.

5. Culver's Root *(Veronicastrum virginicum)*

Tall, stately spires of creamy white flowers glow above dark green whorled leaves arranged in groups of 3 to 7. These lance-shaped leaves have toothed edges and can be up to 6 inches long. This lovely plant should be massed for best effect. Growing 2–6 feet tall, Culver's Root blooms in late summer and is a wonderful perennial border plant as well as a spectacular addition to a moist prairie.

PLANTING REQUIREMENTS: Plant in rich, moist, well-drained

garden loam in full sun. This adaptable plant will also tolerate a dry site once it is established. It is thriving in the alleyway next to my friend's dog kennel.

PROPAGATION: The thick, branched rootstocks can be divided in early spring or fall. Collect ripe seeds and sow outdoors immediately in the fall, or stratify for a month or more. Culver's Root can also be propagated by cuttings.

PLANTLORE: The *New Domestic Physician* by John Gunn, M.D., published in 1857, relates that pills made from the root are "found at all the drug-stores," and when combined with Morphine or Laudanum will "cure any case of dysentery." Called Culver's Physic, the dried roots were also powdered and used as a purgative for intermittent fevers or combined with rhubarb and a little opium as a cathartic for diarrhea and dysentery.

6. Gray-headed Coneflower *(Ratibida pinnata)*

This plant is also known as Yellow Coneflower. Each flower of this 3- to 5-foot medium-tall member of the Aster Family has long, narrow, bright yellow, drooping ray flowers that look like petals with a prominent, tall, cone-shaped center that smells like anise when crushed. It gets its common name, Gray-headed Coneflower, because these centers begin as medium gray, become purplish-brown, and eventually revert to dark gray in fall. The alternate coarse, rough-feeling leaves are finely divided into several leaflets, and the crown-forming roots are thick and woody. This coneflower blooms from June to September.

PLANTING REQUIREMENTS: Gray-headed Coneflower is happiest in sunny, well-drained sites but is tolerant of many growing conditions, including full sun or light shade, dry or moist areas, rich garden loam or heavy clay soil.

PROPAGATION: Direct seeding is the preferred method of

propagation. Collect the dark ripe seed in the fall and sow outdoors immediately for spring seedlings, or stratify in the refrigerator for at least a month for spring planting. You can also increase your stock by dividing the woody, fibrous-rooted crowns with a sharp knife in early spring or fall, but it self-sows readily and division is seldom necessary. This foolproof plant generally blooms in its second year and is an excellent choice for the novice prairie gardener.

PLANTLORE: Native Americans made a tea from the flowers and leaves.

* * *

Six Suggested Grasses

1. Little Bluestem *(Schizachyrium scoparium)*

Little Bluestem, one of the most widespread grasses of the prairie, is native to all states except Washington, Oregon, California, and Nevada. This native grass has been used for hay since early settlement and has provided nutritious grazing for animals. It yields ¾ to 2 tons of forage per acre. Birds love its seeds.

The medium-textured hairy leaf blades emerge a rich bluish-green in spring. This attractive grass turns fiery red, reddish brown, orange-red, or reddish-purple in autumn, remains upright, and keeps its strikingly beautiful tones all winter. The cultivar 'Blaze' has especially nice fall coloration. Fluffy white tufted seed heads appear in August and are striking when they are covered with morning dew in the early morning light. Little Bluestem is usually no taller than 3 feet.

Mass this handsome grass as a ground cover, naturalize it as a transition area at the edge of the woods, or use it for erosion control. Plant a single clump in a mixed perennial border, or locate one in front of a large rock. Site it where you can enjoy its fall and winter color from inside the house.

PLANTING REQUIREMENTS: Plant in full sun in well-drained, average garden soil. Because of its deep roots, it is very drought tolerant once established. It can be grown in heavy soil, but disdains wet soil with poor drainage. It is a good choice for a sand prairie.

PROPAGATION: Plant from freshly ripened seed in the fall, or stratify seed in the refrigerator or outdoors for 3–4 months and plant in spring. It generally self-sows readily. Little Bluestem can also be divided, although the dense root system may be 5–8 feet deep. It is available in the nursery trade.

2. Switchgrass (*Panicum virgatum*)

Switchgrass is probably my favorite native grass because of its delicate, airy appearance. The textured 6- to 18-inch-long blue-green leaf blades, arching gracefully out from a center point, are particularly effective when sited in front of a dark wood privacy fence. The fountain-like growth habit can serve as a focal point in a small round garden, surrounded by colorful, low-growing annuals, or at the edge of a pond. In June, large panicles of seeds, standing 3–6 feet tall, create a purple haze over the grass. In the fall, the graceful foliage turns a soft orange-yellow. Switchgrass remains upright during the winter, but loses its bright yellow color and changes to a soft buff.

It is the larval food source of the Delaware Skipper butterfly. It is eaten by livestock both as green forage and as hay, and seeds can be harvested with a combine.

Several cultivars are available, including some that have red or bright orange fall coloration. 'Rotstrahlbusch' turns an intense red, 'Heavy Metal' has powdery blue summer leaves that turn bright yellow in the fall, and 'Haense Herms' is a shorter, compact, more upright cultivar that becomes reddish-orange.

PLANTING REQUIREMENTS: Plant in average, moist, well-drained garden soil. This plant will tolerate wet feet and can be valuable in erosion control along a streambank where its thick, fibrous roots will extend deep into the ground to form dense sod. It can be used to stabilize slopes and riverbanks or as a ground cover along a road.

Switchgrass is effective as a single specimen or when planted in a mass. Naturalize it at the edge of a woodland to provide cover, homes, and food for birds and wildlife.

PROPAGATION: Switchgrass self-sows and increases vigorously, so once you have it, it is not likely that you will have to agonize about getting more plants. In fact, experts recommend that it be used sparingly in a new prairie planting, as it can easily overtake and exclude other less vigorous plants.

PLANTLORE: Buffalo hunters moved out of Switchgrass areas when they butchered their kill in the field because the sharp spikelets would stick in the meat.

3. Indian Grass *(Sorghastrum nutans,* aka *Chrysopogon nutans)*

Tall, stately Indian Grass provides a background and seasonal interest for a prairie planting. The light to medium-green leaves change to golden apricot and glow in the rains of autumn. The flowers emerge as a tight rod rising 2–3 feet above the foliage. Then late in summer this tight inflorescence opens into a beautiful 4- to 12-inch-long golden-brown plume with protruding yellow anthers. Clumps remain upright in winter, providing food and shelter for birds and wildlife. It is handsome at the back of a border, as a specimen, or planted as a mass. Sod-forming Indian Grass is effective in erosion control. It can be harvested by hand-stripping the seed or with a combine. Livestock eat it as fresh forage or hay.

It has a more upright growth habit than Big Bluestem *(Andropogon gerardii),* and showier flowers. The cultivar 'Sioux Blue' has bright blue-gray summer foliage.

PLANTING REQUIREMENTS: Indian Grass has an extensive root system and thrives in rich, moist garden loam in full sun. It will tolerate drought, heat, sandy soils, and even heavy soils as long as there is good drainage.

PROPAGATION: Propagates easily with seed, root cuttings, or by cutting sections of the short scaly rhizomes.

PLANTLORE: Indian Grass was one of the major grasses of the historic prairie.

4. Prairie Dropseed *(Sporobolus heterolepis)*

This little grass makes a nice swish along the edge of a curved garden near a walkway. Its fine-textured mopheads of bright green foliage will elicit comments and questions from garden visitors. The fountain-like growth habit of Prairie Dropseed lends itself well to massing, edges, or as a clump tucked beside the path. Tiny, delicately airy seed heads appear in midsummer, when this fragrant, sweet-smelling grass takes on the smell of buttered popcorn. Ground feeding birds and small mammals enjoy the seeds. The bright green leaves change to beautiful shades of rich, warm red, orange, and yellow in fall. Like old gardeners, the little mopheads become white-headed in winter.

PLANTING REQUIREMENTS: Plant in moist, rich, well-drained garden loam in full sun. This slow-growing grass grows only about 2 feet tall, although the seed heads rise above the mound. It tolerates heat and drought.

PROPAGATION: Best propagated by seed. Plant fresh, ripe seed immediately or stratify outdoors in winter or in the refrigerator for 3–4 months and plant in spring. Prairie Dropseed does not generally self-sow. Large clumps can be divided in spring or fall.

PLANTLORE: Native Americans dried and pounded the seeds to make flour.

5. Northern Sea Oats *(Chasmanthium latifolium)*

This is one of the few grasses that thrives in shade, making it a good choice for a woodland edge. Plants mature at 3–4 feet and about half as wide. Its graceful, arching habit and oat-like seed heads make a nice accent next to a pond or stream. It is handsome when planted in a mass, naturalizes well, and can be used as a ground cover on a slope.

PLANTING REQUIREMENTS: Northern Sea Oats is an adaptable plant. It prefers light shade, but will tolerate sun if kept moist. It loves fertile, well-drained garden loam, but will also grow in poor soil. If you cut the oat-like spikelets for floral arrangements when they are green, they will dry green. Otherwise they will pass through varying shades of rusts and rich browns before becoming a light buff color after frost. The foliage emerges a lustrous, deep green in spring, becomes lighter green in summer, turns copper in autumn, and climaxes as pale tan in winter.

Why is this grass commonly called Spangle Grass? Who knows? Perhaps a graceful clump of arching oat spikes backlit by the setting sun prompted the name.

PROPAGATION: Propagate by seed, or by division in spring. It self-sows and naturalizes beautifully, but if this is undesirable the seed stalks can be cut and removed. Seed kept in a warm place for 2–4 weeks will germinate more reliably.

6. Bottlebrush Grass *(Hystrix patula)*

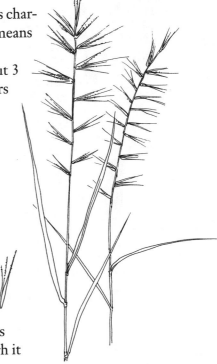

Long, bristly seed heads known as awns give this grass character. Its botanical genus name, from the Greek, means porcupine.

It has an upright, open growth habit and is about 3 feet tall. This grass with dusky green-leaves prefers shade and naturalizes well in woodlands. It can be interspersed with woodland wildflowers or planted near ferns for textural contrast. It makes a good transition at the edge of the woodland when planted as a mass, and also makes an unusual ground cover. Accent the front entry to your home with a small grouping of Bottlebrush Grass or incorporate it into a border garden. In the fall the foliage and flowers turn chestnut brown.

PLANTING REQUIREMENTS: Plant in moist, well-drained fertile garden soil in light or partial shade. It is native to moist, rocky environments and does not appreciate drought or full sun, although it will tolerate a dry shaded site. It can also be grown in quite a bit of sun, as long as it is kept evenly moist.

PROPAGATION: Seeding is the best method of propagation. Mature clumps can be divided in early spring or fall.

*   *   *

Six Suggested Sedges

1. Bottlebrush Sedge *(Carex lurida)*

The cylindrical, brush-like seed heads of Bottlebrush Sedge look like their common name. This sedge, maturing at 1–3 feet, is a slightly smaller, more compact version of Bottlebrush Grass *(Hystrix patula)*. Both species prefer a moist, slightly acid environment. The sedge needs much more consistent moisture than the grass, since it is typically found in all types of wet habitats, including swamps, bogs, sloughs, ditches, and deep marshes.

Consider planting a couple of clumps of Bottlebrush Grass behind one of Bottlebrush Sedge just for fun. Bottlebrush Grass is a resident of the woodlands, so it might not work, but it would be an interesting experiment to try this unnatural Mutt and Jeff relationship in a little corner of the garden.

PLANTING RECOMMENDATIONS: Plant Bottlebrush Sedge in consistently moist soil in sun or partial shade on stream banks, around ponds, in water gardens, or in wet meadows. It is highly recommended for sedge meadow restoration.

PROPAGATION: Divide mature clumps in spring, or plant ripened seed in the fall.

2. Gray's Sedge *(Carex grayii)*

This unique, semi-evergreen sedge grows about 2 feet tall. It is also called Burr Sedge or Morning Star Sedge. Particularly attractive as an accent plant in a garden, it can be massed or used as a ground cover, and colonizes readily. Never let it dry out!

Its distinctive, rounded yellow-green seed heads resemble the spiked maces that medieval knights twirled above their heads in jousting tournaments. These seed heads eventually turn a rich brown color and add interest to a dried floral arrangement. Plant a clump where you can see it from inside the house on a cold winter's day, and enjoy the interesting shadows created by the seed heads as they stand on stiff stems above the leaves.

Gray's Sedge has a narrow, upright form and grows from a short, thick rootstock. The narrow, light green leaves of Gray's Sedge can reach 2 to 3 feet long, but generally remain shorter in hotter climates. Semi-evergreen plants sometimes winter-kill in a severe winter, so Gray's Sedge may need protection, particularly in the more northern sections of the Lower Midwest.

PLANTING REQUIREMENTS: *C. grayii* likes consistently moist, humus-rich soil in full sun or light shade. It is normally found on the banks of creeks, at the borders of swamps, and in rich woodlands.

PROPAGATION: Divide mature plants in the spring, or plant ripened seed in the fall.

3. Plantain-leaved Sedge *(Carex plantaginea)*

Also known as Seersucker Sedge, this clumping sedge has broad, heavily veined bright green leaves that can be up to 1 inch wide. It grows 1 to 1½ feet tall and equally as wide. Arching flower spikes with handsome, nearly black inflorescences emerge before the foliage in early spring. Portions of this sedge, including the base of the flowering stem, are enhanced with a rich burgundy-red.

In *Flora of Indiana*, Charles Deam records that it is usually found in dense shade, "in humus on the wooded sandstone slopes of deep ravines," and is generally in the company of woodland wildflowers commonly found in beech-maple forests. It thrives near ponds or garden pools, and is attractive when interspersed with other woodland plants like Appendaged Waterleaf, Spring Beauty, and Cut-leaved Toothwort.

A cultivar of *C. plantaginea*, 'Dr. Richard Lighty', is almost identical to the species, except that it is smaller, maturing at only 12 inches tall.

Another good choice for the home garden, Carey's Wood Sedge *(C. careyana)*, is similar to Plantain-leaved Sedge, but is slightly taller. This bright green sedge is also typically found in moist, rich beech-maple forests.

PLANTING REQUIREMENTS: Plant in humus-rich, consistently moist, well-drained soil in a shady site. It will tolerate drier conditions if temperatures are moderate.

PROPAGATION: Divide mature clumps or propagate by ripened seed.

4. Black-seeded Sedge *(Carex eburnea)*

According to Charles Deam, this diminutive plant retains its fruit longer than any of our other species. It generally grows less than 7 inches tall, forming symmetrical, 12-inch-wide clumps of soft, exceedingly fine wire-like green foliage. It grows from a rhizomatous rootstock, and is normally found in steep, rocky, well-drained areas, growing with such trees as Pagoda Dogwood, Red Oak, Witch Hazel, White Pine, and Canadian Hemlock. It is also found amid woodland plants like Bloodroot, Hepatica, and Mayapple.

Also called Ivory Sedge, it is a perfect choice to snuggle in close to the base of a tree, tuck into a rock garden, or plant as a ground cover in a small area.

PLANTING REQUIREMENTS: Plant in sun or partial shade in well-drained soil. This particular sedge prefers an alkaline soil that is dry, sandy, or rocky, and is typically found on limestone cliffs and outcroppings, but it has reportedly been grown successfully in neutral or acidic soils as well.

PROPAGATION: Divide mature clumps in spring, or plant ripened seed in fall.

5. Grass Sedge *(Carex jamesii)*

Grass Sedge resembles lily turf and is effective as a border near a path, sidewalk, or driveway. It has soft, narrow, dark green leaves that rise above the insignificant flower stalks. Its natural habitat is rich woods, particularly the steep slopes of deep ravines where the soil is well-drained, and dry woods and thickets. Deam reports that *C. jamesii* is often found with either Hairy Gray Sedge *(C. hitchcockiana)* or Few-fruited Gray Sedge *(C. oligocarpa)*, or both. It also grows in the company of common beech-maple woodland wildflowers, like Spring Beauty, Virginia Waterleaf, False Rue Anemone, Cut-leaf Toothwort, Virginia Bluebells, and *Phlox divaricata*.

PLANTING REQUIREMENTS: Plant in humus-rich, well-drained, neutral soil.

PROPAGATION: Divide mature clumps in spring, or plant ripened seeds in the fall.

6. Palm Sedge *(Carex muskingumensis)*

As befits its common name, this small sedge has a tropical appearance as it creeps and scrambles over the earth, creating an effective ground cover or a massed planting. It forms huge colonies in wet spots in wooded areas, in swamps, or near streams. It is effective in a water garden or near a pond, and grows from a short, sturdy rhizomatous rootstock. This winter-hardy perennial has attractive, fine, light green foliage that becomes straw-colored after the first hard frost in the fall.

PLANTING REQUIREMENTS: Plant in wet, organic, humus-rich soil in medium to deep shade. Although it will grow in sun, the leaves

tend to lighten and bleach in too much light. Keep this sedge evenly moist, and do not allow it to dry out.

PROPAGATION: Mature clumps can be divided in spring; plant ripened seed in the fall.

You shall hear the big gold bees over the red, yellow, and purple flowers, bird song, wind talk, and the whispers of sleepy Snake Creek, as it goes past you.   —*Gene Stratton-Porter, 1909*

10.

Get

Wet Feet

Plants for Wet Places

Softstem Bulrush

Bicycling, like gardening with native plants, has become a popular pastime for many Americans in recent years. In 1899, a twenty-one-year-old African American named Marshall "Major" Taylor reigned as World One-Mile Sprint Champion, capturing the imagination of the country. In 1982, a new $2.5 million outdoor bicycle racing facility in Indianapolis was named in his honor. Each year since the dedication, hundreds of cyclists have raced around the banked, curved track of the Major Taylor Velodrome in Indianapolis.

An unattractive spring-fed area, choked with barnyard grass and ugly weeds, was located near the Velodrome parking lot. This heavily disturbed site was too wet to mow and impossible to maintain; it caused public controversy until an Indy Parks Department land steward remedied the situation by enhancing it with native wetland plantings. His instructions to the plant supplier, a local restoration nursery, specified that the plants must be genotypes native to central Indiana.

Using a large group of Indiana Native Plant and Wildflower Society members,

Sierra Wetland Project volunteers, and university ecology students, he supervised a planting of over 1,600 wetland plants. The planting began early in the summer of 1996, when temperatures were pleasant enough for volunteers to wade in and plant the shallow emergent communities in 1 to 8 inches of water.

Several native bulrushes *(Scirpus* spp.*)* were planted in the center of the wetland, including Hard-stemmed Bulrush *(S. acutis)*, Wool Grass *(S. cyperinus)*, Softstem Bulrush *(S. validus)*, Dark Green Bulrush *(S. atrovirens)*, Three-Square Bulrush *(S. pungens)*, and Red Bulrush *(S. pendulus)*. Prairie Cordgrass *(Spartina pectinata)* and seven varieties of native sedges were installed to help stabilize the area. Sedge meadow communities of wet-mesic grasses, sedges, and rushes, as well as wildflowers chosen for a long season of colorful blooms, were installed around the edge of the water.

Workers installed waterfowl exclusion fence to prevent ducks and geese from gobbling the tender, newly planted shoots and allow the new plantings to become established. The fence was left in place for one year. An additional 750 plants were added in the summer of 1997, most of which were flowering plants. Interpretive signage was installed, explaining the importance of wetlands, and recognizing partnership support from the groups that assisted with this project.

Now, butterflies, dragonflies, and damselflies flit through the flowers, and croaking frogs help to make the site a welcome respite in the midst of urban concrete. This civic-minded environmental project has changed an unsightly problem into a beautiful flower-filled wetland.

Have you ever considered installing a wetland, a pond, a moist meadow, or even a tiny water feature? "But I don't have a place for a wetland in my small suburban yard," you protest. "Why would I want water standing in my yard anyway? Won't that just increase the mosquito population? Besides, that would be just one more thing to clean. And by the way, what does water gardening have to do with native plants? I thought native plants grew on prairies, and in the woods."

If you have enough energy and stamina, plus a willingness to learn, you can dig your own pond, build a meandering woodland stream, or create a bog garden. There are multitudes of ways to use water in your garden. Each requires different initial preparation, and some demand more maintenance than others. Think about what you like in nature and use your imagination. The possibilities are endless.

Why Should I Consider Using Water in the Landscape?

Water is a powerful emotional force in our lives, providing beauty and diversity, calmness and serenity—the inspiration of poets, novelists, artists, and musicians. It stimulates our senses of touch, sound, sight, and even smell. Think of a waterfall's spray against your face as you look up to admire the thundering cascade, the sound of a hard rain on the roof as you lie in bed, or the beauty of a bottomless lake, ringed by towering evergreens and snow capped mountains. Anyone who lives where there is heavy snowfall can attest to the nostalgia produced by the smell of a spring thaw.

Water covers over seventy percent of the earth's surface, and is essential to the survival of every living species present on our planet. Since our bodies are made up of about two-thirds water, we can live for a long time without food, but we will die quickly with no water. Water adds a new dimension to the landscape, expands the diversity of plant selection, creates a habitat for wildlife, birds, and butterflies, and heightens our awareness of the natural world around us. Water affects our climate, our agriculture, our industry, and our transportation, and is the life-blood of our environment. Shouldn't something this important to our very life deserve a place in the garden?

Let me tell you how my friend Dave changed a wet problem area into a wetland wonderland. When a new neighbor brought in a bulldozer to change the contours of his property, the grading disrupted the natural drainage pattern in the corner of Dave's yard. Attempts to eliminate the persistent sogginess were unsuccessful, so he did some research on native plants that prefer a moist habitat and created a small wetland meadow complete with trees, shrubs, flowers, wildlife, birds, and butterflies. He comments, "My neighbor and I share notes on interesting birds that fly in and enjoy watching the seasonal changes in this new garden. It was cheaper than a lawsuit, and besides, I don't have to mow it anymore!"

How Did Dave Create His Wetland?

The existing soil consisted of heavy clay with a thin 1-inch layer of topsoil holding the grass, so Dave had a "ready-made" slow-percolation area.

He removed the sod, dug out about a foot of soil, and tramped down the heavier clay subsoil to compact it as much as possible. Several bales of saturated sphagnum peat moss, compost, the excavated soil, and an equal amount of sand were stirred together and spread unevenly, to create a more natural effect.

Pleasant temperatures gave way to chilly, rainy days, and Dave retreated to the house. About two weeks passed before he was able to resume his task. "In retrospect," he says, "that was probably the best thing that could have occurred, because as the area settled, a small low spot was apparent." He decided that this would accommodate plants needing a damper environment and began by removing the soil mixture from the low spot. He added the excavated soil to one side to create a gentle rise. After digging an irregularly shaped hole about 15 inches deep in the low spot, he added more heavy clay soil and tamped it down. Finally, he filled the basin with sand and worked moistened sphagnum peat into the top 2 or 3 inches.

Now, bright yellow Marsh Marigolds, Blue Flag Iris, and False Dragon's Head *(Physostegia virginiana)* bloom in Dave's natural-looking wetland. But the real highlight occurs in midsummer when a frothy, deep-pink swath of Queen-of-the-Prairie presents a magnificent show just in front of a large stand of statuesque Joe-Pye Weed. Hummingbirds gather nectar from a mass of bright red Cardinal Flower. Monarch and Swallowtail butterflies visit several milkweed species planted here. In late August, the unique flowers of Blue Gentian near delicate Pink and White Turtlehead flowers create a late "summer spectacular" in the lightly shaded part of the meadow.

Dave purchased plants because he commented, "I am too old to wait for seeds to mature. I want it all to be beautiful *now*." In general, this is the wisest choice for most wetland projects. If you purchase seeds, plan to start them in pots or flats and tend them as you would any new seedling until they are large enough to transplant into your wetland, meadow, or marsh.

What Are Some Examples of Simple Water Gardens?

Gardeners use a variety of containers for colorful summer annuals to brighten the corner of the deck or patio, create interest near the front of the house, make a small yard seem larger, or beautify an out-of-the-way spot. Container gardens are easy to maintain, relocate, and simply enjoy. It is possible to create small water gardens in much the same way. Nearly any container that can hold water can be used, as long as it is large enough to fulfill your needs.

Adding a water garden to your yard can be as easy as setting up a watertight wooden half-barrel to hold a single waterlily or a few native aquatic plants on the corner of the deck or patio. Sink a container full of Arrowhead and Blue Flag Iris into the ground and surround it with a mass of colorful meadow wildflowers. Rigid or flexible fiberglass pre-formed containers to create an in-ground water garden are readily available from garden centers in a variety of sizes, shapes, and prices, and are easy to install. Turn an existing, unused hot tub or swimming pool into a large pond, or create a haven for waterlilies and fish in an old metal stock watering-trough sunk into the ground to the rim.

Install a brick or stone divider into a long trough-like container and fill half of the container with water for aquatic plants. In the other half, put moist sand or saturated, cheap, generic cat litter for wonderful pond-like "gravelly muck," and plant some species that normally grow on the water's edge.

Help children learn about native carnivorous bog plants by nurturing a few in a watertight windowbox. (Check the Resources section for nurseries that carry aquatic plants.)

Regardless of what water feature you choose, also consider adding some type of birdbath for the sake of our feathered friends. You will enjoy their antics as they splash and dunk and flip water about, chattering incessantly, much like teenagers in a swimming pool.

My first water garden was a 15-gallon, flexible rubber hog-feeder purchased at a local hardware store for $15, and sunk into the brick-paved patio near my outdoor swing. In this tiny water garden I have a single pot of Marsh Marigolds, and two goldfish to eat mosquito larvae. I left a 5-inch border of soil around the container to cover the roots of several native ferns and some shade-tolerant dwarf impatiens, which provide color all summer long. This is my favorite retreat after an afternoon of weeding, where I come to swing gently, read the mail, rest, and enjoy a cup of coffee. Few things equal the happy chirping of birds in the soft summer breeze, the reflection of the sky in the water, and the lovely fragrance of nature.

How Do I Install a Pre-Formed Container for a Pond?

1. Mark the shape on the ground, using your container as a pattern.
2. Dig the hole 2 inches deeper than the container.
3. Level the bottom dirt and fill the hole with 2–3 inches of sand.
4. Smooth the sand and level with a carpenter's level.
5. Set the container in the prepared hole.
6. Fill the container ³/₄ full of water, pack sand around the edges to stabilize and firm it, and fill with water to 2 inches from the top.
7. Cover the edges with rocks, limestone slabs, or some other type of material to hide the edge and make the pool look more natural.
8. Plants can be added after 48 hours. Set pots on bricks or concrete blocks to bring the crown of the plant just above the water.
9. Let the water "age" for two weeks before adding fish. Add no more than 1 inch of fish (not counting the tail) for each 2 square inches of surface water.

What Other Factors Need to Be Considered?

To grow aquatic plants successfully, any water garden must be sited where there is sunlight. Most of these plants need full sun. Some will tolerate light partial shade and produce adequate foliage, but will not bloom as well—or at all. Waterlilies need 8 hours of sunlight, and 4 to 6 hours of direct sunlight, to bloom. They like still water and don't appreciate fountains or other vigorous water-circulating devices. Wild Calla *(Calla palustris)* is one of the few plants that can survive in stagnant, mucky water. Research and understand the cultural needs of the native plants you choose.

To control breeding mosquitoes, it is important to add fish to ponds with still water. I seldom feed the two goldfish in my little outside container pond, but they grow and remain healthy as they keep the mosquito larvae under control. Hardier varieties of tropical fish like guppies or swordtails can live in outdoor pools and will also control mosquitoes. Koi are popular for large outdoor ponds, but nonnative fish should never be used in a stream or wild area that is not totally contained. Even for large, contained ponds, consider using native fish or minnows as a less expensive option. Check with a nearby fish hatchery, or ask the individual who stocks the local lake or fishing pond about a possible source. Then if a Great Blue Heron flies in for lunch, you can appreciate his beauty instead of chasing him wildly around the yard as he swallows your expensive Koi.

For a pond that will be stocked with fish, be sure to use a container or pond liner that is not toxic. Heavy, black PVC rubber roofing material had been installed on the flat portion of our roof just before we built a pond outside our living room. We used a large scrap of this material for the pond liner and waited two weeks for the water to cure before adding a dozen handsome 3-inch goldfish. The aquatic plants were not affected, but every fish died within 24 hours. I added goldfish again after about three months, and they, too, promptly died. If we want fish in that pond, the liner will have to be replaced with a non-toxic PVC liner specifically manufactured for outdoor fish ponds.

A friend bought a large children's swimming pool for her expensive collection of Koi while her outdoor pond was being drained and repaired, and within 24 hours all the Koi were dead. Many of these portable swimming pools carry a warning label, but inquire before you kill off your fish.

A pond must be at least 18 inches deep if you plan to leave the fish in it during the winter months, or they may not survive. The goldfish in my little container-pond spend the winter in the indoor aquarium.

What Maintenance Is Necessary for Water Features?

Keep the pool or pond free of leaves, because as leaves decay, the water will become fouled, and fish and plants may die. Small ponds may need to be siphoned empty, cleaned, and refilled in the spring.

Weeds and undesirable plants may intrude in and around a pond or stream. Pull these in the spring when they are still young and small, and when the ground is wet. Be diligent about removing seed heads from unwanted plants before they have a chance to relocate on the ground.

Marginal water's edge plantings should be kept well watered and not allowed to dry out, or the plants may die. If there is a drought for over three weeks, let the hose run slowly into any wetland-type area until it is well-watered.

What if the Site Is Too Shady?

Our friends' suburban home, built on a half-acre lot, is surrounded by towering beech, oak, and maple trees. They realized that a large pond was not feasible in their yard because the abundance of falling leaves would require intensive maintenance, so they created three small water features, each of which will work well for a shady garden—a pebble pool, a small waterfall, and a dry stream.

A Pebble Pool

A wet, glistening pebble pool is easy to make by simply sinking a container to its rim into the ground. Jim used a plastic 5-gallon pail, but a trash can or any similar container can be used as a water reservoir. Cover the top of the sunken reservoir with something to hold the pebbles, such as metal hardware cloth, wire mesh, or the half-inch plastic mesh used for fluorescent light fixtures available at most hardware stores. Cut the covering 4 to 6 inches wider than the top of the reservoir. Lay the covering across the top of the reservoir at ground level, and anchor it with bent coat-hanger wires. You can also drill holes in the cover of the pail, or in a trash can lid, to hold the pebbles. Put a small pump into the bottom of the pail to recirculate the water over large rocks for a gentle waterfall, or install a jet for a small bubbling fountain (see diagram).

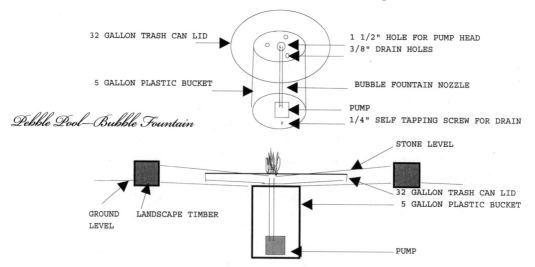

Pebble Pool—Bubble Fountain

A Small Waterfall

Jim purchased a twin to my 15-gallon rubber hog-feeder at the hardware store to use as a reservoir, and sank it into the ground. At a local quarry, he found a handsome, medium-sized boulder with a natural concave "v." He buried the bottom third of the boulder to make it look "like it had always been there," facing the "v" toward the reservoir.

A small pump, one that will pump 15 gallons in a half hour, rests on a brick in the bottom of the bucket to keep it free of debris. Heavy aquarium tubing is snaked from the pump in the reservoir, around to the back of the rock and over the top, camouflaged by a small rock set on top of the boulder, so that a gentle trickle of water continuously runs over the face of the boulder like a small waterfall, falling into the reservoir, where it is recycled (see diagram). Because the rock does not hang over the reservoir, some of the water initially ran under the rock, so he used a small piece of bent metal as a lip, fastened underneath the rock with epoxy. When the water hits the lip it falls over the edge, so that now all of the water returns to the reservoir. A strip of plastic could also be used for this purpose.

Small Waterfall

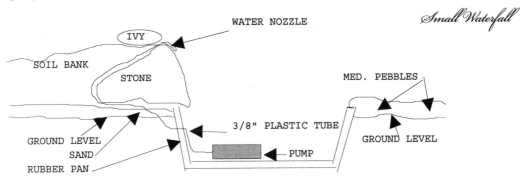

WATER NOZZLE

IVY

SOIL BANK

STONE

MED. PEBBLES

3/8" PLASTIC TUBE

GROUND LEVEL

GROUND LEVEL

SAND

PUMP

RUBBER PAN

A Dry Stream

In nature, dry streams occur where early spring rain and floods cut a channel to carry excess water away. As the season progresses, the stream dries up and disappears, leaving behind a litter of rocks and debris. Typically, moisture-loving native shrubs and trees grow along the banks of these areas. The dry stream concept has been used decoratively for many years, probably most effectively in Japanese gardens.

Some friends who were running out of space for their extensive hosta collection decided a dry stream could create a natural-looking gardening area, so they dug a meandering trench that varied from 5 inches to 2 feet deep along the entire width of their back yard and lined it with black plastic garbage bags punctured to allow drainage. They installed a layer of coarse sand and gravel to hold the plastic in place, and then added rocks over the entire area to cover the sand (see diagram). Some gardeners prefer multiple styles and sizes of rock combined for a more natural effect; others like the look of dark gray stream cobbles.

Dry Stream   LINER

If there is a future possibility that you may want to convert your dry stream to a real stream, prepare the channel following stream specifications. Usually this means adding a layer of sand to cover a PVC pipe and an underground electrical wire, and using 32-mil liner instead of garbage bags or weed cloth. With this preparation any water moving capacity can be added later without disturbing the streambed.

For a shady water garden site, try planting shade tolerant, moisture-loving natives such as Jack-in-the-Pulpit and its cousin, Green Dragon. Acid-loving Wintergreen or Checkerberry *(Gaultheria procumbens)* is a pretty, evergreen, low-growing ground cover with bright red berries and shiny leaves. For areas at higher elevations, or farther north, the prostrate Creeping Snowberry *(Gaultheria hispidula)* can accent the edge of a pool with tiny leaves and white berries. To provide a suitable growing habitat, see the suggestions in this chapter for marginal plants that thrive at the water's edge.

As I play the piano in the living room, I can look out through floor-to-ceiling windows into a small, shaded outdoor atrium. Beyond the atrium, in the area that separates our house from the neighbor's, are native ferns, young evergreen Eastern Hemlocks, and several tall Sugar Maple and Cherry trees. In the spring, early crocus and yellow daffodils complement a variety of native wildflowers. In the heat of the summer, finely textured leaves of Blue Cohosh *(Caulophyllum thalictroides)*, Doll's Eyes

(Actaea pachypoda), and Greek Valerian *(Polemonium reptans)* contrast with large-foliaged hostas to create a cooling scene. Nonnative Japanese Pachysandra is a utilitarian, unexciting, evergreen swath of ground cover. There is a path between the two homes. Even though this spot is only a way to get from the front yard to the back, I longed for something more interesting outside the window.

Stacking up several huge rocks on one side of the atrium helped, but somehow wasn't quite what was needed. A metal sculpture? Too formal. Next I planted some native ferns and hollies, thinking that the foliage and red berries might make a nice contrast to the pachysandra. Still not enough. A friend with a good eye for design suggested a small pond. Questioning the wisdom of such a major installation in such an out-of-the-way spot, I debated about it for nearly a year. Then one day I simply began digging a hole next to the rocks, working toward the center of the atrium, piling the dirt into the garden cart. With my husband's help, we completed the project over the weekend. The new pond, only about 6 feet in diameter, has varying depths, with "shelves" on the sides to hold aquatic plants.

At last there was something interesting outside the windows of the living room, but it was not until winter arrived that I realized why this tiny little pond pleases me so much. One afternoon as I sat at the piano, I suddenly realized that it is a "mirror in the ground," reflecting fleecy white clouds and stark, black branches of naked trees against a brilliant blue winter sky. Just as a large mirror enlarges a small room, my little pond reflects the surroundings above and around it, making the entire area seem larger, brighter, and more intriguing.

How Do I Build a Pond with a Flexible Liner?

1. Lay out a garden hose to mark the shape. Once the shape is determined, excavate at least 18 to 24 inches deep. Cut the sides at a gentle angle, neither too steep nor too shallow, toward the center as you deepen the area.

2. Level a flat area around the outer edge about 12 inches wide at ground level, for rocks, stones, or used bricks, to hold the liner in place, camouflage it, and make a natural-looking edge.

3. As you excavate, leave ledges of dirt for shelves to hold aquatic plants. Our shelves are about 8 to 12 inches below the level of the sur-

rounding soil and 9 to 12 inches wide. Placing a board on the dirt under the pond liner makes it easier to level the shelf.

4. Dig a small "well" at one side 12 inches deeper than the rest of the pond. Fallen leaves collect in the lowest spot and will make cleaning easier. When you drain the pond, it is easier to bail the last water out of this small deep area.

5. Remove any rocks, dirt clods, tree roots, or other debris from the hole and spread 2 or 3 inches of fine sand over the entire excavation, including the shelf areas. Place ¾-inch plywood boards on the dirt shelves and level with a carpenter's level. Old indoor/outdoor carpeting or dampened newspaper also works in place of sand. Commercial underliners are available for purchase. We used 2 inches of sand and then draped "splush" carpeting upside down over the sand, smoothing it to fit.

6. Drape a PVC pool liner that is rated safe for fish and plants over the entire excavation. EPDM (ethylene propylene diene monomer) is another safe choice. To determine how much liner to purchase, measure the widest width, the longest length, and the depth of the excavation. The formula is simple:

Depth x 2 + widest width + 2 feet = width of liner.

Depth x 2 + longest length + 2 feet = length of liner.

My pond is 2 feet deep, 6 feet wide, and 7 feet long, so I had to purchase a piece 12 feet wide x 13 feet long. The additional 2 feet added to width and length measurements provides a 1-foot overhang all around the edge of the pool for anchoring the liner.

7. Weight the edge of the liner with rocks placed along the flat rim of the pond, covering the 1-foot overhang, and slowly fill the depression with water, smoothing the liner as the pond fills.

8. To install native marsh plants around the edge of the pool, dig a trench 14–18 inches deep around the perimeter of the flat area and line it with more of the PVC liner, or even heavy plastic garbage bags. Puncture a few random holes for drainage, and fill with a mixture of saturated humus-rich soil, organic matter, and sharp sand. Wet generic cat litter has the consistency of coarse gravelly muck. When it is mixed into the soil, it will help retain moisture. If you need an even more muddy planting medium, try the clumping cat litter. Some plants will grow in plain cat litter, or in sand, as long as the planting medium is kept consistently moist. After setting the plants in the soil, water and cover with a 2-inch layer of pea gravel.

Pink Turtlehead, Royal Fern, and Cinnamon Fern will grow lush in a moist environment. Marsh Marigold and Swamp Milkweed provide bright color and typically grow in damp spots at the edge of a pond or stream, or in a marshy environment. Many water's edge plants are also found growing in those moist environments that are sometimes inundated with water, but also experience drier periods throughout the growing season.

What if I Already Possess a Natural Water Feature?

Those fortunate few with an existing pond, stream, wetland, or moist area on their property should identify its characteristics, determine which types of plants typically grow in these places, and avoid compounding environmental problems due to poor plant selection. Purple Loosestrife and Canary Reed Grass are two examples of exotic plants that create terrible problems in wetlands.

Safe choices include native plants that grow naturally in comparable nearby environments. However, even some native plants can cause problems, so careful research is crucial. Cattails can quickly colonize a wet area. White Waterlily, one of my six suggested aquatic plants, can grow rampantly if not containerized. A friend told me that he had to remove it with a backhoe from his pond, and warned the horticulture director at the Indianapolis Zoo about its aggressive tendencies. It is a lovely waterlily, but needs to be in the right setting so that it does not take over the world! Yellow Lotus is another beauty that can become a beast in an uncontained area. In fact, it is probably wise to enjoy waterlilies in man-made water features and use less aggressive plants in the wild.

Begin by taking an inventory of existing trees, shrubs, and other plants. Eradicate any undesirables by hand weeding, grubbing out, or girdling. Or cut the stems and paint the wounds with glyphosate herbicide to kill the plant. Next, list native plants that are commonly found in your region in this type of environment and determine what you want to include in your natural wetland. A professional wetland specialist or a member of the Department of Natural Resources can help you with federal or state guidelines. Use started plants rather than seeds. Maintenance is necessary for the first few years to ensure that undesirable plants do not reappear, but once natives are established, the maintenance should be minimal.

When early settlers came to the New World, they feared and avoided low, marshy areas because of unexplained diseases that prevailed in these soggy environments. In the late 1800s many farmers began installing clay drainage tiles to claim these primarily flat, fertile areas for agricultural use. Government agencies encouraged this practice early in this century, and by the 1970s over 35 percent of our nation's wetlands had been drained.

Unfortunately, draining wetlands has created problems with pollution, flooding, and loss of wildlife habitat. After the wetlands surrounding Lake Maxinkuckee in northern Indiana were drained for agriculture and development, this large natural lake became polluted with agricultural chemical runoff. Concerned citizens and government agencies have worked together in recent years to restore some of these vital wetlands and, in turn, the quality of the lake.

We are beginning to understand the value of these unique ecological communities. Wetlands store and hold excess water and release it slowly, helping to prevent flooding. They boast the greatest plant and animal diversity of any habitat; provide erosion control; are valuable recreation areas for hunters, fishermen, birders, boaters, and nature lovers. Because they filter pollutants and cleanse our water, they are like the kidneys, without which the body soon dies.

Once considered a liability, wetlands are now known to be an asset worthy of protection. These are some of our most threatened environments, and public education is probably the key to their preservation. As Margaret Mead wrote, "Never doubt that a small group of thoughtful, committed citizens can change the world; indeed it is the only thing that ever has."

*　*　*

Six Suggested Aquatic Plants

1. White Waterlily (*Nymphaea odorata*)

Commonly known as Sweet-scented Waterlily, it has fragrant, showy 3- to 5-inch white flowers that bloom all summer and into the autumn. The

bright white petals taper to a center
of bright yellow stamens. Flowers open in the morning and
close in the afternoon. The
broad, round green leaves have
a hint of purple underneath. This
waterlily can be aggressive, so it is wise to

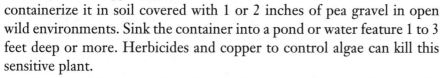

containerize it in soil covered with 1 or 2 inches of pea gravel in open
wild environments. Sink the container into a pond or water feature 1 to 3
feet deep or more. Herbicides and copper to control algae can kill this
sensitive plant.

Beaver, muskrats, nutria, and some diving waterfowl consider the rhizomes a delicacy. For control, contact Fish and Wildlife authorities to
live-trap and relocate the offenders, or build an underwater metal barri-
cade to keep them out.

PROPAGATION: Propagate by rhizome division with an intact 2-
to 3-inch growing tip or purchase from a nursery specializing in aquatics.

2. Arrowhead *(Sagittaria latifolia)*

The triangular arrow-like leaves of Arrowhead contribute
to its tropical look. Arrowhead has lovely, white three-
petaled flowers with bright yellow stamens that bloom on
long stems all summer long. These interesting flowers
march up the tall stem in whorls of three. Arrowhead is a
colonizer and will fill in shallow ponds, mucky soil, or a
half-barrel on the deck, and will even grow happily in a
container of mud or wet kitty litter on the patio. It likes
still, standing water.

This plant is commonly known as Duck Potato because of its potato-like root. Beavers and muskrats eat it
as part of their staple diet, and it is a favorite of waterfowl.

PLANTING REQUIREMENTS: Plant in very moist
or saturated soil at the water's edge, or directly into a pond 1–8
inches below the surface of the water. Sink a pot in a small pool
in full sun. It blends nicely with Pickerel Weed and Cattails and is
a good accent for a water garden filled with waterlilies.

PROPAGATION: Propagate by division, or with seed planted in moist soil, or purchase plants.

3. Marsh Marigold *(Caltha palustris)*

Marsh Marigold is one of the earliest wildflowers to bloom in spring. It is found in wet, marshy areas with Skunk Cabbage and brightens up a dreary, rainy day. Each shiny yellow flower has 5 to 9 yellow sepals. It grows 12–18 inches tall. The long-stalked heart-shaped leaves get larger after the flowering ceases and can become 4–8 inches across. These leaves grow from a fleshy, stringy, crown-forming perennial rootstock.

PLANTING REQUIREMENTS: Marsh Marigold thrives in full sun or high open shade in rich, fertile, wet soil that is neutral to slightly acid. It requires constant moisture during the growing period but will tolerate a drier site after going dormant in midsummer.

A single Marsh Marigold can be planted in a container filled with rich soil and covered with 2 inches of pea gravel. Sink the pot with the water level about 1 inch above the rim in a small pond or water garden container.

Space multiple plants 1–2 feet apart, spreading the roots on a small mound of soil. Cover the top of the crown with about 1 inch of soil.

PROPAGATION: Plant fresh, ripe seeds in wet or evenly moist soil. It generally takes one to two seasons before the plants will bloom. Established clumps can be divided immediately after blooming or just after the plant becomes dormant by separating the soft, thick crowns. Available from specialized mail-order nurseries.

PLANTLORE: Early settlers and Native Americans cooked young green leaves of Marsh Marigold and Skunk Cabbage in "three waters." They covered the leaves with water that had been brought to a boil. The water was drained, replaced, and brought to a boil again. After the third treatment, the leaves lost the toxic alkaloid and were pleasant to eat as cooked greens. Marsh Marigold was also used to treat spring coughs and convulsions, and as a spring tonic.

4. Soft Rush (*Juncus effusus*)

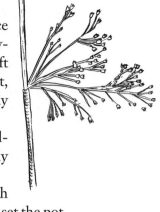

This upright plant grows 18–24 inches tall and makes a nice vertical accent in a small water garden or a small pond, or growing along the edge of a large pond or stream. The relatively soft foliage will break and flop in too much shade. It forms a neat, tight, stiff-looking clump in a sunny location, and will stay nearly evergreen in many parts of the Lower Midwest.

PLANTING REQUIREMENTS: Plant in the soil in shallow water in full sun, or in wet, mucky soil that is consistently moist.

Soft Rush can also be containerized in a large pot filled with rich soil. Cover the top of the soil with 1 inch of pea gravel and set the pot 1 inch below the water level in a small pool or pond.

It is also possible to grow Soft Rush in a container on a sunny patio. Mix saturated soil with kitty litter to help retain moisture.

PROPAGATION: Divide large established clumps in early spring, or purchase started plants.

5. Pickerel Weed (*Pontederia cordata*)

Pickerel Weed typically grows at the edge of a pond or lake, where the water is shallow and still. Its handsome, glossy, arrow-shaped leaves look like an elongated heart. The large spikes of striking pale-blue to violet flowers have an extended bloom period in midsummer. It grows 2 to 3 feet tall, and each plant spreads about half as wide. *Pontederia cordata* 'Alba' is the white flowering form. The iris-like rhizome grows near the surface of the soil. Pickerel Weed acts as a filter, so it is a particularly valuable plant to include in a pond. Its air-filled stems are buoyant, and mosquito-eating damselflies and dragonflies will often lay eggs in them.

The name comes from the Pickerel fish that are often found swimming nearby.

PLANTING REQUIREMENTS: Plant directly into the soil 1–8 inches below the water surface in a pond, lake, or water garden, or at the water's edge in saturated, constantly wet soil. Plant the iris-like rhizome in a pot filled with rich soil and covered with 1 inch of pea gravel. Set the pot an inch or two below the water surface.

PROPAGATION: Plant fresh, ripe seeds in constantly moist soil, or divide the rhizome leaving at least two eyes. Available from many nurseries, especially those specializing in aquatic plants.

6. Yellow Lotus (*Nelumbo lutea*)

The large, beautiful, light yellow flowers of Yellow Lotus are spectacular as they rise high above the surface of the water. These delightfully fragrant flowers can be 5–10 inches across, so that they are nearly as large as the 1- to 2-foot upright, blue-green leaves. The huge, bowl-shaped leaves have a sturdy stem attached to the center. Interesting seedpods follow the flowers; these are often used in floral arrangements. Each flat-topped fruit has several small holes in its upper surface, with a marble-sized seed found in each. Yellow Lotus can produce 30-foot runners, so this plant should be containerized, and not be used at all in an open wild environment. The tubers are "filet mignon" for beavers, muskrats, nutrias, and some waterfowl.

PLANTING REQUIREMENTS: These aggressive plants can crowd out other aquatics if they are not contained. Fill a huge pot half full of rich soil and lay the tuber horizontally on the soil with the growing tip facing upward. Carefully add more soil, leaving the growing tip exposed. Cover the soil with 1 inch of pea gravel and drop the pot to the bottom of the pond. A 15-gallon rubber stock feeder is an excellent container for these giants.

Yellow Lotus requires full sun, and prefers still or sluggish slow-moving water. It will grow in water depths of 8 inches to several feet, but since it takes more energy to reach the surface in a deep pond, plants bloom more prolifically in shallower water.

PROPAGATION: Propagate by carefully separating an entire banana-shaped tuber from the mother plant. Be gentle so the growing tips are not damaged. Yellow Lotus is available from nurseries specializing in aquatic plants.

*   *   *

Six Suggested Moist-Area Plants

1. Monkey Flower *(Mimulus ringens)*

The snapdragon-like flower of this plant resembles a grinning monkey face. Pinch the sides of the flower and the monkey will laugh! These lavender or pinkish flowers have bright yellow throats and grow in opposite pairs on long petioles on a 3-foot square-stemmed ridged stalk. The sessile leaves are narrow and lance-shaped, and clasp the stem. The fibrous thin-rhizomatous roots form dense mats. Monkey Flower blooms from midsummer to autumn.

    PLANTING REQUIREMENTS: Plant in full sun or partial shade in moist or wet soil at water's edge or in a boggy area. Space plants 12 inches apart. Spread the roots over a mound of soil and plant with the growing tip just at soil level. Mulch well. Monkey Flowers are attractive massed by a rock near a stream. Several sources caution never to let this plant dry out. However, I have observed it flourishing in normal garden soil in a typical perennial border.

    PROPAGATION: Divide the white fibrous-rooted plants in the spring to maintain good bloom. A two-lobed seed capsule produces many tiny fine seeds that can be scattered on moist soil in late fall or in early spring.

    PLANTLORE: *Mimulus*, from the Latin, means "small monkey face." Early Americans used the leaves as salad greens.

2. White Turtlehead *(Chelone glabra)*

Large, white two-lipped flowers resemble the head of an open-mouthed turtle. *Chelone* is from the Greek meaning tortoise. Early settlers called it Snake Head and Bitter Herb, and in the 1850s this herb was available at most drugstores. Flower clusters are at the top of each leafy stem and bloom from late in the summer to early fall. The two-celled oval seed capsules are attractive and contain many small winged seeds. Turtlehead grows 3–4 feet tall and demands constantly moist soil.

PLANTING REQUIREMENTS: Plant in full sun or very light shade in moist or wet soil. White Turtlehead is particularly effective when planted as a mass. Space plants 12–18 inches apart, spreading the coarse, fibrous rhizomes over a mound of soil. The crown should be placed barely below the soil, since it will rot if it is planted too deep. Mulch well. To create bushier plants, pinch back a few in late June for later flowering.

PROPAGATION: Plant fresh, ripe seeds immediately, divide rhizomes, or take stem cuttings in midsummer. Turtlehead self-sows readily if the ground is moist.

PLANTLORE: In his 1857 book *New Domestic Physician*, John Gunn, M.D., refers to *Chelone glabra* as Balmony and recommends combining it with equal portions of Poplar Bark and Goldenseal to "strengthen the system." He writes, "an even to a heaping teaspoonful may be taken two or three times a day." It was also reputed to give relief from internal parasites.

Chelone glabra is the larval food source for the Baltimore Checkerspot butterfly *(Euphydryas phaeton phaeton)*. A stamp honoring this butterfly was issued June 6, 1977.

3. Blue Flag *(Iris versicolor)*

Beautiful violet-blue flowers enhanced with gold and white appear in June. These small, delicate flowers resemble Siberian Iris more than they do the perennial garden iris. The 2- to 3-foot graceful sword-like leaves are identical to those of garden iris and provide a vertical interest all season.

PLANTING REQUIREMENTS: Plant rhizomes just covered with water in wet or moist average soil in full sun. Leave 1 foot of space between them. Blue Flag is found naturally in swampy ground and wet meadows, and by the edges of creeks and ponds. It will even grow in standing water.

PROPAGATION: Divide the rhizomes after blooming or in late summer and replant. It is possible to grow Blue Flag from seed, but seeds must be kept moist. Seeds will germinate the following spring, and the seedlings should bloom in three years.

PLANTLORE: The root was valued as an anti-mercurial and anti-venereal remedy and was generally made into a syrup or tincture. A powdered form was prescribed for dropsy. A concentrated extract of Blue Flag root, known as Iridin, was combined with Leptandrin to treat liver afflictions.

4. Great Blue Lobelia *(Lobelia siphilitica)*

Each 2- to 3-foot stalk of Great Blue Lobelia is topped with an impressive spike of thickly set bright sky-blue flowers. The flower stalk grows from a basal rosette of dark green leaves that has overwintered. These interesting tubular flowers have two lips above and three below, with prominent striping under the lower lip. Broken stems exude a yellowish milky sap. Great Blue Lobelia is longer lived and blooms longer than its cousin *Lobelia cardinalis*.

PLANTING REQUIREMENTS: Lobelia accepts full sun or light shade as long as the soil is rich and constantly moist. A native resident of damp environments, it typically grows along streams, in wet meadows and prairies, in damp woods, or at the edge of a swamp.

PROPAGATION: Rosettes can be divided in early spring or fall and replanted. Plant fresh seed or stratify over the winter and plant in the spring.

PLANTLORE: Americans in the 1800s used the roots as a diuretic and as a remedy for worms. It was also believed to heal the sores of syphilis.

The botanical name *Lobelia siphilitica* was originally assigned to Red Lobelia, also known as *L. surinamensis*. Red Lobelia is native to the West Indies and reportedly was used there to treat cancer, scrofula, and syphilis. The patient was to drink up to a quart of the decoction each day. *Lobelia siphilitica* was also used to treat breast cancer. The patient was to drink "a wineglassful three or four times a day, and apply to breast or cancer a poultice made of equal parts of Elm bark and the powdered root (or leaves)."

5. Queen-of-the-Prairie *(Filipendula rubra)*

Frothy rose-pink flower clusters 4–10 inches across and nearly a foot long rise above large, deeply divided leaves, marking this plant as truly the Queen of the Prairie. This regal lady grows 2–6 feet tall and stands head and shoulders above many of the shorter prairie plants. It makes a strong statement in any garden and is particularly effective when planted as a mass in the center or front of a border or along a walkway. It grows wild in boggy areas and moist meadows or prairies. It is a wonderful plant to naturalize because once it is established, its creeping rhizomes take over and complete the job.

'Venusta Magnifica' is a beautiful 5- to 6-foot tall cultivar with deep pink flowers.

PLANTING REQUIREMENTS: Plant in full sun in moist, fertile, rich garden loam. Keep the soil evenly moist throughout the growing season. This plant should be mulched. Space rhizomes 1–2 feet apart and plant them with the growing tip at soil level.

PROPAGATION: Divide rhizomes in spring or fall, sow fresh seed immediately, or refrigerate and plant in spring. Readily available from mail-order nursery sources.

PLANTLORE: Like willow, Queen-of-the-Prairie contains salicylic acid, which was used as an aspirin substitute. Native Americans and settlers used it as pain medication for arthritis, rheumatism, and fevers. Because it also contains tannin, it was used as an astringent and cleansing agent.

6. Joe-Pye Weed *(Eupatorium purpureum)*

Swallowtail butterflies flock to Joe-Pye Weed. This tall, stately plant towers over nearly every other plant as it grows 8–10 feet tall. Whorls of four

The seed heads of Bottlebrush Grass do resemble miniature bottlebrushes. This grass is a good choice for a shady nook.

Airy panicles of Switchgrass catch the early morning light.

Fiery russet tones of Little Bluestem signal the onset of autumn. This small grass is particularly valuable in the winter when it brightens a gray wintry landscape (photo by Ruth Ann Ingraham)

THE WEA PLAINS

Granville cemetery was once part of the great Wea Plains and still contains many species of the original prairie vegetation. This is one of the last remnants of the Indiana prairies that covered much of Tippecanoe County. It is preserved and managed as a memorial to the Indians and early settlers to whom these grasses and flowers were once familiar.

Historic prairie remnants are scarce, but a few have been preserved in old cemeteries. Coneflowers bloom beside a squat tombstone at Granville Cemetery near Lafayette, Indiana (top left). A sign about the heritage of the Wea Plains (top right) and a tall grave marker (bottom left), accented by more coneflowers and Little Bluestem grass, denote a small segment of the Great Prairie of the past. Near West Branch, Iowa, spring wildflowers bloom profusely at the Rochester Cemetery (bottom right, photo by Rolland Wehner).

Native plants in public plantings in the Indianapolis area (clockwise from top left): a biker on the Monon Trail; Smock Golf Course (photo by Don Miller, Indy Parks); Goldenrod in front of an antiques store; the educational prairie garden at Holliday Park.

The nectar of Bee-balm or Wild Bergamot attracts butterflies and bees. This striking plant will grow in sun or shade.

Wherever Cardinal Flower grows, hummingbirds are sure to abound as they seek out the nectar found within its brilliant red flowers.

In July, 1922, Jens Jensen submitted a landscaping design for the F. D. Stalnaker estate. These Blue Flag iris are growing on the site of that original planting designed by Jensen (photo by Emily Daniels).

A close-up view of the rosy-red flowers that cover Swamp Milkweed shows the interesting flowers and tiny, unusual buds on this moisture-loving plant.

Native Americans and early settlers used the abrasive plant material of Scouring Rush to scour their cooking pots. Fossil remains of gigantic prehistoric *Equisetum* species have been discovered by archaeologists.

Beautiful flowers and unusual seedpods rise above the cupped leaves of the American Yellow Lotus.

Marsh Marigolds are easily grown in a container set in a small pond. They bloom gaily in early spring.

Two small water gardens enhance an outdoor patio. A waterlily grows happily in a small free-standing container (right); goldfish and aquatic plants thrive in a buried container camouflaged by Vinca (left).

One of the first wildflowers to emerge in the spring, Bloodroot's ethereal white flowers carpet the forest floor.

Delicate Hepatica flowers bloom above last season's leaves.

If you plant Mayapples on a hillside you will have a unique view of the underside of the large leaves and the flower that hangs beneath (photo by Rolland Wehner).

Also called Crane's-bill or Prairie Pointers, Shooting Star sends up a dainty flower stalk from a cluster of basal leaves.

Jack-in-the-Pulpit is a distinctive woodland plant that children delight in spotting as they wander through woodlands.

An unusual pink-flowered specimen of Virginia Bluebells nods daintily.

Seldom are we fortunate enough to find a whole field of Prairie Trillium like this one!

Rust-colored berries of False Solomon Seal create an interesting late summer scene.

Baneberry or Doll's Eyes has stark white berries with black dots resembling eyeballs on bright red stalks that persist after the fruit falls.

The sparkling red, notched petals of Fire Pink are unforgettable. Native-plant enthusiasts hope to convince the legislature to replace the Peony (from China) with Fire Pink as the state flower of Indiana.

Small raspberry-like berries sit atop Golden-seal's distinctive leaves; a mass of these plants makes a beautiful ground cover.

If it is attention you want from garden visitors, plant Indian Pink. This underused flower will stop people in their tracks!

Swallowtails flock to Joe-Pye Weed, a tall wood-land plant with beautiful rose-mauve domed flower clusters.

A newly emerged Monarch butterfly dries its wings near its spent chrysalis.

One of the best butterfly attractants, Butterfly Weed can create a brilliant orange spot in any sunny well-drained garden.

(opposite) The huge, silk-filled seedpods of Common Milkweed were collected and the fibers used to fill life preservers during World War II.

Royal Catchfly is on the threatened species list in several states. However, it is easily propagated from seed and thrives in normal garden soil in a sunny location. Its presence guarantees hummingbirds!

The fruit of Red Osier Dogwood is consumed by over 45 species of wildlife. Its gleaming, bright red stems brighten a wintry landscape.

Three invasive exotics: Garlic Mustard (opposite, large photo), which is usurping and eliminating our native wildflowers, and Multiflora Rose, an introduced species that creates impenetrable brambles; and (this page) Buckthorn, a shrub or small tree that is taking over many woodland areas.

A fourth undesirable, although a native: Poison Ivy, a plant that can cause much grief (and itching!).

leaflets march up the stem, which branches near the top. This section holds huge domed clusters of dusty-rose flowers.

The common name comes from an Indian medicine man in colonial New England named Jopi or Joe Pye, who used this plant to treat his patients. Some historians think the word "jopi" may have been the word for typhoid fever used by Native Americans in that area, who called the plant "jopiweed."

PLANTING REQUIREMENTS: Joe-Pye Weed prefers moist, well-drained, rich garden soil in full sun or light shade. It naturalizes well and makes a good background for a border garden. It is also handsome in a corner that needs a special accent.

PROPAGATION: The fluffy seedheads will scatter and ensure a good crop of this plant. For more control gather the fresh seed and plant or stratify in the refrigerator over the winter and plant in the spring. Divide large clumps with a sharp knife in early spring or late fall or purchase plants from a mail-order nursery.

PLANTLORE: A concentrated resinous extract called Eupurpurin comes from the root. It is reportedly a powerful diuretic, and was once used for dropsy and kidney disorders. The root was also used as a tonic, stimulant, and astringent. Gunn's 1904 *New Domestic Physician* recommended "three or four ounces of the root boiled briefly in as many pints of water, and given in doses of from a half to a teacupful three or four times a day."

*   *   *

Note: For information on sedges, see chapter 9.

11.
Stroll in the Shade

Developing Woodland Gardens

The kindliest thing God ever made,
His hand of very healing laid
Upon a fevered world, is shade.
— *Theodosia Garrison, 1910*

The spring wildflower garden is my favorite garden, for these small early plants signal the return of spring and the rebirth of nature after a long period of dormancy. When winter aconites and snowdrops push up in the spring, we know that it is time to begin to watch for spring wildflowers. Austria greets its Edelweiss; the Lower Midwest's "blossom of snow" might be the tiny white Snow Trillium, or the delicate white flowers of Bloodroot, two of the first natives to brave the early spring chill each year.

How Can I Establish a Woodland Garden?

Solomon's Seal

If you have any shade at all, it is possible to create a woodland garden, although you will probably have to amend the soil before you plant. This garden can be just a few spring wildflowers under a tree, or a large wooded area with trails and paths. Try to begin planning early in the year, not long after Valentine's Day, because many of the woodland wildflowers are spring ephemerals. Ephemerals are plants that emerge from the ground before the trees leaf out, bloom, and then die back to the ground, having stored enough energy in their roots for the following spring.

Towering trees surround our home, which is less than seven miles from downtown Indianapolis. This is an area that naturalists call a beech-maple forest. As developers subdivided lots for individual dwellings, they left as many of the native trees as possible. In this dense shade, few plants flourish. Only filtered sun reaches the ground except in a few places, so the ground beneath the Sugar Maples, ash, and beech trees was nearly barren when we first moved here in 1984.

Even spring ephemerals need light and moisture to survive, so we removed a number of small saplings, limbed up several of the larger trees, and marked a path through the woods. Unlike a meadow or prairie, which can be enjoyed and appreciated from afar, woodland plants require observation at close range. My family and I are inveterate tent campers and love the quiet solitude of the woods, where we can hike, listen to the birds, and try to identify the vegetation. Our neighborhood was originally a large, dense woods, so I decided to attempt to recreate a small replica of this quiet peacefulness, where we could escape from the hubbub of the city, and encourage wildlife, birds, and butterflies to join us.

False Solomon's Seal

My first task was to mow a proposed path with the lawn mower, and then walk the path to be sure it felt comfortable, was wide enough for two people to stroll together, and led where I wanted it to go. I flared the path at the entrance, so that this wider area said, "Welcome. Please come into my garden."

After I cleared and established the pathways, I dug and disposed of all the unwanted vegetation, and designated "rooms" within the area to make design and planting tasks more manageable (see chapter 2). With trails, transplanted ferns, and wildflowers, we have transformed our yard into a woodland that resembles the hiking areas found near campsites. Our small granddaughter loves to tromp around the trails in our woods trying to spot wildflowers. One day when she and I were walking through a nearby wooded state park, she delighted me by exclaiming, "Grandma, look! There is a Bloodroot leaf. Now, where do you suppose the flower went?"

Should I Rake the Leaves in the Fall?

Before I just say "no," let us consider maintenance practices and their results by conjuring up two imaginary neighbors. The first homeowner hires a raking crew to remove every leaf and twig from the yard in the fall and complains about the compacted, poor, and infertile soil, where virtually nothing grows except the large, fertilizer-dependent, water-guzzling lawn.

Instead of raking the leaves, the second homeowner uses a mulching mower, and in places where mowing is not feasible, he rakes off just enough leaves to keep the plants from smothering, allowing the rest to return to the soil. He also mulches annually with wood chips. This neighbor's yard is filled with a constant display of wildflowers, bulbs, and perennials. Although he has a small amount of turf grass, he cuts down on mowing, and protects his trees and shrubs with an underplanting of ground cover.

Are these results as imaginary as our example? Not at all. Think about the existing soil in the woods. Woodland plants grow in rich loose soil that has been naturally amended over the years with fallen leaves, the kind of soil you can almost dig with bare hands. In fact, it is often possible to dig down several inches with your fingertips due to the wonderful loam created by decomposing leaves over many years. In a natural forest, the tree leaves fall, decay, and decompose, creating what naturalists refer to as "duff." The flowers push up through this duff, which provides nutrients, conserves moisture, and serves as a natural mulch in the forest. Soil is the most important factor for success with woodland wildflowers. Check the pH (most woodland wildflowers prefer neutral to slightly acid soil), and amend accordingly to create a moist, well-drained, humus-rich loam.

We have been conditioned over the years to rake, burn, bag, and remove leaves from our property to make it neat and tidy. If you feel compelled to rake, then compost the leaves and return them to the garden the following year. However, if you have a wooded area rather than a place you consider a garden, try to reprogram yourself to let the leaf litter lie and amend the soil in its own natural way. One compromise is to mow the leaves after the last one has fallen to keep them from blowing into a neighbor's yard. They will break down faster if the pieces are smaller, and will mulch and protect the plants over the winter.

What about Planting?

Plants growing in the wild generally grow in drifts or colonies. Even when a plant of a particular species is growing all by itself, you will find another not far away. When you plant your wildflowers, group your plants. The old uneven rule—one, three, five, seven, nine—gives a more pleasing effect than even lots. Plan and plant a swath of a given variety. Plants do not grow in straight lines in the wild and should not in your garden. When you rescue plants, or hike in the woods, observe how these plants grow naturally, what plants are found together in the same location, what kind of light and moisture is available, and what type of soil is prevalent.

Be aware of a plant's idiosyncrasies before incorporating it into a woodland or garden. Mayapples, for example, are colonizers. If you plant a few, you will soon have a multitude; be sure that you want them where you plant them. Once I planted four or five Mayapples in a hosta bed, because the foliage is a nice complement to hosta foliage. For the first two years they stayed just where I had planted them, but in the third year they began to cover a much larger area than I wanted. In late summer, before they became dormant and while I could still locate each one, I dug and transplanted them all to a back corner of my woods where they could multiply freely. The following spring the Mayapples dutifuly appeared in the new bed, but to my consternation, I also found twice as many as I had removed growing happily in the hosta bed. For each small rhizome I had broken and left behind, a new plant grew. I could almost hear them sniggering! If you want only a few Mayapples, plant the rhizomes in a bottomless five-gallon pail. Otherwise, be content to let this willfully aggressive wildflower follow its nature and colonize the site.

Can I Grow Woodland Wildflowers from Seed?

Most woodland wildflowers are more difficult to grow from seed than prairie or meadow wildflowers. Many need to have cold-moist or warm-moist stratification. Tough seed coats may need to be scarified before germination can occur. Some wildflower seeds, like trillium seeds, can take two years to germinate. However, if you enjoy a real challenge, try to learn what a particular wildflower seed needs in order to germinate. Sometimes you *can* fool Mother Nature. For example, if you plant a trillium seed and place the container in the humidrawer of your refrigerator for six weeks, then take it out and give it light for six weeks, then replace it in the humidrawer for another six weeks, and at last put it under lights or plant it outdoors, the seed will believe it has been through "two winters" and will probably germinate. But not always!

It generally takes at least three years for a woodland garden to become established. If you have access to a large number of plants, or can successfully raise a good crop from seed, you may be able to have an established look more quickly, but it still takes these plants about three seasons to settle in and begin to increase. As with any perennial, remember, "The first year they sleep, the second year they creep, and the third year they leap."

Woodland wildflowers can give pleasurable seasonal interest from early February throughout the spring and early summer. The easiest and most dependable native woodland wildflowers are those that grow naturally in your area, so do some research before acquiring plants. Good sources of information include native plant organizations, the county extension agent, the public library, bookstores, the Department of Natural Resources— Division of Nature Preserves, and members of local garden clubs.

Where Can I Get Woodland Wildflowers?

As gardening with natives becomes more popular, species become more readily available. Most of the native plants discussed in this book are available in the nursery trade as plants or seed, either locally or by mail order. The most difficult species to obtain are woodland wildflowers; unfortunately, this has created an ethical dilemma. It is not acceptable to dig from natural areas that are not threatened. Horror stories abound of overzealous nurseries digging wildflowers from undeveloped natural areas, public property, or even others' private property. Reputable nurseries purchase the plants they sell from wholesale propagation sources, or do their own propagation. There is a decided difference between nursery-grown and nursery-propagated plants. Wild-collected plants grown for a year or two at the nursery can be advertised as nursery-grown.

The selling price of a native plant can be another indication of wild collection. For example, a trillium can take up to two years to germinate and 5–7 years to bloom. If a nursery offers trillium or other uncommon woodland plants for an exceedingly low price, they may be wild-collecting their stock, or purchasing it from wild-collecters. Wild collection depletes and destroys natural populations, so be a wary buyer, ask questions, and purchase only from reputable nurseries who increase their stock by acceptable methods such as seeding, layering, division, or tissue culture.

Is Wild Collection Ever Acceptable?

When a site is destined for development, I believe that plant rescue is not only permissible but necessary. Without it, the existing plants would be destroyed by the bulldozers.

Nearly all the plants in my woodland were rescued from two construction sites. These sites covered several acres of pristine forest teeming with wildflowers. The first site was a veritable wonderland with massive drifts of wildflowers that commonly inhabit beech-maple forests. The second had as many wildflowers, but in addition was distinguished by over an acre of Nodding and Drooping Trillium, Wild Hyacinth, Goldenseal, Twinleaf, and Puttyroot Orchid. Huge trees shaded these native wildflowers, and wildlife abounded. Then the bulldozers arrived, and now those same sites are only concrete, glass, and masonry, with turf lawns, parking lots, sterile landscaping, and a few token trees. Instead of the hum of bees, the songs of birds, and the quiet respite of the shade, there is the roar of huge riding mowers.

Thanks to organized plant rescues, many of the doomed woodland natives from those two sites are still thriving and blooming dependably in several city parks, in shady educational gardens near local schools, along bike and walking trails, on the grounds of the art museum, and in the woodland gardens of many volunteers. It is gratifying to save wildflowers from certain death. It is also a good way to add hard-to-get species to your own woodland.

Be responsible as you rescue wildflowers and native plants. Rescue only from construction sites and never from natural areas. If you hear of a site destined for construction, seek permission from the owner of the property to dig and relocate native plants. Communicate your plan to the owner, enlist a crew of volunteers, or at least one other person beside yourself. Never go alone. Probably the most important thing to remember is that in order for the rescue to be successful, it is crucial to find or establish a similar planting environment nearby in which to transplant as soon as possible after removal. If such an environment is not available, your time will be wasted, as the plants will not survive.

When I first began rescuing native plants, I carried small plastic dishpans into the woods. It didn't take me long to realize that dishpans filled with rescued plants were unwieldy and very heavy to carry out of the woods. Jumbled plants mixed with dirt were difficult to separate properly when I arrived home. When you go to the grocery store in the spring and the clerk inquires, "Paper or plastic?" choose plastic. These lightweight plastic grocery bags are the perfect tool for plant rescues. They have cut-out handles and hold an amazing amount of weight. You can stuff dozens of these small bags into a single bag and attach them to your belt. Plants can be separated by species, and planted in colonies, just as they grow naturally. You can also water the rescued plants right in their bags as soon as you return home.

When rescuing plants, bring a spade, a trowel, and a good supply of plastic grocery bags. Wear protective clothing and sturdy, waterproof boots. Don plastic disposable medical gloves, and then add strong gardening gloves. Stick some mosquito repellent in your hip pocket. I generally also carry a film canister filled with white vinegar. A few drops will neutralize the bite and relieve the itching. Know what Poison Ivy looks like and avoid it. If you get into it, a product called Technu is effective if used up to 8 hours after exposure. Shower, and wash your clothing as soon as possible.

When I return home, I put several plastic bagsful of rescued plants into a dishpan, fill each bag about ¼ full of water to cover the roots, and leave the plants in water several hours, or even overnight, before planting. This seems to alleviate some of the transplant shock.

Dig a planting hole, amend the excavated soil with moistened sphagnum peat moss and compost, and arrange the roots of the transplant over a small mound of the amended soil at the base of the planting hole. Fill the hole with water, let the water drain, fill the hole with amended soil, tamping firmly around the roots to be sure there are no air pockets, and water thoroughly. Mulch the new transplant to help retain the soil moisture, and keep the plants well watered for three to four weeks until they become established. During the entire first growing season, new transplants need at least one inch of water per week, so if the natural rainfall isn't adequate, additional watering will be necessary to prevent stress and possible loss. Finally, be sure to water adequately before winter sets in.

When you rescue a plant, it is your responsibility to tend and nurture it until it can survive on its own. Then, if the planting site was properly prepared, these transplanted wildflowers will show their appreciation by increasing and spreading throughout your woodland garden.

What Ephemerals Should I Plant?

One of the first spring ephemerals to appear in the woodland is Harbinger-of-Spring *(Erigenia bulbosa)*, a diminutive member of the Parsley Family. The tiny white flowers with dark anthers give rise to one common name—Pepper-and-Salt. The leaves are very similar to Italian Parsley; crushed, they emit a parsley-like scent. These little plants are only 3–4 inches tall. A very small bulblet lies about 2½ inches under the ground. The plants transplant easily. After the flowers die, the leaves continue to grow as the plant stores energy for another season. Plant a mass of this tiny ephemeral close to the path to enjoy as you stroll through your woodland garden.

Nivale, the specific epithet of Snow Trillium *(Trillium nivale)*, means "white or snowy." This minute white-flowered Trillium often peeks through snow when it begins to bloom with Bloodroot and Hepatica in late February or early March. It grows only 3–5 inches tall and is often found next to a fallen log. The small rhizome can be found about 1–2 inches underground and is slow to increase. Plant it in well-drained, humus-rich, slightly acidic woodland soil. If it is happy in the environment, it will flourish and multiply, sometimes forming nice-sized colonies. If conditions are not quite to its liking, it will languish and disappear. Although I have not discovered the reason, I have had more trouble establishing this little trillium in my woods than some of the larger trilliums.

Fragile, delicate stems hold the little flowers of Rue Anemone *(Anemonella thalictroides)* to create a tiny bouquet. The pink and white flowers of this dainty ephemeral open in late March or early April, when early tulips and daffodils begin to bloom in the Lower Midwest. Rue Anemone blooms for over a month. Its rounded leaves resemble a small paw. It is generally found as a solitary specimen or in a small group. Clusters of tiny tubers are found 1–2 inches below the ground.

False Rue Anemone *(Isopyrum biternatum)* is a vigorous colonizer, forming large drifts of pretty little white flowers with miniature columbine-like leaves. It has a sturdy fibrous root system. This ground-hugging ephemeral is striking when planted with Virginia Bluebells. At Indiana's Turkey Run State Park these blue and white flowering plants grow en masse in front of high rocky cliffs, creating an unforgettable picture.

False Rue Anemone is easy to distinguish from true Rue Anemone. Just remember the letters *ff* and *tt*. False Rue Anemone has only five flower sepals; there are five letters in false. Rue Anemone has six to twelve sepals; rue rhymes with "true."

Wood Anemone *(Anemone quinquefolia)* is another colonizer that will cover huge areas of the forest floor with bright white flowers. It has three-parted leaves and grows from a crisp, reddish-brown, horizontal rhizome that can be found an inch or so below the soil.

In 1988, I planted about a dozen good-sized Virginia Bluebells that a friend dug from her huge colony. These have multiplied to create a spectacular spring display. I have also planted over 100 daffodil bulbs each year since we moved here in 1984, and when spring breezes blow, the wooded area in front of my house becomes a sea of blue and yellow.

When we first moved to Indianapolis, a lawn service salesman arrived just as the Toothwort was in full bloom and told me he could rid my lawn of "those little white flowers." Needless to say, I did not hire him or his lawn service! Toothwort naturalizes easily in a lawn, or in a woodland setting. Many lawns in the Lower Midwest sport a spectacular carpet of flowers in early spring of white toothwort, purple violets, pink and white Spring Beauties, interspersed with naturalized electric-blue squills *(Scilla siberica)*, or colorful crocus. In a few weeks, the foliage of the ephemerals and the nonnative early spring bulbs dies back and disappears until the next spring. (Unfortunately this is not the case with violets, so if you dislike violet leaves in your lawn, do not encourage them because they are extremely difficult to eradicate.) If you plant these early spring flowers in your lawn, be sure to let the foliage yellow and die before the first mowing. Since they become dormant after the foliage dies back, they do not seem to be injured by lawn fertilizers or broad-leaf sprays applied later in the season.

Toothwort has a relative called Crinkleroot or Two-Leaved Toothwort *(D. diphylla)* with similar growing requirements and shallowly rooted tubers that grow just under the mulch. However, this species is not ephemeral; it colonizes, and reportedly retains a ground cover–like green foliage all summer. It prefers more acidic, dry soils. I am not familiar with this plant, although I understand it is easy to grow.

Early settlers used the tubers of Spring Cress *(Cardamine bulbosa)* as a substitute for mild horseradish. Unlike many members of the Mustard Family, it is not invasive. Spring Cress has a cluster of pink or white flowers that bloom in midspring. It grows from a small tuberous root. Members of the Mustard Family are called "crucifers" because the four petals of their flowers form a cross.

I am often asked to identify the foliage of Trout Lily *(Erythronium albidum* and *E. americanum)*, also known as Dogtooth Violet, Fawn Lily, and Adder's Tongue. Each plant has two lance-shaped, mottled leaves and occasionally either a yellow or white flower. Their small lily-like leaves can blanket a site. Unfortunately, this ephemeral does not bloom profusely. *E. americanum* (yellow) is common in eastern states. *E. albidum* (white) becomes more prevalent as one travels west. Both species grow in my woods. Trout Lily grows from a small bulb 6–7 inches deep in the ground. Admire the flower, but don't pick it. It takes seven years for this plant to mature and reach blooming size, but if two leaves and the flower are picked the plant may die.

Do an inventory in your woods to identify existing ephemerals. Because these small, delicate plants disappear, it is crucial to mark their location, or plant them where you will not garden later in the season, or unwittingly you will destroy them.

After the Ephemerals Go Dormant, What Then?

Intersperse ephemerals with perennial native wildflowers that retain their foliage all summer, like Wild Geranium, Celandine Poppy, and Baneberry.

Ferns fill spaces left by ephemerals, creating a calm coolness. Plant colonies of each variety of fern in various parts of the woods, spacing them 2–3 feet on center so that each fern can be appreciated, or plant them closely to form a mass. Massed areas of Wild Ginger, Foamflower, Jacob's Ladder, or Trilliums will bring an elegance to the woodland garden.

Jack-in-the-Pulpit *(Arisaema triphyllum)* is one of the most widely recognized woodland wildflowers. My grandchildren love to lightly squeeze the bottom of the pulpit (spathe) and rotate it back and forth. This makes a squeaky noise— the sound of Jack (spadix) preaching. Jack-in-the-Pulpit and trillium both have three leaves so identification of young seedlings can be confusing. Trillium leaves are equally spaced. Jack-in-the-Pulpit leaflets resemble a "T." Two opposite leaflets form the top, and the third leaf is like the stem of the "T." Bright red pulp-covered seed clusters attract hungry birds, which spread the digested seeds around the woods. You can easily remove the pulp and plant the seed in the fall. It usually germinates the following spring, but takes several years to grow large enough to produce a Jack.

This member of the Arum Family grows from a deep fat corm containing crystalline calcium oxalate which, when eaten raw, produces a stinging needle-like sensation in the mouth. Native Americans and early settlers boiled these corms in "three waters" to get rid of the calcium oxalate and used the boiled corms as a starchy vegetable.

Another member of the Arum Family, Green Dragon *(A. dracontium)*, has a long dragon-like tongue and a 1–2 foot wide leaf that looks like the huge claws of a dragon. This unusual plant is another favorite of little people. My grandson thinks it makes a great sentinel posted at edge of the path leading into the woods. Its roots are clusters of corms. It can grow over 3 feet tall, and plants of varying heights make an interesting grouping.

If you photograph wildflowers, get the camera poised and ready the moment the beautiful creamy-white flower of Twinleaf *(Jeffersonia diphylla)* opens, because its beauty is fleeting. It looks like the flower of Bloodroot, and generally lasts only a day or two. However, the large butterfly-wing leaves are reason enough to plant this lovely vase-shaped plant in a place of honor where it can be appreciated by all. It is handsome in a colony, as a specimen, or interspersed with trilliums, Hepatica, and Maidenhair Ferns. Mature clumps can be separated by cutting apart the heavy rootstock. It self-sows moderately. The seed capsule is often described as "an upside-down pear," but it reminds me of the Monarch Butterfly's lime-green chrysalis.

Jacob's Ladder *(Polemonium reptans)* and Greek Valerian *(P. caeruleum)* are so similar that the names are often interchanged by gardeners and there is confusion over which is which. I believe I have Greek Valerian in my woods, but some insist the two species are one and the same. According to several popular field guides, Jacob's Ladder has protruding stamens; Greek Valerian does not. Both have ladder-like compound leaves and blue flowers, and grow from a fibrous rootstock. Either makes an effective border along the edge of a garden or along a woodland path. They can also be planted as a specimen, in a colony, or interspersed with a variety of other woodland wildflowers.

There is no better vertical accent in the woodland garden than Solomon's Seal *(Polygonatum biflorum)*, found commonly throughout the region. Great Solomon's Seal *(P. commutatum)* is taller. Annual scars on the white rhizome are said to resemble the seal of King Solomon of the Bible. Solomon's Seal has graceful, arching leaf stems with insignificant white bell-like flowers that hang under the stalk. The dark blue pea-sized berries are favorites of the birds, so this plant self-sows readily.

False Solomon's Seal, also called Solomon's Plume *(Smilacina racemosa)*, is actually showier with its feathery white plume at the tip of the leaf stalk, and is impressive when planted in mass. A cluster of rusty-red berries appear at the end of each stalk in the fall. This plant is shorter and not quite as upright as Solomon's Seal.

Wild Blue Phlox *(Phlox divaricata)* is commonly called Sweet William. This little gem is one of the few blue flowering plants in the woodland. It is one that is fussy about being transplanted, so keep it well watered until it is established. It grows 10 inches tall from a fibrous rootstock. To purchase Wild Blue Phlox, ask for it by its botanical name—Sweet William is also the common name of an unrelated garden flower. An area filled with Blue Phlox and Wild Geranium in full bloom is truly a photographer's paradise.

White Baneberry *(Actaea pachypoda)* is a good choice to intersperse with ephemerals. Rounded white flower clusters are followed by the red-stalked white seeds, each with a single black dot, that give this airy plant the common name of Doll's Eyes. When my two-year-old granddaughter heard the name, she stared at the plant wide-eyed and asked, "Why are the dolly's eyes on that bush?" It looks nice massed or planted in threes. It is pretty combined with clumps of Giant Star Chickweed (*Stellaria pubera*) that are profusely covered with star-like white flowers, or with shorter wildflowers like lavender-blue flowering Jacob's Ladder at its base.

Baneberries seldom need dividing, but can be propagated by dividing the coarse rootstock, leaving 2–3 eyes on each piece, or by planting cleaned seed in the ground. Red Baneberry (*Actaea rubra*) has shiny red berries. The fruits of both Red and White Baneberry are poisonous. Both are woodland plants, grow 2–4 feet tall, and thrive in partial to full shade. Baneberries need moist, well-drained, humus-rich soil, but Red Baneberry prefers a more acidic soil and cooler temperatures.

Blue Cohosh (*Caulophyllum thalictroides*) has a similar growth habit, but the attractive, lobed leaves are smooth-edged rather than serrated like those of Baneberry. Tiny, insignificant, greenish-yellow flowers appear in early spring, followed by inedible blueberry-like berries. It grows about 2–3 feet tall from a thick, scarred rootstock with fibrous rootlets.

What Woodland Plants Bloom Later in the Season?

We generally hike through natural woodlands in the spring because later in the season these areas become full of dense foliage and undergrowth. Surprisingly, there are many plants that bloom later in the summer in the woods. As long as you have paths, the woodland garden can be lovely to wander through all summer.

The lavender-pink flowers of Wild Bergamot (*Monarda fistulosa*) thrive at the edge of a woodland garden and draw in myriads of butterflies and hummingbirds to sip the sweet nectar. Mint Family plants, such as this, can be identified by their square stems, opposite leaves, and herbal scent. They generally spread rapidly by thin, underground stems and are easy to transplant.

Many consider Daisy Fleabane (*Erigeron annuus*) "just a weed," but the white aster-like flowers are actually quite pretty when grown in a mass. This plant was once used as a flea repellent.

A interesting plant for an open area is Wild Leek (*Allium tricoccum*).

In spring, thick, strappy leaves grow from an onion-like bulb. These leaves die back, and in midsummer a ball-shaped umbel of white flowers on a naked stalk rises out of the ground. Commonly known as Ramp or Ramps, it can spread vigorously to colonize an area, but is not really invasive. It prefers damp, rich, well-drained soil. Long treasured as a food source, it is still eaten by wild food aficionados.

I always leave a few yellow or orange Jewelweed *(Impatiens pallida* and *I. capensis)* planted as a mass in the woods to attract hummingbirds, but I must caution you: Be wary of Jewelweed. Another common name is Touch-me-not because its capsules explode when they are touched and propel the shiny black seeds quite a distance. As a result, it can spread rampantly through the garden, especially if children are around! It has shallow roots, so it is not difficult to pull—just time-consuming.

Jewelweed has watery stems similar to those of our common annual Impatiens. One afternoon, our neighbor's child ran through a large patch of Stinging Nettle in the woods behind his home and came screaming to his puzzled father. I knew that the juice of Jewelweed's watery stems was reputed to prevent the rash from Poison Ivy *(Rhus radicans)* and to alleviate the pain caused by Stinging Nettle *(Urtica dioica)*. I yanked out a few plants and rubbed the broken stems on Jason's legs. The next day he reported to his preschool classmates, "Did you know there is a jewelry-plant that makes the 'owie' go away?"

American Bellflower *(Campanula americana)* is a tall biennial with fascinating sky-blue flowers with a long tongue-like style that protrudes from its center. Combine it with equally tall Woodland Sunflowers *(Helianthus divaricatus)*. Their yellow flowerheads have yellow centers of disc flowers, and spread by thin, creeping rhizomes just below the surface of the soil.

Jerusalem Artichoke *(H. tuberosus)* blooms later in the summer with large yellow flowers. History relates that in 1805, Sacajawea brought edible tubers, probably from this tall, rough-leafed plant, to feed Lewis and Clark and their party. The tubers taste a little like a water chestnut.

Even in the fall, a woodland garden can be pretty. White Snakeroot *(Eupatorium rugosum)* looks like a white flowering shrub when it is planted in a mass, and makes a beautiful sight at the edge of the woods. It looks weedy until it blooms, so tuck it into the woods, where it looks "like it belongs." This is the plant that reportedly killed Abraham Lincoln's mother. When cows eat White Snakeroot, their milk is tainted with a poisonous substance called tremetol that causes Milk Sickness. In the 1800s, whole villages would move away in terror, believing the "haunts" were prevalent in the area. The cause of this malady was not understood until after 1900. A planting of its relative, Hardy Ageratum (*E. coelestinum*), with its fuzzy blue flowers, is also lovely in autumn. Since it spreads aggressively, either containerize this native or plant it where there is a natural barrier (like the driveway!).

The bright blue flowers of Closed Gentian (*Gentian andrewsii*) signal the end of the growing season and the beginning of fall. These beautiful bright blue flowers grow in a whorl in the axil of the leaves and never open. This dainty plant generally grows less than two feet tall. Plant it near the edge of the woods, or close to a path in an open area where it can get sunlight, so that its fragile beauty can be appreciated close up.

*   *   *

Six Suggested Spring Ephemerals

1. Spring Beauty (*Claytonia virginica*)

Tiny flowers of Spring Beauty blanket the ground in early spring and bloom for 2–3 weeks. The five-petaled flowers may be pink or white, and each petal has darker pink veining. The flowers close on cloudy days.

Fleshy, grass-like leaves clasp the stem halfway between the ground and the flower. These leaves are opposite and usually not more than 3–5 inches in length. Sometimes a third single leaf will be present at the base of the stem. After this small ephemeral sets seed, the leaves yellow and die back to the ground until the next spring.

PLANTING REQUIREMENTS: Spring Beauty needs good moisture during its brief growing season. It grows best in light shade at the edge of the woods or in open areas, but can take a fair amount of sunshine. The tubers thrive in well-drained woodland-type humus or good garden loam. Plant the tubers 2–3 inches deep in clusters, just as you would plant small spring bulbs. This lovely ephemeral colonizes in lawns or woodlands and is easy to transplant.

PROPAGATION: A tiny potato-like tuber with eyes lies at least 3 inches under the ground, which is quite deep considering the size of the tuber. Small white fibrous rootlets grow out of this little tuber. They are too small to divide successfully, so it is better to propagate this wildflower by seed. Shiny black seeds self-sow readily and are often propelled a fair distance from their small capsule when they ripen. Because of this trait, Spring Beauty will spread throughout a large area if growing conditions are favorable.

PLANTLORE: Native Americans and pioneers called the tiny tubers Fairy Spuds or Wild Potato and ate them raw or boiled. Wildlife commonly root up and eat the tubers, and also nibble the leaves, since these are some of the first green leaves to appear in spring.

This little spring ephemeral is of interest to botanists because the number of chromosomes varies from plant to plant. Charles Deam writes, "It is extremely variable in all of its parts except the seed." Linnaeus named this interesting plant after his friend and fellow botanist John Clayton.

2. Dutchman's Breeches (*Dicentra cucullaria*);

Squirrel Corn (*Dicentra canadensis*)

Dutchman's Breeches and Squirrel Corn are nearly impossible to tell apart unless they are in bloom. They grow together in similar environments, although Squirrel Corn may begin to bloom just a little later than Dutchman's Breeches and is not as common. The fern-like leaves are finely divided, and plants rarely exceed 8 inches in height. Each three-parted leaf is found at the top of a long petiole (stem) which grows from a common point near the surface of the ground.

Dutchman's Breeches takes its common name from the ¾ inch pantaloon-like flowers which look like a line of upside-down Old World

Dutchman's Breeches

breeches, each attached at the crotch of the pants to the arching flower stem. Squirrel Corn flowers are heart-shaped, can be white, pinkish-white, or pale lavender, and bloom a little later.

PLANTING REQUIREMENTS: Both prefer well-drained, moist, humus-rich, woodland soil and often grow on slopes in high or open filtered shade, where dappled sunlight highlights the tiny flowers and warms the forest floor early in the spring.

PROPAGATION: The fruit in both Dutchman's Breeches and Squirrel Corn is an oblong pod or capsule that splits in half to its base when the seeds are ripe. The seeds should be planted immediately and barely covered with soil. However, I have found it faster and easier to propagate these wildflowers by dividing the mature tubers just after the plant becomes dormant. Division and transplanting is also possible in the fall, if you can find the tubers. Both plants will self-sow moderately.

Dutchman's Breeches grows from a round pinkish-tan tuber composed of many tiny individual bulblets that are easily broken off. Handle the tuber gently and try to plant the entire ball intact. Each individual bulblet will eventually produce a new plant, but it takes several years to reach blooming size. When transplanting, cover the tubers with about 1 inch of soil or less. They are not normally found very deep under the soil and can often be found poking through at ground level just under the mulch. If some of the tiny bulblets break off the Dutchman's Breeches tuber, barely cover them with soil. As they grow and mature, they will seek their own level.

Squirrel Corn

Squirrel Corn's tubers are bright yellow and look like several tiny kernels of corn forming a small round ball. These are not as fragile, and although each kernel will eventually form a new plant, plant the entire tuber intact if possible. Squirrel Corn tubers are generally found a little deeper in the soil, but should still only be covered with 1 to 1½ inches of soil when transplanting.

PLANTLORE: The pioneers used parts of Dutchman's Breeches to treat urinary disorders. The tubers of both plants are poisonous and occasionally cattle will eat enough to get "blue staggers", a disorder which causes labored breathing and trembling. *Dicentra* means "two-spurred" or "two-lobed."

3. Cut-leaved Toothwort (*Dentaria laciniata*)

White or pink-tinged four-petaled flowers perch jauntily atop 6–12 inch stems above the leaves. Each palmate leaf is deeply cut into 3–5 narrow leaflets, and the edges are serrated. Three of these leaves grow in a whorl just below the flowers, and after the bloom cycle, another, similar set of leaves with five leaflets grows from the base of the plant not long before it begins to yellow and go dormant.

PLANTING REQUIREMENTS: Tooth-wort grows well in high, open shade or part sun. The leaves bleach in full sun. It prefers humus-rich, moist well-drained soil and often can be found along streambanks. However, I have it growing in profusion in my lawn where the soil content is primarily clay.

PROPAGATION: The long, thin seed-pod is a 1½ inch capsule that contains many seeds. As soon as the capsule splits, the ripe dark brown seeds are flung out. To collect seeds, attach a piece of nylon pantyhose around the capsules to catch them, or collect the capsules as soon as you observe dark brown seeds in any of them and place them in a paper bag or plastic container. Sow the seeds immediately, or store in a zipperlock bag with damp sphagnum peat moss in the refrigerator until they can be planted.

The roots of *D. laciniata* are small, tan, horizontal tubers that connect one to another with a fragile joint that is easily broken. The tubers are found 2–3 inches below the surface. Unfortunately, Toothwort is not readily available from wildflower nurseries. It is easy to identify on a plant rescue, is only moderately difficult to transplant, and self-sows readily. The biggest challenge is digging deeply enough to locate the small neck-lace of tan tubers. Each tuber will produce a new plant, but if you can leave several tubers connected, it will not take as long to get a nice display of flowers.

PLANTLORE: Because of the shape of the roots, this plant was be-lieved to help with toothache. Pepperroot is another common name for this member of the Mustard Family. It has a peppery, sharp flavor similar to a radish and was used by the pioneers in cooking.

4. Virginia Bluebells *(Mertensia virginica)*

Clusters of nodding blue trumpet-like 1-inch bells nod gracefully above 18-inch-long stems. The smooth-edged alternate leaves are broad and oval shaped. Bluebell flowers first emerge as a vivid pink bud and open into a delicate blue bell, although occasionally pink or white specimens can be found in the wild.

PLANTING REQUIREMENTS: This lovely wildflower prefers humus-rich, loamy woodland soil, but will tolerate the heavier clay soils of some areas in the Lower Midwest. Bluebells are often found growing in flat, open high-shade areas not far from a stream and will also thrive in full shade. Space bluebells at least 15–18 inches apart and strive for a "drift effect." Because they are spring ephemerals and disappear in late spring, intersperse them randomly among plants that keep their foliage, such as Doll's Eyes, Perfoliate Bellwort, Wild Geranium, Meadow Rue, or various ferns.

PROPAGATION: The rootstock reminds me of a black, misshapen piece of fungus. This strange, gnarled rhizome is very brittle and breaks easily if you hit it while you are digging. The inside of the rootstock is white. Several tiny white eyes signal next year's growth. You can divide these rhizomes to increase your stock as long as you leave 3–4 eyes per division. The rhizomes are usually found 3–5 inches below the surface of the ground, and when transplanting, the eyes should be covered with at least 1½–2 inches of soil.

Each individual flower produces four tiny nut-like seeds. Sow the ⅛ inch wrinkled, brown seeds immediately or dry the seeds and store in a film canister in the refrigerator. Bluebells self-sow readily if there is enough moisture.

PLANTLORE: When pioneers first arrived, they observed that bluebells were similar to the rough, spotted-leaved shade garden plant that we call Pulmonaria or Lungwort, and tried to use it to alleviate lung problems. However, *Mertensia virginica* is in a different family, so it was not effective (and I do not know if Lungwort was effective either!).

5. Bloodroot *(Sanguinaria canadensis)*

A blood-like liquid will stain your hands if you break a rhizome of Bloodroot. The botanical name, *Sanguinaria,* literally means "bleeding." This lovely early spring wildflower emerges from winter slumber tightly wrapped in a leaf cloak. The 8–12 bright white poppy-like flower petals alternate from large to small and accent the vivid yellow of the stamens. Bloodroot is usually 6–10 inches tall.

The distinctive, deeply cut leaf of the Bloodroot is probably the most enticing feature in the woodland garden. This plant grows in colonies and is most effective as a ground cover. Plant in drifts for best results, or tuck in a little group at the base of a tree.

PLANTING REQUIREMENTS: Bloodroot grows well in a high-shade area, where early spring sunlight casts dappled light on the forest floor. Give it slightly moist, well-drained soil that is rich in humus. The emphasis is on the word "well-drained" for if the soil remains too wet, the rhizome will rot. Bloodroot is often found on hillsides or on slightly elevated hillocks.

Bloodroot is not a true ephemeral, but when the soil dries out in late summer, the plant goes dormant until the next season, so in planning your garden, include some other perennials to fill the void.

PROPAGATION: Bloodroot is one of the earliest wildflowers to bloom, and the 2–4 inch white flowers last about a week depending upon the weather. The flower petals fall revealing a capsule-like light green seedpod filled with pale green seeds that slowly ripen to a dark brown. It takes about four weeks for the seeds in the capsule to ripen after the petals drop. If you keep the ground surrounding the plant free of mulch, leaves, and debris, the capsule will split and the seeds will fall naturally and "plant themselves." This is the easiest way to propagate Bloodroot, because the seed needs to be planted immediately after ripening for best viability.

The root system of Bloodroot includes a $^1/_2$ to 1 inch thick pencil-like horizontal rhizome which grows 1–2 inches below the surface of the ground. These rhizomes have bud-eyes. You can break a rhizome into pieces, leaving a bud-eye on each piece, and replant 2 inches deep.

PLANTLORE: Several Indian tribes used Bloodroot as body paint and insect repellent. Both Native Americans and pioneers combined it with oak bark, which provided tannin as a mordant, to dye clothing. A substance similar to morphine is present in this member of the Poppy Family, and parts of the plant served medicinal purposes. Early Americans dripped the red liquid onto a lump of sugar to ease sore throats and coughs. It is an ingredient in Viadent toothpaste. Bloodroot is pollinated exclusively by pollen-gathering insects since the plant produces no nectar.

6. Mayapple *(Podophyllum peltatum)*

The broad umbrella-like leaf of the Mayapple is strong and handsome and can be as wide as one foot across at the top of a stalk 12–18 inches high. It is deeply cleft into 5–8 parts and makes a strong statement in a woodland.

Single-leaved Mayapples are immature. In order to bloom, the Mayapple must have two leaves, borne on a Y-like stalk. Mayapple flowers bloom on a short stalk (peduncle) in the axil of this "Y." These lovely white waxy flowers have 6–9 petals and are 1$^1/_2$–2 inches across, but because they are under the huge leaves they are not as noticeable as many of the spring wildflowers. Unless you locate the plants on a hillside above your path, you plant Mayapples for the striking foliage.

Mayapples sometimes develop rust. Yellow and light green dots mottle the top of the leaf opposite fuzzy, powdery, rust-colored patches underneath. Rust is a fungus, like blackspot on roses, and there is no cure. Prevention and cleanliness are the only treatments. Untreated plants will eventually weaken and die. Remove infected leaves and destroy. Do not compost them. You can treat the area with a fungicide to prevent the disease. Spray according to directions on the bottle, beginning in the spring when new foliage first emerges, and reapply as directed. Supposedly dusting with baking soda helps roses avoid blackspot. Would it work on Mayapples? It might be worth a try.

PLANTING REQUIREMENTS: Mayapples grow in high shade and open areas and are sometimes are found in deeper, more densely shaded woodland areas. They need moist soil and will go dormant early if conditions become too dry. Mayapples normally disappear in midsummer when it gets hot, but will reappear in duplicate the next season!

PROPAGATION: Once established, the thick, pencil-like rhizomes run ruthlessly underground, colonizing an area. The easiest method of propagation is to break these rhizomes into pieces, and replant them horizontally about 1½ inches deep and 12 to 15 inches apart, with the eyes pointing toward the surface.

The seeds are in a 2 inch egg-shaped fruit. Remove the seeds from the fruit and plant immediately.

PLANTLORE: All parts of the Mayapple except the fruit are poisonous. Various parts of the plant have been used medicinally for many years. The rhizome is a cathartic and has been used to treat a wide variety of medical disorders, including diarrhea, venereal warts, skin disorders, snake bites, and syphilis, and it is currently being tested for anti-cancer properties.

Pioneer women made jelly from the ripened fruit, and although I have a recipe, I have never collected enough fruit to try making it. Some mushroom hunters insist that Morels are found where Mayapples grow.

Six Suggested Spring Non-Ephemerals

1. Hepatica (*Hepatica acutiloba; H. americana*)

Hepatica is one of my favorite woodland wildflowers because of its unique tri-lobed leaves and its compact, neat growth habit. It awakens early in the spring and parts are covered with fine hairs to protect it from the cold. Each plant has multiple flowers with pink, white, lavender, or purple sepals and looks like a miniature bride's bouquet. The flowers last 2–3 weeks and close when the sun hides its face. Hepaticas and species crocus bloom together in early spring.

Charles Deam reports that while white Hepaticas are constant, colored forms can change color from year to year, but my hepaticas have always retained their original hue.

PLANTING REQUIREMENTS: Hepaticas often grow on an east or south-facing slope, which indicates that they like early spring sunlight and good drainage. They need rich woodland humus, are generally found pushing their way up through the forest duff, and appreciate being mulched. When you transplant Hepaticas, plant them about 8–10 inches apart, since the clump increases in size each season.

I have had greater success transplanting Hepaticas in the spring, with soil left on the fibrous roots. Dig a hole about 3 inches deep and 6 inches wide, and amend the planting hole with humus. Place a small mound in the center of the hole and spread the roots over the mound, making sure the crown is not below the soil level. Water and wait until the water has drained away. Then fill in the hole, tamp the soil around the base of the Hepatica, and water again. Keep the plant well watered for at least 3 weeks after planting until it becomes established.

PROPAGATION: When growing conditions are favorable, Hepaticas will self-sow. The tiny seeds drop close to the plant just before the leaves totally unfurl in spring. If you keep the mulch moist during this time, germination will be improved. It usually takes 3–4 years from seed to bloom. Small seedlings can be moved and transplanted after the second or third season.

It is possible to divide Hepatica like any other fibrous rooted perennial, but I have not had very good success with this method of propagation and sometimes lose both pieces.

PLANTLORE: Hepatica is one of the Doctrine of Signatures plants.

According to medieval physicians, each plant had a signature, indicating what ailments or diseases it would cure. Because of the liver-shaped leaves, Hepatica was believed to be a cure for diseases of the liver. Early physicians also used it to treat lung diseases and mild depression. However, it has no known medicinal properties.

2. Prairie Trillium *(Trillium recurvatum)*

Prairie or Appendaged Trilliums are most impressive when massed. Generally 8–9 inches tall, this plant can range from 6–18 inches. A single upright three-petaled dark red flower blooms atop the rigid unbranched stem just above the leaves. Occasionally a yellow-green flower form is found. Three mottled green and brown leaves with short stems (petioles) curve downward. The rhizome is medium sized and found 3–4 inches deep.

Trillium leaves are easily identified, even when they are young and very small, because the three leaves are evenly spaced in a whorl at the top of the stem, unlike the Jack-in-the-Pulpit, which has two opposite leaflets above and one pointing straight below. Leaf edges are smooth.

PLANTING REQUIREMENTS: Trilliums need moist, well-drained, humus-rich woodland soil in a shaded location. If they are planted in a garden border, the soil should be amended with as much compost and sphagnum peat as necessary to make a humus rich soil, or they will be short-lived. Trilliums appreciate a good layer of mulch to help retain soil moisture and need additional watering if the soil becomes too dry.

The root system of trilliums can best be described as corm-like rhizomes, being more rounded than long. Rootlets grow out of the rhizome, which grows 3–4 inches below the surface of the ground and seeks its own level as it matures. Rhizomes planted too deep require too much energy for the plant to emerge above ground, and plants may be weakened or rot. Some experts recommend a little sand under the rhizome to encourage good drainage, as is often done with tulip and daffodil bulbs.

PROPAGATION: After the flower fades, the seeds ripen over a period of 6–8 weeks in a pulpy three-parted fruit. The seeds, within this rather pointed fruit (about the size and shape of a very large chocolate chip), mature from white to dark brown and each seed has a little tail-like appendage scientifically known as the *elaiosome*. If this appendage is allowed to dry out, the trillium can take several years to germinate, so plant trillium seeds immediately if possible. The elaiosome contains oils and serves as a food for ants, which aids in seed dispersal.

To propagate trilliums from the roots, carefully uncover the rhizome in late summer or early fall after the top foliage has died back and the plant is dormant. It is not necessary to remove the rhizome from the ground; just uncover enough of it so that you can wound it with a sharp knife by cutting a "v" or a small "u" groove along the top of the rhizome. Dust the cut with sulfur or a rooting hormone containing a fungicide and replace the dirt. Small offset corms with tiny rootlets will grow on the wounded area which can be carefully removed the following fall and replanted. It usually takes more than two years for these new corms to reach blooming size.

PLANTLORE: Trilliums were known as Birthroot because Indians and pioneers both used a tea made from the pounded roots to aid in childbirth. An antiseptic wash for wounds, burns, insect bites, and eye problems also came from parts of the plant.

3. Celandine Poppy *(Stylophorum diphyllum)*

There are a few native plants which have such unique leaves that once you have learned their individual characteristics, you should be able to identify them in any season. These plants include Celandine Poppy, Wild Geranium, and Bloodroot. The leaves of Celandine or Wood Poppy are deeply lobed and remind me of oak leaves. This plant has large four-petaled bright yellow flowers in mid-spring, and will rebloom off and on all summer long.

PLANTING REQUIREMENTS: Plant in humus-rich, moist, well-drained soil in partial to full shade. Celandine Poppy leaves will become yellow and ugly with too much light but can be cut to the ground and new leaves will sprout.

PROPAGATION: Seed capsules are fat and fuzzy and are filled with seeds which spring out when the capsule explodes. Seedlings appear in profusion near a mother plant, but are easily weeded out or lifted to be transplanted elsewhere. The root is a yellow-brown, brittle rhizome with eyes and fleshy rootlets which is found 1–3 inches deep and can be divided when dormant in spring or fall. Leave 2–3 eyes per division and cover with an inch of soil.

PLANTLORE: Because the flowers are yellow and the broken stem exudes a bright yellow liquid, the Doctrine of Signatures proclaimed that Celandine Poppy would cure jaundice. It is used in Russia as a cancer treatment.

4. Wild Geranium *(Geranium maculatum)*

Wild Geranium's leaves have a distinctive shape: palmate, cleft deeply into 5–7 parts. Each leaf has smooth margins and prominent teeth on the ends of each partition. The hairy stem and leaves of this plant feel rough to the touch. Wild Geranium grows 1–2 feet tall and forms a clump about the size of a small peony bush. The delicate flowers are soft pink, rosy-lavender, or occasionally white with bright yellow stamens in the center. The flowers are usually about 1½ inches wide and bloom for 2–3 weeks between late March and May.

This versatile wildflower fills in areas that would otherwise be barren once the spring ephemerals disappear, since its leaves remain green throughout the season. Although it is a handsome specimen plant at the base of a tree or at the edge of the woods, a massing of this plant in an open woodland is spectacular. It is also pretty in the center of a border garden. As long as it gets enough moisture, it will accept a fair amount of sun and remain beautiful all season long. It is probably the most useful of all woodland plants in any native planting.

PLANTING REQUIREMENTS: Wild Geranium will bloom profusely when it is planted where it receives more sunlight. Moist, rich soil is necessary to keep it from going dormant too early in the season so you need to keep it well watered during periods of drought. Space young Wild Geranium plants at least 10 inches apart.

PROPAGATION: Another common name for Wild Geranium is Cranesbill because the pistil becomes beak-like once the seeds have formed. Each seed capsule has five segments with one seed in each. When the capsule splits, there is a recoil action that flings the seeds quite a distance from the mother plant, so that it readily increases when conditions suit it. The small, smooth seeds are dark brown when they are ripe, but are difficult to collect unless you cover the seed capsule with a paper or nylon stocking bag to catch them as they catapult. Young plants have a small rhizome and will bloom 2–3 years after germinating.

As Wild Geranium ages, the thick, knobby, brittle rhizomes multiply and intertwine to form a rhizomatous mass the size of a large dinner plate which grows about 1½ inches below the surface. To increase your stock, divide this clump of rhizomes in early spring or fall. Be sure to leave two buds or more on each division. After division, plant about 1 inch below the surface. As the rhizome ages, it will seek its own level.

PLANTLORE: Wild Geranium's rhizomes and leaves contain tannin; they were used by early pioneers for tanning hides. Native Americans and pioneers made a tea from the root to treat diarrhea, stomach disorders, and sore mouths. Indian women in some tribes drank this tea for birth control.

5. Perfoliate Bellwort *(Uvularia perfoliata)*

Perfoliate Bellwort looks as if some "wilde fairie" had taken her needle and stitched the stem through the base of each leaf. Unlike Solomon's Seal and

False Solomon's Seal, which have only a single stem per rhizome, Bellwort can have a forked stem which grows 6–20 inches tall. The twisted bell-like yellow flowers appear on only one of the two branches and generally open between April and May. The plant continues to grow taller after flowering. The triangular green seedpods are about ³/₈ inch long.

PLANTING REQUIREMENTS: Bellwort can be added wherever spring ephemerals abound. It performs best in light, high shade, in moist, rich, well-drained woodland soil. I have it in a mass in one area of my woods, but prefer the solitary specimen next to the path at the entrance to my back yard because the unique "stitched" leaves are a conversation piece for visitors.

Large-flowered Bellwort (*U. grandiflora*) has larger orange-yellow 2 inch flowers and is often called Merrybells. The leaves of Wild Oats or Sessile Bellwort (*U. sessilifolia*) clasp the stem and are not perfoliate.

PROPAGATION: Bellwort is easily propagated by rhizome division in the spring or when dormant. The white horizontal rhizome of Bellwort lies 1¹/₂ to 2 inches underground and has stringy white roots.

PLANTLORE: The ancient Doctrine of Signatures indicated that Bellwort would cure diseases of the throat because the small twisted drooping flower resembled the small drooping membrane at the back of the throat called the uvula.

6. Wild Bleeding Heart *(Dicentra eximia)*

In the nursery trade, Wild Bleeding Heart is also called Fern-leafed Bleeding Heart and Fringed Bleeding Heart. It is in the same family as Dutchman's Breeches and Squirrel Corn and is easy to grow. This lovely fern-like plant grows in a compact, bushy shape about 10–18 inches tall, 12–30 inches wide, and is a dependable wildflower to fill in spaces when spring ephemerals become dormant. Heart-shaped 1 inch flowers dangle from long racemes and continue to bloom on and off all summer long. The flowers are usually a delicate pink, but can be found in shades ranging from lavender-pink to hot pink.

Although it is not native to the northern states of the Lower Midwest, planted specimens flourish here. It grows wild in the woods of some of the more southern states, including Tennessee. This plant is readily available from many garden centers and catalogs, self-sows profusely, blooms periodically all summer long, and is a wonderful addition to any wildflower garden.

PLANTING REQUIREMENTS: It does well in both high, filtered shade and heavy, dense shade. If there is too much sunlight, the leaves will become yellow and ugly. Plant in moist, humus-rich, loamy well-drained soil.

PROPAGATION: Seeds form in light green capsules which look like thin, bumpy peapods, and fresh flowers, spent flowers and seedpods can occupy the same drooping raceme. Because this plant blooms intermittently all summer, seed capsules also continue to form. The shiny ripe seeds are small and black and need moist cold stratification for at least 4 weeks in order to germinate. Seeds can be planted immediately and will germinate the next season, or you can hasten germination by storing ripened seeds in moist sphagnum peat moss in a zipperlock bag in the refrigerator for at least four weeks, then plant. Cover with a fine layer of soil and keep moist until germination occurs. These seedlings can be carefully transplanted to a permanent location in about three or four months. However, because Wild Bleeding Heart self-sows easily, you may prefer to let nature take its course and use the little seedlings around the mother plant to increase your stock.

As the plant matures, the short, carrot-like rhizomes multiply and become intertwined to form a coarse, fibrous rootstock of multiple crowns with eyes for the following season's growth. Divide mature plants in early spring or fall after three years to keep them blooming well.

You can't change the world, but you can change
    your heart . . .
No, you can't change the whole world, but you
    can change your own part.
And you can't change the world, but you can
    make a start.
The problem is so massive . . . are we equal to
    the task?

—Verlene Schermer, 1996

It is an absolute delight to watch huge
Pileated Woodpeckers march up and down
the elm tree, or a fat, rat-tailed opossum
waddle across the patio. Squirrels chase
each other, racing up and down trees with
abandon, and at night as I lie in bed, I hear
the Barred Owls hoot, "Who cooks for
you? Who cooks for you all?" In this chapter, the primary emphasis is on gardening
to attract butterflies or birds, but you will
probably find that other wildlife will move
in as well.

A small family-run heating and air
conditioning company near downtown
Indianapolis received a Backyard Wildlife
Habitat Certificate for landscaping around
its new offices. The property was previously a barren canal-side coalyard and rail-
way line, established shortly after the Civil
War. It had been a favorite spot to dump
trash and garbage. Aside from a few resi-
dences across the street, it is surrounded
by pavement. Commercial buildings rising nearby create a steamy summer environment, inhospitable even for humans.

The company created a meadow
planted with native perennials and grasses

12.

Be Wild
and Woolly

*Wildlife, Birds,
and Butterflies*

Pussy
Willow

between the office and the canal, which employees and clients can enjoy from the large picture windows. There was initial resistance from neighbors, who expressed concern that rats would move into the meadow. City officials sent out fliers and talked to the residents about the values of meadow plantings. Pointing out that rats would be more apt to come to the former trash site, they quelled the opposition.

Now the barren area is a lovely flowering meadow. A huge clump of Big Bluestem helps support a tall yellow sunflower-like Cup Plant, and serves as a backdrop for plantings of blue New England Asters, purple Dense Blazing Star, Blue False Indigo, Purple Coneflowers, yellow Gray-headed Coneflowers, Black-eyed Susans, and rosy-pink Queen-of-the-Prairie. Prairie plants bloom successively from early spring until fall, and several native trees and shrubs soften the formerly bleak landscape, creating a sense of enclosure and privacy. A variety of native grasses create movement and sound. A large patch of Purple Coneflowers suddenly appeared in a spot frequented by ground-feeding birds.

A city employee, amazed at the vigor of the plantings because he knew the subsoil was full of coal dust and rubble, commented, "You are accomplishing bio-remediation on this poor landscape with your native plantings." Since the plantings on this property have become established, the owners have recorded over 60 species of birds. Squirrels and chipmunks have moved in, butterflies and dragonflies dance over the colorful flowers, and passersby stop to ask questions.

The Ronald McDonald House in Cleveland, Ohio, was recognized in a special dedication ceremony on August 23, 1997, as the 20,000th recipient of a Certified Backyard Wildlife Habitat certificate (requirements listed at the end of this chapter). The habitat contains a pond with a waterfall, trees, and shrubs to encourage wildlife. It is a special place for families of children with serious illnesses to enjoy nature. Children can observe birds and butterflies as they sit inside a full-sized tepee covered with grape vines, scarlet runner beans, and Dutchman's Pipe. One of the originators of this habitat said, "I thought it was a wonderful way for [my children] to learn about nature and to realize that we all have a responsibility to take care of our world."

If it is possible to create viable habitats for wildlife in the center of major metropolitan areas, how much easier it should be to persuade wildlife to take up residence in our suburban yards! Unfortunately, sterile, water-guzzling "property-line to property-line" grass lawns primarily appeal to "lawn-mower salesmen" species, rather than birds, butterflies, and small mammals.

So what needs to change in the typical American suburban landscape to encourage these intriguing flying or four-footed friends to take up residence? As you contemplate that question, don't forget a few givens: in order to have butterflies, you also need caterpillars that eat holes and chunks out of leaves; spraying is a no-no; plants cannot be picture perfect. Raccoons can tip over your garbage, deer may eat your favorite hosta for an evening snack, and an abundance of birds might necessitate washing the family car more often. However, plants usually grow new leaves after the caterpillars devour their share, those masked raccoon bandits are a delight to watch, there are few thrills equal to seeing a deer in the neighborhood, and the coin-op car wash is probably not far off.

How Can I Attract Wildlife to My Property?

Decide what you really want to invite into your yard, and study the habitat components necessary for the survival of that particular species. If you provide these, the wild ones will respond. And before you begin to plot out the habitat area, go into the house. Be sure you will have a view of these little guests from your easy chair or the kitchen table.

The four basic needs for wildlife survival are similar to our own: food, water, shelter, and individual space. Our natural environment is composed of communities which are interdependent. Plants, animals, birds, and butterflies and other insects depend upon each other for survival, so as one species is pollinated, another is fed. Diversity and variety of plant material are more effective than a monoculture, and create a healthier landscape. Plant diversity is particularly important to ensure that these basic requirements will be met during every season of the year:

Food: Choose a variety of plant specimens for an ongoing, year-long supply of nectar, berries, nuts, and seeds to attract small mammals, supplement bird feeders, and encourage a greater variety of birds. Winter and early spring are the most difficult times for wildlife to find food, so include specimens that hold fruit throughout the winter. Hawthorn, crabapple, juniper, Black Chokeberry, Snowberry, or American Highbush

Cranberry are good choices. Consider including vines like Bittersweet or Virginia Creeper as well. In addition to food, many birds need grit or gravel to grind their food and dust to "bathe" in. Place a small bed of sand and gravel near shelter so that they can quickly escape if danger threatens.

Water: At a minimum, you should have a birdbath for your feathered friends, plus a broad saucer filled with pebbles and water, or constantly moistened sand, for butterflies to puddle in. Small pools, ponds, and streams, and even water-filled containers will bring a variety of wildlife, including damsel flies and frogs.

Shelter: Do you remember the scene in the Disney movie *Bambi* when the forest creatures crept from the edge of the woods into the open meadow? Wildlife need cover to hide or escape from predators. Winter birds are more apt to visit a feeder if they can fly to nearby evergreens and eat the morsel of seed in relative safety. Trees, shrubs, vines, or grasses provide midday shade, shelter from the wind, a place to rest, and nesting sites to raise young.

The middle or understory is the layer that is most often missing from the modern landscape, except near the foundation of the house, and may be the most important component you can add to help birds and wildlife. Consider planting a variety of small trees and shrubs to create a biohedge for food and shelter (see chapter 5). Property lines are often chosen for siting these hedges, but another small grouping near the patio can help bring wildlife closer to the house for viewing.

Dead trees or "snags" are wonderful apartment houses for woodpeckers, raccoons, owls, and a variety of other wildlife and birds. Snags also house a multitude of insects to tempt wildlife to stop for lunch. Instead of getting carried away with the chain saw to make things neat, plant a vine at the base, and just enjoy watching the inhabitants of this low-income housing unit.

Individual Space: Don't you feel happier and healthier when you have personal space? Territory is an important component of individual health and survival for wildlife, too, and dominance determines the pecking order. Since males challenge other males in the same species for a mate, nesting sites, and first rights to food, territory needs to be considered when designing flower borders and hanging bird houses and feeders.

If two wren houses are too close to each other, a couple will build nests in both and defend both, but raise its family in only one house. I hang a wren house on each side of our one-acre property, and different wren or chickadee families usually occupy at least three of the four. All summer, the wrens' beautiful, lilting warble and the happy chick-a-dee-dee-dee song keep me smiling as I work in my gardens.

Enough space between feeders will help attract larger numbers of birds of the same species, and give those lower in the pecking order a chance to be fed. Hummingbirds can be fiercely territorial; feeders are located on each side of our house to cut down on fights which otherwise occur as the dominant male chases other males away from "his" feeder.

What if I Don't Want So Many Gardens?

Gardening for wildlife can actually reduce that overwhelming feeling of "too many gardens." Closely planted shrubs and trees create a wildlife-friendly area. Pruning tasks and leaf clean-up can be reduced if you accept the idea that excessive neatness may deter wildlife from taking up residence in your yard. By excessive neatness, I am referring to closely clipped lawns without a twig or leaf in sight, and heavily pruned foundation plantings which do not welcome wildlife. Instead, plant the trees and shrubs with enough space for them to grow. Incorporating ground cover under the trees and shrubs will fill in spaces, cut down on weeding, and give cover and nesting sites.

Evergreen and deciduous trees and shrubs can form a wonderful living privacy fence around your yard, while providing food, shelter, and space for wildlife. Established native plants and less turf grass means less maintenance—and more time to relax! Obviously, the use of insecticides and herbicides should be discontinued, since these chemicals will destroy the very lives you are trying to attract.

How Can I Attract Wildlife to My Typical Suburban Lot?

Create a small wild area toward the back of the property. It can be allowed to look wild, or maintained in a more civilized fashion, as long as you don't get carried away with extreme neatness. Be sure to locate it where you can easily observe it from the windows of your home.

Begin with small trees and add some flowering, berry-producing shrubs like deciduous holly, chokeberries, or some members of the large family of viburnums. Encourage a native ground cover like Green and Gold or Wild Ginger. Put down mulch, and plant shade-tolerant annuals like impatiens or wax begonias to fill in the spaces until the ground cover is established. The more spaces you fill with mulch and plants, the less weeding you have to do. If there is a privacy fence, consider covering at least part of it with a native vine like Crossvine or Virginia Creeper, which reportedly attracts 39 species of wildlife.

Prairie grasses and sun-loving flowering forbs can lure a large number of birds, butterflies, and small mammals by providing food as well as shelter, cover, and nesting sites. A grouping of short-grass prairie plants such as Little Bluestem, Prairie Dropseed, Columbine, Coreopsis, and Purple Prairie Clover can be planted as a typical perennial border, but will encourage wildlife to visit. Include butterfly magnets like Whorled Milkweed, Butterfly Weed, and Common Milkweed. The colorful flowers of Purple, Green-headed, and Gray-headed Coneflowers are filled with sweet nectar and, later, supply nutritious seed.

Tall, yellow-flowered silphiums such as Rosinweed, Prairie Dock, Cup Plant, and Compass Plant can be combined with airy Switchgrass or the taller, more upright Indian Grass to provide food and shelter and give structure and "bones" to the back of a larger garden. Cup Plant can even hold rainwater in the unusual cupped perfoliate leaves.

Will Planting for Wildlife Encourage Undesirables?

How about rats? You can assure your neighbors and family that rats are residents of wharves, sewers, old buildings, and garbage dumps, and are attracted by meat scraps, bones, and huge food storage sites like grain elevators. You can safely plant any size prairie or meadow on your property, and put kitchen vegetable scraps in compost bins, with little fear of attracting rats.

In most small home meadows or prairies, the only rodents you are likely to see are seed-eating chipmunks and squirrels. Neil Diboll of Prairie Nursery told me that he enjoys watching tiny Jumping Mice (*Zapodidae*) in his extensive Wisconsin prairies, and sees chipmunks, squirrels, field mice, and an occasional gopher or groundhog. As for moles and voles, a conventional garden will attract just as many.

What about snakes? I have planted native plants in wooded areas and in my small prairie garden for many years, and I have yet to see a snake, although I certainly have rock, brush, and wood piles strategically located should one ever want to move in. Snakes generally dislike meeting humans as much as the reverse, so they tend to stay out of sight most of the time, and I suppose it is possible that some unseen helpers live in the yard without my knowledge.

A friend recently bemoaned the death of a huge black rat snake that had lived on her property for years. This fellow had kept the area free of moles, shrews, voles, mice, and other so-called "pests." A new neighbor had recently moved next door and was not told about "Wilbur." Startled when he unexpectedly met Wilbur face to face, the new neighbor unceremoniously lopped off the snake's head with his spade. My friend hunted unsuccessfully in the nearby woods for a replacement for Wilbur, and even checked at the nearby pet store, but was informed that it is illegal to sell rat snakes. The pet shop employee commented, "But if it was legal, even a small rat snake would probably cost over $60." My friend, who still hasn't located another snake, sighs, "Even if I find one, what will keep it from visiting my neighbor and getting beheaded?"

If you are fortunate enough to have a snake take up residence on your property, name it "Wilbur" or "George" or "Penelope." Then if either of you should happen to meet the other unexpectedly, simply take a deep breath to regain your composure and say, "Oh, hello there, Penelope. Thanks for helping," and go on your way, knowing the pest problem is minimized thanks to this quiet, unobtrusive friend. And remember to communicate with your neighbor!

Learn to identify the very few venomous snakes in the Lower Midwest, but remember that there is nothing to fear from the vast majority of useful and non-poisonous species.

Will my wild area attract bugs? Probably, and that is not all bad. There are good bugs and bad bugs. In a healthy environment, the good guys keep the bad guys under control. Many insects are helpful pollinators. Plants like Wild Ginger and Red Trillium are pollinated by carrion beetles that mistake the reddish-brown flowers for rotting meat and climb in to investigate.

Even the so-called bad bugs have a purpose. When my small grandson asked, "Why did God make mosquitoes?" I replied, "Well, probably so that birds could have something to eat beside worms and seeds." Mosquitoes are actually a very important link in the food chain. They breed in standing water. After a good rainstorm, there will probably be more standing water in a sterile landscape than in a natural garden of native plants. Ten days are needed to hatch a brood of mosquitoes, so patrol your property and dump any standing water. If you have a still pond or pool, stock it with small fish to eat the mosquito larvae before they have a chance to develop.

Problems arise when we grab the nearest aerosol can of insecticide or spray randomly with a broad-spectrum chemical that kills all the insects except the ones that have developed resistance, which, unfortunately, are more often the destructive ones.

The good guys include spiders, who are the "lions" of the insect world and do a great job. My mother used to say, "You know that you have a healthy house if there are spiders." The nervous system of a spider is so delicate that they are the first to be destroyed in a chemical attack, or if the environment is unhealthy. Do you have a healthy house? I do!

Praying Mantis and Walking Sticks are fantastic insects to observe as they slowly march up and down a shrub, camouflaged so well that you need to look twice to determine why that leaf or twig is moving. Butterfly caterpillars enjoy eating many plants and will reward your generosity with a lovely fluttering insect later in the summer.

Small flying and crawling insects help pollinate the beautiful flowers; birds are attracted to feast on the insects. One of the great things about providing a wild habitat is being able to watch nature in action every day, right in your own back yard.

How Do I Attract Birds and Butterflies?

If you plant nectar sources, Ruby-throated Hummingbirds, Orioles, and butterflies will be attracted to the garden. Hummingbirds are also voracious insect eaters, and they are after the insects in the nectar-laden plants in addition to the nectar itself. Seed-eaters like chickadees, Tufted Titmice, cardinals, goldfinches, and blue jays are a few of the species that can be lured with seed-bearing plants. They will peck seeds out of many of our flowering native plant species like Purple Coneflowers, sunflowers, and asters, so don't be too eager to deadhead. Your generosity may be rewarded by a "surprise" planting of wildflowers, like the Purple Coneflowers at the beginning of this chapter. Trees and shrubs with berries and fruits attract a variety of birds and animals, including Orioles and Rose-breasted Grosbeaks, who love a dessert of berries and fruits to top off a tasty meal of tent caterpillars!

Purple Martins are efficient bug-zappers since their diet consists entirely of insects. However, remember that these birds need a large space to dive and swoop as they catch their favorite food—mosquitoes!—so if your suburban area is blessed with trees, you will not be blessed with Purple Martins. Martins, our only black-bellied swallows, prefer a home near water with large open areas. If you live in a rural area and can incorporate a small pond or homemade stream into your landscape, you may be able to entice them to move in and reduce your mosquito population. These birds were appreciated by early Native Americans, who reportedly constructed houses to encourage them to stay. Purple Martins are so popular that there is an active society organized in their honor!

Purple Martins winter in South America. In early spring, scouts arrive to check out the territory and find suitable accommodations for the flock, which arrives 2 or 3 weeks later and stays until around Labor Day. To attract these sociable, communal birds, erect a martin house with many apartments in an open area. If you build the house, construct each individual compartment about 8 x 8 inches and drill a 2-inch-diameter entrance hole. The house should be 15–20 feet above the ground. Many commercially made martin houses include telescoping poles for ease in cleaning. English sparrows are the biggest problem, since they move into any available space. Some homeowners use corks to stop up the entrance holes to deter sparrows, removing them only in spring when martins have been sighted.

Did you know that one bat can eat 3,000–7,000 mosquitoes and other insects in a single night? These creatures of the night are much more efficient than any bug-zapper you can purchase, and do not like to tangle themselves in human hair. Honest! In fact they are highly unlikely to come anywhere near you as they swoop and fly, because they are equipped with echolocation, one of the most sophisticated navigating systems in the animal kingdom. Bats are nocturnal, coming out just at dusk to catch and devour mosquitoes. Consider adding a bat house to your bird house collection. Bats will be more likely to find the house and move in if it is attached to a pole or building, rather than to a tree. Paint it black, and mount it 15 feet above the ground. It should face southeast to get as much sunlight as possible.

What Trees or Shrubs Will Attract Songbirds?

The light blue berries of the Red Cedar (*Juniperus virginiana*) are an excellent food source for wildlife, and this evergreen attracts more than 40 species of songbirds. However, it is an alternate host for the cedar-apple rust and should not be planted near hawthorn, apple, crabapple, and certain members of the Rose Family. Purchase rust-resistant species of the latter plants if there are existing Red Cedars on the property.

American Highbush Cranberry (*Viburnum trilobum*) entices the Eastern Bluebird, the Brown Thrasher, and the Cedar Waxwing with its pretty red cranberry-like fruits. Serviceberry is a favorite of birds like the Wood Thrush, Red-eyed Vireo, and Rose-breasted Grosbeak. The fruit of our beautiful dogwood species is relished by a variety of birds. Flowering, Pagoda, and Red Osier Dogwoods are sought out by Summer Tanagers, Eastern Bluebirds, and Catbirds. Northern Bayberry (*Myrica pensylvanica*) attracts Yellow-rumped Warblers and Tree Swallows. Black Cherry, Spicebush, and Holly are other desirable trees that will bring a variety of birds.

Will Bluebirds Nest in My Area?

Bluebirds are fruit and insect eaters and need about five acres of space per pair. This beautiful bird, with an indescribably bright blue back and a rusty breast, is the state bird of Missouri. They prefer open areas with short vegetation, so a short-grass prairie planting may tempt them. Valuable fruiting native plants to encourage Bluebirds include Red Osier Dogwood, Gray Dogwood, Pin Cherry, Elderberry, and Downy Serviceberry. Civic-minded groups often install nesting boxes along "bluebird trails" in field windbreaks and along fence lines. Bluebirds also nest in dead-tree cavities and may choose abandoned woodpecker holes, but one pair will not nest closer than 100 yards—the length of a football field—to another pair.

How Do I Attract Hummingbirds?

Hummingbirds are like tiny helicopters as they hover, dart, and fly in any direction, including backwards! These feisty little birds love red and orange more than any other color, which you will learn in a hurry if you wear a red shirt in their vicinity. Some birding experts insist it is contrasting colors that attract them, rather than red per se, so include sky-blue asters and purple liatris in your red and orange hummingbird garden.

Wild Columbine and Solomon's Seal will tempt them to stop off and eat as they return from their long migration early in spring. In addition to entertaining us with their antics, these tiny birds are responsible for pollinating many of our plants. To keep them coming back, cover a chain-link fence with tubular-flowered Trumpet-Creeper, mass some Cardinal Flower in a border garden near the kitchen window, or plant bright red Bee-balm behind daylilies, coralbells, and annual red Salvia. Indian Pink (*Spigelia marilandica)* has a magnificent red trumpet with a bright yellow interior and is easily grown from seed.

Hummingbirds love the flowers of the *Silene* species. Fire Pink blooms early in the summer, and Royal Catchfly continues the red show in mid-summer. Fire Pink is a short-lived perennial about 6–8 inches high that hugs the edges of the woods, thrives on well-drained soil, and will put on a spectacular show on a gravelly hillside. Royal Catchfly is a threatened species in several states; native plant gardeners can assist Mother Nature by planting the easily germinated seeds and growing these stately red beauties in the home garden.

Hummingbirds also visit artificial feeding stations. To make hummingbird nectar, combine one cup of sugar with four cups of water. Bring the mixture to a boil, and stir to dissolve the sugar. Red coloring is neither necessary nor good for the little birds. Most hummingbird feeders have bright red plastic flowers anyway. Never use honey in place of sugar, because honey can cause a fatal fungal infection. Replace the syrup at least once a week, oftener in hot weather. I usually do this task every Sunday afternoon, so I don't forget. If ants are a problem, try smearing petroleum jelly on the wire. Clean the feeder with vinegar and water.

I Want Butterflies. Is a Flower Border All I Need?

Butterflies are drawn to large areas of color and fragrance as they flit through your property. Plant masses of diverse colorful nectar and larval food plants in a sunny flower border. If you add a few well-chosen trees, shrubs, or vines, a place for them to puddle, and sunning rocks for basking, a variety of butterflies can be enticed to declare your property home. Butterflies need a safe place to hide, rest, and retreat from the midday heat or to get out of the wind.

Our region is blessed with several large, eye-catching members of Lepidoptera, including Swallowtails, Monarchs, Fritillaries, and Mourning Cloaks; many smaller species such as the colorful Red Admiral, Buckeye, Painted Lady, and Viceroy; plus a host of other moths and butterflies.

Nearly any of the prairie species can be combined to create a wonderful color palette of nectar plants. Butterflies actually prefer yellow, purple, blue, pink, and orange flowered nectar sources over red flowers, and massing colors in the garden will entice a variety of these beautiful insects to stop in for a snack. Begin with purple Liatris, Black-eyed Susans, and Gray-headed Coneflowers. Add groups of hot pink and lavender-pink Monarda. Plant tall blue or white asters next to deep purple Ironweed at the back of the border, and Purple and Yellow Coneflowers at the center and front. Be sure to include at least one of the milkweeds, the favorite all-around plant of many butterflies.

There is a milkweed species for nearly any soil and moisture condition. Butterfly Weed (*Asclepias tuberosa*) demands sharply drained soil or it will rot, while Swamp Milkweed (*A. incarnata*) and Red Milkweed (*A. rubra*) prefer moist soil. Common Milkweed (*A. syriaca*) grows along roadsides and in dry fields, and the deep magenta-red flowers of Purple Milkweed (*A. purpurascens*) can be found in woods and thickets. Study the requirements to select the species that suits your property, and work within the limitations of your site.

In addition to nectar sources, butterflies need host or larval food plants for the caterpillar stage. Design your flower garden with nectar plants in front of larval food plants to camouflage the caterpillar salad-bar.

What Larval Food Sources Can My Landscape Provide?

Surprisingly, larval food sources for many butterflies come from vines, trees, or shrubs that are readily available from the local garden center. A kitchen herb garden will attract and feed the larvae of many butterfly and moth species, so plant enough to share.

Swallowtail larvae need host plants from members of the Parsley Family; in addition to the herb-garden variety, wildflowers in this family include native Golden Alexanders *(Zizia aurea)*, with bright yellow flowers in spring and early summer, and Rattlesnake Master *(Eryngium yuccifolium)*, which looks like a large yucca plant with unique ball-like flowers. This historic native plant will feed Swallowtail larvae and never fail to spark the interest of your human garden visitors.

Nettles and thistles also provide larval food for butterflies and moths. Two weedy Parsley Family wildflowers produce those nasty seeds that stick to your clothing and your pet's fur. Sweet Cicely *(Osmorhiza claytoni)* has needle-like seeds that smell like anise, and Black Snakeroot *(Sanicula spp.)* contributes velcro-like, round, stick-tight burs. Queen Anne's Lace is an invasive, alien wildflower in the Parsley Family which originated in Europe, and some nettles "sting." But don't destroy all those weeds—leave a few for the butterfly larvae. Simply remove the flower heads to keep them from seeding and taking over the garden.

There are other native plants, including trees and shrubs, that are larval hosts for individual butterfly species. With a little simple research and planning, it is possible to attract a wide variety of butterflies as you beautify your property.

How Long Do Butterflies Live?

Some adult butterflies live only a week or two; a few live as long as 18 months. The egg-larva-pupa-butterfly metamorphosis can take up to several weeks or even months. A number of butterflies hibernate, and most of these species hibernate in the third or chrysalis (pupa) stage, although a few hibernate as butterflies or caterpillars. If you want a yardful of butterflies, you need to be less diligent with leaf clean-up in the fall.

Using the Monarch as a model: the adult butterflies mate; the female lays her eggs on the host (larval food) plant; and the eggs hatch into tiny larvae (caterpillars), which increase in size as they eat the leaves of the host plant. Monarch larvae eat until they are round, fat, 2-inch-long caterpillars. When the larva has grown to the appropriate size, it attaches itself at one end to a leaf or twig and hangs down, forming a "J." It develops into a chrysalis (pupa), and hangs for the appropriate number of days, at which time the chrysalis splits and a butterfly emerges to seek a mate and begin the cycle again. This is the general pattern of metamorphosis for other species of butterflies and moths. A few also spin a cocoon, and some fold themselves in leaves.

How Do I Recognize the Caterpillar Stage of a Butterfly?

Ugly gray cutworms and the so-called "winter-predicting" Woolly Bear Caterpillars are easy to identify, but whenever I see an unidentified caterpillar, I wonder if it is headed off to munch my hostas and ravish my tomatoes and vegetables, or if it is the larva of some beautiful butterfly. I usually look, wonder, and watch as it inches its way to safety, and do nothing, except continue to wonder.

Books about butterflies, complete with colorful drawings or photographs of these lovely winged insects, are easy to find, but few tell what butterflies need to eat in their larval period, and even fewer describe the appearance of these larvae. Before a beautiful butterfly emerges from its chrysalis, it is first a fat caterpillar, whose only task is to be an "eating machine" that voraciously devours a multitude of leaves. If you want the "beauty," you must first entertain the "beast."

In The Butterflies of Indiana, Ernest M. Shull includes precise descriptions of butterfly larvae. Some of the butterfly field or nature guide books, such as Peterson and Golden, have drawings of larvae. Below are four of the largest "beauties" common to our region, and some information about their caterpillars to help protect those essential "beasts."

Great Spangled Fritillary

If you see a black caterpillar, look closely to see if it has branching spines that are orange at the base. It may be the larva of a Great Spangled Fritillary, a beautiful coppery-orange butterfly with black markings and a huge wingspan of 3 to 4 inches. This species generally has one and sometimes two broods a year. After the fall hatching, the larva hibernates until spring, when it emerges to feed on violets at night (so to attract these lovely fellows to your yard, please don't nuke the violets). Plant a Passionflower vine to attract them in the summer. Fritillaries love to gather nectar from flowers of deep purple Blazing Star (*Liatris* spp.) and brilliant orange Butterfly Weed, as well as from Ironweed, Black-eyed Susans, Gloriosa Daisy, and Verbena, and prefer the proximity of a damp meadow or marshy spot.

Another striking member of the Fritillary Family is the Diana. The male is considerably smaller than the female in this species, with wide orange edging its dark brown-black wings, while the larger female edges her wings with aqua and white. The black, spiny larva, which is similar to the Great Spangled, also feeds on violets. This lovely butterfly actually prefers a manure pile to the flower border; mix up some manure tea to tempt it to puddle in your yard.

The mottled brown, ridged Fritillary chrysalis attached to a host tree or shrub blends with twigs and branches to give good camouflage.

Mourning Cloak

Familiar Mourning Cloak butterflies begin as velvety black larvae covered with tiny, delicate white specks. The larva has a row of interesting raised red spots on the back, several rows of branched bristles, and fat, rust-colored legs. The Mourning Cloak larva's conspicuous attire deters birds from choosing it for a tasty meal.

Consider incorporating some water into the landscape if you would like to invite this enchanting butterfly into your yard. Dressed in a deep purple-brown "widow's cloak" beautifully trimmed with bright blue spots and edged with buttery yellow, Mourning Cloaks can be observed sipping nectar from asters, goldenrod, and milkweed species. They prefer streams, but my little garden pools made from 15-gallon hog-feeders must be adequate, because I have a congregation each summer.

I have none of their preferred native willows to serve as host plants, but my woods are filled with many maple trees, and even a few elms. Mourning Cloaks also lay their eggs on aspen, birch, cottonwood, hackberry, hawthorn, and poplar. These conspicuous customers will chomp many tree leaves before they pupate, but don't be alarmed—most trees grow new leaves within the same season with no ill effects. The chrysalis of the Mourning Cloak looks like a light brown leaf with thorns, and is hard to spot.

Mourning Cloaks may live up to 10 months, usually have two to three broods each summer, and often hibernate in piles of leaves or brush, under tree bark, or under the eaves of nearby buildings. Try filling a large coffee can with leaves and twigs to tuck into the crotch of one of their favored host trees to encourage hibernation in your yard, rather than purchasing a fancy butterfly house, and don't be a "clean-freak" in the fall with the leaf rake!

Mourning Cloaks appreciate nectar sources from Purple Coneflower, a variety of milkweeds, and dogbane (*Apocynum* spp.). They love to feast from a saucer of rotting fruit, although this will also be tempting to ants, bees, wasps, and flies.

Monarch

Pictures of the distinctive larva of the Monarch butterfly are readily available, and the 2-inch-long caterpillar is easy to recognize, with threadlike appendages at each end of its wildly striped black, white, and greenish-yellow body. Milkweed is the host plant for this orange and black butterfly, and a planting of milkweed species will almost guarantee a population of Monarchs. The small jewel-like chrysalis is lime-green studded with gold, not much larger than ¾ inch, and once the caterpillar pupates, a period of 9–10 days is all that is needed before a Monarch is dancing across your yard. To keep them there, plant goldenrods, marigolds, lantana, and dogbane, along with the milkweed.

Swallowtail

I have spent many hours chasing and photographing magnificent Swallowtails. These brilliantly colored butterflies, in shades of yellow, black, and blue, are probably our region's largest and best-known butterflies, and the ones most often admired in the garden. At least six Swallowtail species frequent the Lower Midwest. The two largest are the Pipevine and Giant Swallowtails, with wingspans of up to 5 inches or more.

If you plant one of the pipevines (*Aristolochia* spp.; for more on them, see chapter 6) instead of the traditional English Ivy to dress up a tool shed or fence, Pipevine Swallowtails will likely appear to grace your yard and lay their orange eggs. The larvae of this large, beautiful butterfly are dark purplish-brown, with three rows of paired tentacles, which are longest on the head. Pipevine Swallowtails are distasteful to birds due to their larval food, which includes Dutchman's Pipe, Wild Ginger, and weedy species like Virginia Snakeroot (*Aristolochia serpentaria*) and Knotweed or Smartweed (*Polygonum* spp.). Palatable females of several other Swallowtail species, including Eastern Black, Tiger, and Spicebush, avoid becoming bird food by mimicking the dark-colored Pipevine, much as the Viceroy mimics the Monarch.

The Giant Swallowtail larva is olive or dark brown with creamy white or buff markings and a broad saddle around the middle of the body. Orange scent horns diffuse a very strong odor when the caterpillar is startled or provoked. Its preferred host plants include cultivated citrus leaves, Prickly Ash (*Zanthoxylum americanum*), and Hoptree (*Ptelea trifoliata*), and these larvae need a constant supply of leaves.

Other larval food sources for Swallowtail species include Spicebush, Sassafras, Sweet Bay, Pawpaw, Wild Cherry, Tulip Tree, willow, poplar, parsley, parsnip, celery, and carrot. A friend of mine in Nashville, Tennessee, lost her entire planting of dill to a host of Swallowtail larvae, but thought the trade-off was worth it when all those elegant butterflies emerged.

Most Swallowtail larvae are dark brown with a white saddle when they are first hatched, but they change according to the species as they grow and mature. An Eastern Swallowtail chrysalis looks like a little lime green dragon with two yellow "eyes" and a double row of beautiful bright yellow dots marching down its back. At the rear of the chrysalis, there are noticeable ridges on the unmarked underside.

In late summer, my garden is alive with Swallowtails busily sipping nectar from Joe-Pye Weed with its large rose-mauve flowers. Swallowtails also flutter around gardens with masses of orange Butterfly Weed, zinnias and marigolds, lantana, and phlox.

Schull's larval descriptions of other commonly observed Swallowtails in the Lower Midwest include:

Eastern Black Swallowtail: *(2.6–3.5" wingspan): young larva is brownish black with a white saddle, resembling a bird dropping. The mature larva is leafy green, with each segment crossed by a black band dotted with tiny, round yellow spots.*

Spicebush Swallowtail: *(3.5–4.5" wingspan): dark green larva with two eyespots on the metathorax and two less prominent spots back of the hump.*

Tiger Swallowtail: *(3.1–5.5" wingspan): Green and swollen in front; it has large false eyespots of orange and black.*

Zebra Swallowtail: *(2.4–3.5" wingspan): Smooth, pea-green larva with yellow and black cross-bands, widest and darkest in the thoracic region.*

How Can I Tell if It Is a Butterfly or a Moth?

Butterflies flit about during the day, while most moths are nocturnal. Butterflies generally hold their wings erect when resting. Moths may hold their wings horizontally, or draw them back over the abdomen. A moth's body may appear furry as compared to the smooth body of a butterfly. Butterflies have small round knobs, like little boxing gloves, at the tip of their antennae. A moth's antennae lack these knobs and are often feathery. The chrysalis of a butterfly usually hangs unprotected from a twig or branch. Moths may pupate underground, in leaves or debris, or on trees or shrubs. Few butterflies are considered pests, but many moths, such as armyworms and tent caterpillars, are extremely destructive. Few destructive moths are attractive, and butterfly field guides should help identify undesirable moths.

How Can I Get These Insects to Stay Still for Photographs?

Butterflies and moths can often be observed feeding on sap oozing from a tree trunk. Ernest Shull describes a time-honored technique called "sugaring." An old recipe recommends combining "four pounds of sugar, a bottle of stale beer, and a little rum." Schull advises, "The following formula works even better: two pounds of brown sugar, one pint of beer, several tablespoons of Karo white syrup, and a half-dozen crushed, ripe bananas." Mix the chosen recipe ingredients well and let ferment for a few days. Stir and brush onto the trunks of trees within sight of your windows. Butterflies will arrive during the day and moths at night, and they can be easily photographed as they partake of this intoxicating feast.

What Is the Backyard Wildlife Habitat Program?

This program was started in 1973 by the National Wildlife Federation to acknowledge people who were "gardening for wildlife," whether their property was a large acreage, a minuscule city lot, or a commercial business as detailed earlier in this chapter. By providing appropriate food, water, shelter, and nesting sites, you can create a backyard habitat for a variety of wildlife, birds, and butterflies to qualify for this program. Order an information packet from the National Wildlife Federation, P. O. Box 50281, Hampden Station, Baltimore, MD 21211, call for information at (703) 790-4434, or check the website at http://www.nwf.org Submit the completed application form with the required fee. Qualifying applicants receive a special Backyard Wildlife Habitat certificate, and may purchase a handsome, permanent, recycled aluminum sign for a small fee.

Gardening for wildlife can accomplish many things: Lower-maintenance gardening with more trees and shrubs for seasonal beauty and privacy; a beautiful flower border of colorful native perennials; less raking; no herbicides or insecticides; less watering—all of which gives you more time to relax on the garden bench to enjoy the sounds and sights of all the creatures who thankfully reside on your property!

*　　*　　*

Six Suggested Trees and Shrubs to Attract Wildlife

1. White Pine *(Pinus strobus)*

White Pine is one of the fastest-growing evergreen privacy screens, will lend a beautiful, bluish-green backdrop to a perennial bed, and can provide a home to over 47 species of wildlife and birds. Seeds in the abundant pine cones are relished by Crossbills, Pine Siskins, and Red Squirrels. It makes a tightly knit hedge if planted in a zigzag, and is easily identified by its soft-textured needles in bundles of 5. Once settled in, it can grow 3–4 feet in a single season.

PLANTING REQUIREMENTS: Provenance is important; try to purchase locally grown stock. This state tree of Michigan is susceptible to air pollution, but in a clean environment can reach 80–100 feet tall. It thrives in a sunny site with loamy, moist, well-drained soil, but will tolerate most soil and moisture conditions. It should not be planted near gooseberry or currant bushes, which are the intermediate hosts of White Pine Blister Rust.

PROPAGATION: White Pine is easily grown from seed, or it can be transplanted as a seedling, or as a balled and burlapped specimen in spring or fall. It develops a taproot as well as spreading lateral roots.

PLANTLORE: The scientific name *strobus* originates from Greek and Latin words for pine cone, and White Pine produces pine cones in abundance. The wood is regularly used for many building purposes and may be the most economically important wood in North America. The bark was used in cough syrups, and Indians used the inner bark of the White Pine as a survival food.

2. Eastern Hemlock *(Tsuga canadensis)*

The graceful Eastern or Canadian Hemlock is one of the few evergreens that will tolerate shady growing conditions. This slow-growing, long-lived tree is a handsome specimen that can grow as tall as 60 to 80 feet. It can be pruned as a hedge, used as a windbreak, or planted as a background. Many wildlife species use this beautiful evergreen as shelter, and several birds enjoy the tasty seeds in the small reddish-brown cones, which generally hang on over winter. The needles are flattened, arranged in two ranks, and tend to be darker above and whiter beneath.

PLANTING REQUIREMENTS: Often found on north- or east-facing slopes, hemlocks prefer a somewhat protected site out of strong winds in moist, well-drained soil. They need at least partial sun to become full and dense and are particularly handsome when planted as a mass. Because they are so slow-growing, they are easily maintained as a 4- to 10-foot hedge by pruning early in the spring and again in midsummer.

PROPAGATION: Seedlings must be grown in moist, shaded conditions and are difficult to establish, so cuttings are generally preferred if you elect to start your own trees. Because of their slow-growing nature, nursery-grown seedlings or balled-and-burlapped specimens are generally recommended for transplanting in early spring. Once established, hemlock has few problems although it has been attacked by the Woolly Adelgid on the East Coast and occasionally gets scale or mite infestations.

PLANTLORE: Indians used the leaves to brew a tea. In 1921, Charles Deam wrote, "Hemlock [wood] is of no economic importance in Indiana. The bark is much used in tanning." Many huge trees were felled for the tannin-rich bark and then sadly left to decay.

The drink that killed Socrates was Poison Hemlock *(Conium maculatum)*, an entirely different species, which is a member of the Parsley Family.

3. Red Osier Dogwood *(Cornus sericea,* formerly *C. stolonifera)*

This shrub is of particular interest in the winter, when its bright red stems contrast with the stark landscape. Creamy white flowers bloom in late spring and may rebloom in midsummer. The flowers produce bluish-white berries that attract a multitude of wildlife species. Leaves turn orange-red in fall, making this a handsome plant year-round. It is an ideal choice for a mixed biohedge or to define the edge of your property.

The cultivar 'Flaviramea' has yellow stems, and 'Silver and Gold' sports variegated creamy-white edged leaves and yellow stems.

PLANTING REQUIREMENTS: Red Osier Dogwood can grow 5 to 9 feet tall and equally as wide. It spreads by suckers, which may be pruned with a spade from time to time. It will tolerate a wide range of soils, but prefers a moist, rich, well-drained, sunny location.

PROPAGATION: It is easily propagated by softwood or hardwood branch cuttings or by suckers, and transplants easily. This plant is readily found in the nursery trade.

PLANTLORE: Early settlers boiled the bark of the root to make a tonic for ague, as well as an astringent.

4. Downy Serviceberry *(Amelanchier arborea)*

The various Amelanchier species may be the most valuable wildlife plants you can choose. These shrubs or small trees generally do not grow over 25 feet tall, and provide food and shelter for more than 40 species of wildlife, including many songbirds, red fox, ruffed grouse, and raccoons. Downy Serviceberry is wonderful naturalized at the edge of a woods, massed, or used in mixed borders. In the spring, the delicate white flowers are among the earliest to emerge. In summer, the plant is covered with glossy, rich green leaves. The delicious deep purple blueberry-like fruits

are equally appealing to wildlife and humans. Downy
Serviceberry contributes a vibrant fall accent in the landscape, with colors ranging from yellow, orange, or
apricot to a deep maroon-red. The streaked gray
bark is attractive in winter. This disease-
resistant understory plant is also called
Juneberry, Shadbush, or Service Tree.
Other good Amelanchier species for the
landscape include Allegheny Shadblow (*A.
laevis*), Shadblow Serviceberry (*A. canadensis*),
and Low Shadblow (*A. humilis*).

PLANTING REQUIREMENTS: Plant in
rich, well-drained soil with adequate moisture in sun
or part shade, although it will tolerate fairly dense shade.

PROPAGATION: Downy Serviceberry is easily propagated from
fresh or cold-stratified seed, softwood cuttings, or rooted suckers dug in
the fall. It transplants well as a seedling or as a balled-and-burlapped nursery specimen.

PLANTLORE: The name Shadblow was reputedly affixed to this
plant because it blooms at the same time the Shad fish swim upriver in
the East. The berries were a favorite food of Native Americans and early
settlers.

5. Coralberry *(Symphoricarpos orbiculatus)*

Coralberry is also commonly known as Indian Currant. The berries are sought after by a variety of birds and wildlife, and the leaves
are a butterfly larval food source. Deer won't eat this shrub, but
hummingbirds and bees love the nectar in the small clusters of
white flowers tucked into the axils of the opposite leaves. The
tiny yellowish-white flowers have a hint of pink, and bloom in
midsummer. Coralberry is handsome in autumn, with fiery red
leaves and profuse dark crimson berries lined thickly along the
branches. The berries persist well into winter, enticing birds to
stop for a snack. It grows 2 to 5 feet high and nearly twice as wide.
It can be pruned in late winter. It is a good choice for a biohedge, a
shrub border, or a small city garden.

PLANTING REQUIREMENTS: Plant in fertile, well-drained ordinary garden soil in sun or shade. Coralberry needs good air circulation, as it is susceptible to mildew. However, it is a sturdy shrub, withstands pollution, and will tolerate nearly any planting environment. It suckers heavily and naturalizes well, providing both food and cover for wildlife.

PROPAGATION: Remove a rooted sucker in early spring or fall and replant. Soft or hardwood cuttings root easily. The seeds have a tough outer coat. Plant fresh ripe seed immediately or store in a warm, moist place for three months and then in a cold, moist place for 3–4 months. Started plants can be purchased from a nursery.

PLANTLORE: Thomas Jefferson prized white berries in the winter, and Coralberry's relative, Snowberry *(S. albus)*, was one of his favorite shrubs. Lewis and Clark helped to bring Snowberry into cultivation in America. It grows to 6 feet tall and is tolerant of alkaline soils, and I recommend it also.

6. Ninebark *(Physocarpus opulifolius)*

In *Dirr's Hardy Trees and Shrubs*, Michael Dirr comments, "This species is adaptable to all conditions, probably even nuclear attacks, and once established requires a bulldozer for removal." Needless to say, this is a sturdy shrub!

Ninebark is covered with small, white, ball-like flowers in early spring, followed by interesting reddish-brown inflated pod-like fruits, and has exfoliating shaggy bark for winter interest. It grows 5 to 8 feet tall and equally as wide. Ninebark's arching, spirea-like growth habit can create a dense hedge or a good privacy screen, or it can be incorporated into a mixed shrub border.

The nectar in Ninebark's flowers attracts hummingbirds and bees and its dense foliage provides good cover for wildlife.

PLANTING REQUIREMENTS: This tolerant shrub will thrive in full sun, partial shade, or full shade, in wet or dry environments, and will accept any soil conditions as long as the area is well drained.

PROPAGATION: Plant fresh seed immediately. No treatment is necessary. Softwood cuttings taken in midsummer root easily.

*   *   *

Six Suggested Nectar Plants

1. Stiff Goldenrod *(Solidago rigida)*

Botanical names are crucial in ordering goldenrod seeds; some species make better garden plants than others. *Solidago rigida* is just that—rigid. Its stiff stems remain upright and don't need staking. It has huge, slightly rounded clusters of beautiful bright yellow flowers in late summer and fall. But best of all, it is not invasive, as are so many of the Solidago species. It is generally 3 or 4 feet tall, although it can rise as high as 5 feet. Its flowers attract butterflies and hummingbirds. Birds love its seeds. It is wonderful when planted in a mass at the back of a border or naturalized into a prairie or meadow.

Other desirable species of *Solidago* include large flowered Showy Goldenrod *(S. speciosa)*, flat-topped Ohio Goldenrod *(S. ohioensis)*, and shade-tolerant Zigzag Goldenrod *(S. flexicaulis)*. The latter is an interesting woodland plant with a zigzag stem and small flower clusters that grow in the axils of the leaves.

PLANTING REQUIREMENTS: Most *Solidago* species need full sun and well-drained average garden soil. They also do well in sandy soil. Plant Stiff Goldenrod where you want it to stay, because its roots can extend nearly 5 feet into the ground.

PROPAGATION: Sow ripe seed immediately or divide mature clumps. Stiff Goldenrod also self-sows. Its roots are long and fibrous.

PLANTLORE: *Materia Medica*, published in 1832, reports that the leaves are gently astringent. The flowers were used to remove obstructions of the urinary organs or to heal ulcerations of the bladder. The leaves were also used to treat intestinal problems.

The sticky pollen of goldenrod is not the villain that causes hay fever.

That culprit is Ragweed (*Ambrosia* spp.), which sends up inconspicuous green flower stalks full of airborne pollen and is anything but ambrosia for allergy sufferers.

2. Royal Catchfly (*Silene regia*)

Striking bright red flowers top 3- to 4-foot-tall stiff stems and keep hummingbirds returning regularly to the garden. This beautiful plant is aptly described by its species name, *regia*, which means regal. Charles Deam wrote, "A very local plant, mostly of a dry, prairie habitat." It has become rare, but seeds heavily and germinates readily in a home garden situation. The stalkless leaves are opposite and clasp the stem.

PLANTING REQUIREMENTS: Plant Royal Catchfly in average to sandy garden soil that is well drained. This plant develops a taproot that will rot with too much moisture. It requires full sun and will be short-lived in partial shade. Sometimes it may need to be staked.

PROPAGATION: It is easy to grow from seed. Plant ripe, fresh seed immediately. Do not cover the seed, or let the planting medium dry out. Store dry seeds in an envelope or film canister in the refrigerator and plant in the spring.

Fire Pink (*S. virginica*), a smaller member of the *Silene* genus, blooms earlier than Royal Catchfly. It is happiest within or at the edge of the woods and is seldom over 2 feet tall. The bright red petals are notched. This short-lived perennial can be encouraged to stick around by lifting and transplanting some of the ground-hugging rosettes in early fall. Plant a few seeds for insurance. Fire Pink will self-sow if it likes its environment, but will decline and die if conditions are not quite satisfactory. Mulch lightly for winter protection. Remove the mulch early in the spring to prevent rot.

3. New England Aster (*Aster novae-angliae*)

Bright golden-centered violet flowers cover large shrubby New England Asters in late summer and early fall to complement the multitude of yellow goldenrods and other composites. These giants of the aster world can reach 3 to 5 feet in height, with a spread half as wide. They naturalize well, and can be used as a background planting for a perennial border or massed. They need good air circulation to prevent mildew and occasionally need staking, especially in a shady site. Butterflies, bees, and moths will seek out this plant for its sweet nectar.

Other desirable species include shade-tolerant woodland asters such as Heart-Leaved Blue Wood Aster (*Aster cordifolius*), Side-flowering Aster (*A. lateriflorus*), and Short's Aster (*A. shortii*). Smooth Aster (*A. laevis*), Heath Aster (*A. ericoides*), and Shining Aster (*A. firmus*) are sun-loving and prefer a meadow or prairie setting. Swamp Aster (*A. puniceus*) is true to its name and needs moist or wet soil.

PLANTING REQUIREMENTS: Plant in full sun or light shade in moist, rich garden soil that is well drained. Shear off about half of the top growth in early summer for a bushier plant. Mulch heavily to keep the soil cool and moist.

The roots are heavy rhizomes with many fibrous rootlets that need to be divided every 3 or 4 years to keep the plant neat and blooming profusely. Space divided plants 1 or 2 feet apart, with the growing tip just below the soil level.

PROPAGATION: Nursery stock is reputedly the most vigorous. Tip cuttings will produce small plantlets in midsummer. Plant fresh, ripe seed immediately, or stratify in the refrigerator for 4 to 6 weeks, then plant outdoors.

PLANTLORE: *Aster* is from the Greek and means "star." There are over 200 varieties of asters that grow wild in our natural prairies, meadows, and woodlands. Native Americans brewed a tea from the leaves, and some tribes smoked the pulverized root in a pipe to attract game.

4. Wild Columbine (*Aquilegia canadensis*)

Pretty little drooping flowers of red and yellow nod over delicate foliage. This plant tolerates a wide variety of environments, and will grow on rocky cliffs, in deep woods, and near streams. It is particularly effective at the edge of a woodland pond, or massed at the base of a large tree. It grows 12–30 inches tall.

Columbine has an exceptionally long bloom period and is a favorite nectar source for hummingbirds. Plant some of these graceful, airy beauties where you can watch from the window to see the lovely little winged visitors enjoying a sweet treat. Columbine is also the larval food source for the Columbine Duskywing butterfly, so be prepared to share.

PLANTING REQUIREMENTS: Plant in moist, well-drained, humus-rich garden soil in full sun or light shade. Leave 18–24 inches between plants. Cutting back the foliage after flowering will produce a new mound of neat-looking foliage that will persist throughout the summer. Leaves damaged by Leaf Miners should be removed.

PROPAGATION: Columbine has a coarse, short, thick, carrot-like rootstock with many fibrous roots that twist and turn, making it difficult to divide successfully. Transplant small self-sown seedlings, or propagate by seed. Cut the dried seed heads and shake into a paper bag, or sprinkle the shiny black seed on moist, unmulched soil. Seed can be planted immediately, or given a moist-cold treatment for 2–4 weeks in the refrigerator for faster germination, then planted outdoors. Do not cover the seed.

PLANTLORE: Thomas Jefferson grew columbine on his grounds at Monticello. Native Americans rubbed the seeds between their palms to be more persuasive in the war council or with a loved one. The tough, woody roots were a food source during famine.

5. Bergamot (*Monarda fistulosa*)

Clouds of butterflies and bees hover over the unique flower heads when Bee-balm or Monarda is in bloom. Hummingbirds delight in sipping nectar from the tubular shaped flowers.

Monarda fistulosa is a delicate lavender-pink. Other desirable monardas to incorporate into the native garden include *M. didyma*, with brilliant red flowers; *M. media*, which has deep red-purple blooms; and *M. clinopodia*, with white flowers. Each monarda has a square stem to identify it as a member of the Mint Family, and the crushed leaves have a definite herbal aroma. It grows 3–5 feet tall and naturalizes well. It spreads quickly by thin, underground stems, but is easy to pull. It tends to be somewhat short-lived, so replant some of the excess plants rather than composting them all.

PLANTING REQUIREMENTS: Plant in moist, well-drained garden soil in full sun or partial shade. This plant is particularly effective planted as a mass. Good air circulation is important or Monarda will mildew. It loves a site where the ground is consistently damp.

PROPAGATION: Plant seeds as soon as they ripen. Transplant seedlings in spring or early fall, leaving 12–18 inches between plants with the thin rhizome about 1 inch below the surface. Stem or tip cuttings taken when the plants are actively growing in midsummer are generally successful as long as the cuttings are misted several times a day and kept evenly moist.

PLANTLORE: Native Americans and pioneers brewed the leaves of this mint-like herb into a tea to calm an uneasy stomach or to open stuffy nasal passages.

6. False Sunflower *(Heliopsis helianthoides)*

False Sunflower's 2- to 4-inch yellow, daisy-like flowers bloom nearly all summer long and attract nectar-seeking butterflies. The brightly colored dome-like yellow disc flowers are surrounded by yellow ray flowers. Birds enjoy the ripened seed. Clusters of flowers may abound on a branched stalk, or there may be a solitary specimen at the top of the sturdy stem. The plant grows 3–6 feet tall.

PLANTING REQUIREMENTS: Plant in full sun

or partial shade in average, well-drained, moist garden soil. Space plants 1–3 feet apart. Mulch well. Once settled, it tolerates drought, and even grows happily on gravel, although it will increase more rapidly in fertile soil. Clumps should be divided every 3–4 years. Provide adequate air circulation to prevent powdery mildew.

Several improved cultivars are available, including 'Summer Sun', which is shorter and more compact, and 'Golden Plume', with double flowers. An early variety called 'Scabra' is sturdier and coarser than the species plant.

PROPAGATION: Plant ripened seed immediately for spring germination. The plant will self-sow sparingly. Divide large clumps by cutting apart the stocky rhizomatous rootstock with a knife, leaving at least two or three eyes in each division.

PLANTLORE: The scientific names describe this plant. *Helios* is Greek for "sun." *Heliopsis* means "sun-like appearance," and *helianthoides* describes *Helianthus*, "the sunflower." The long-lasting flowers are popular with floral arrangers.

*   *   *

Six Suggested Butterfly Larval Food Plants

1. Hackberry *(Celtis occidentalis)*

In 1921, in *Trees of Indiana*, Charles Deam reported a Hackberry in Gibson County that was 120 feet tall. Hackberry trees generally mature between 40 and 75 feet. It is one of the most resiliant trees in the Lower Midwest and will thrive where others succumb. Hackberry is fairly fast-growing, and once established grows 2–3 feet per year. This long-lived tree can live 200 years or more.

The Hackberry is an excellent shade tree and is one of the best native trees for wildlife. It is the only larval food source of the Snout, Tawny Emperor, and Hackberry butterflies.

Mourning Cloak and Question Mark butterflies also spend their larval stage munching Hackberry leaves, but new leaves soon reappear. Small, insignificant flowers bloom in early spring and are followed by dark purple-brown berries that are sought after by mammals and seed-eating birds. Some claim these edible pea-sized fruits are sweet and taste slightly like dates. Others think "they taste awful." You be the judge. This hardy tree has interesting whitish-chartreuse fall foliage, and its knobby bark gives winter interest. It is easy to grow from seed or transplants. It is handsome in all seasons. There is also a Dwarf Hackberry *(Celtis tenuifolia)* that is nice for smaller gardens.

PLANTING REQUIREMENTS: Hackberry trees will accept nearly any growing conditions, including rich loamy soil, sandy soil, or clay. They will tolerate sun or partial shade, wet or dry soil, and will even survive poor drainage. Plant balled-and-burlapped specimens or bare-root plants in spring or fall. The cultivar 'Prairie Pride' is resistant to nipple gall and witches' broom, which often attack the species but do no harm.

PROPAGATION: Purchase nursery stock or root softwood cuttings in early summer. Plant fresh, ripe seed immediately, or stratify 2–3 months, then plant outdoors.

2. Highbush Blueberry *(Vaccinium corymbosum)*

Connoisseurs of blueberry pie, jam, or fresh blueberries over ice cream should consider planting a Highbush Blueberry. This shrub is handsome in all seasons. Small, white urn-shaped flowers bloom in May, followed by luscious deep blue fruit in July. Just try to beat the birds to it! Fiery red foliage makes this shrub an "autumn spectacular," and in winter the multiple stems of yellow-green and dark red look stunning against the snow and brighten up a drab winter day.

The leaves of Highbush Blueberry are a larval food source for the Spring Azure and Hairstreak butterflies. Its fruits are prized by 53 species of wildlife, including many songbirds, butterflies, red fox, and grouse.

PLANTING REQUIREMENTS: Plant in full sun in acid soil (a must!) that is moist, well-drained, and humus-rich. Site this shrub along the property line as a living privacy fence, at the back of a border, or in a mixed biohedge.

PROPAGATION: Purchase nursery specimens for fastest results. To start from seed, remove the seeds from the pulp and plant immediately. No stratification is necessary but any seeds that will not be planted immediately should be stored in the refrigerator. Softwood cuttings taken in late summer or hardwood cuttings in early spring will root.

3. Swamp Milkweed (*Asclepias incarnata*)

A large cluster of rosy-red flowers bloom in midsummer at the top of a rigid stem, above dark-green lance-shaped leaves. Swamp Milkweed likes wet, swampy areas, as its common name indicates. It grows 3 to 5 feet tall from a thick rhizome. The seeds resemble parsnip seeds and are attached to silky strands that float through the air to sprout in hospitable locations. Monarch and Spring Azure butterflies depend on this species for the larval stage, and if you plant it they will come. 'Ice Ballet' is an attractive, snowy-white cultivar.

PLANTING REQUIREMENTS: Plant in full sun in moist or wet humus-rich garden soil. Mulch well. Naturalize in a prairie or meadow, plant in the middle of a border, or mass.

PROPAGATION: Propagate from seeds planted immediately, or divide the sturdy rhizome, leaving several eyes in each section.

PLANTLORE: In Greek mythology, Asclepias was a god of healing and medicine. Milkweed has been used for medical purposes for centuries. The roots are reportedly a powerful diuretic. Early physicians boiled "half a pound of dry roots, bruised, in six quarts of water, down to two quarts." The recommended dose was half a teacupful three or four times a day, or added as drops to gin. Native Americans also used parts of the plant as food.

4. Spicebush *(Lindera benzoin)*

The small, round greenish-yellow flowers of Spicebush are some of the earliest to brave the spring chill. These interesting spiky flowers attract early insects. Spicebush Swallowtail depends upon this shrub during its larval stage.

Bright red berries are accented by clear yellow leaves in autumn and are borne on female plants. The entire shrub (wood, leaves, twigs, and berries) has a spicy, agreeable, aromatic flavor. This multi-stemmed shrub or small tree grows 6 to 12 feet tall and naturalizes well. Blend Spicebush into a mixed shrub border or plant multiple shrubs in a mass.

PLANTING REQUIREMENTS: Spicebush grows well in sun to partial shade, but has a more airy, open growth habit in a shadier location. Plant in moist, humus-rich, acidic soil with good drainage. It does not tolerate drought.

PROPAGATION: Remove the flesh from the small berry and plant fresh, ripe seed immediately in the fall. It will germinate in spring.

PLANTLORE: Early Americans brewed the leaves and twigs and drank the tea as a tonic or stimulant. It was also administered to patients with fevers to induce sweating. Liniment was made by combining crushed berries and sweet oil in a glass bottle. The mixture was allowed to steep in the sun for several days, strained, and used as a rub for bruises, sprains, or rheumatism.

5. New Jersey Tea *(Ceanothus americanus)*

New Jersey Tea was well known as "Red Root" on the western prairies, since the large, hard, woody root is dark red. The twisted, convoluted roots reached deep into the ground, and made early sod-busters work a little harder as they plowed the prairie.

This 3-foot shrub has long-stalked 1- to 2-inch panicles of fluffy white flowers that look like small plumes. It blooms in early to midsummer. It is a larval food source for the Mottled Duskywing butterfly. The pubescent 2- to 3-inch leaves are finely toothed and have three prominent veins.

Charles Deam describes the fruit capsule as "generally crested or roughened on the angles; seed more than 2mm long, smooth." New Jersey Tea fixes nitrogen in the soil via bacteria that live in its roots.

PLANTING REQUIREMENTS: Plant in well-drained average garden soil in full sun or light partial shade. This shrub normally grows in dry or rocky areas and is tolerant of harsh, dry conditions.

PROPAGATION: Collect fully ripened seed and soak in hot water before planting. Cold stratify 2–3 months and plant in spring. Softwood cuttings root well.

It is difficult to transplant. Purchase it balled and burlapped, or buy specimens in containers.

PLANTLORE: The American colonists used the leaves as their primary tea substitute during the dispute with Great Britain in 1773 over taxation. When the plant was in full bloom, the leaves were gathered and dried. This tea should not be steeped very long, because harmful alkaloids may be released with long brewing.

Pioneers made the bark of the root into a decoction used as a remedy in early stages of consumption, or to treat whooping cough.

6. Pawpaw (*Asimina triloba*)

Unusual dark reddish-brown flowers, like strange upside-down flared wooden cups, hang on stark naked branches before the large, drooping leaves emerge. This small understory tree, commonly known as "Indiana Banana," grows 10 to 40 feet tall and is almost tropical looking. The 2- to 6-inch soft banana-like fruit has yellow flesh with embedded black, wrinkled seeds, and ripens in late summer. It is a favorite of squirrels, birds, and raccoons, who usually get it before we do.

Zebra Swallowtail larvae munch the leaves and will reward your generosity with beauty later in the summer. The long oval-shaped leaves turn intensely golden in autumn.

PLANTING REQUIREMENTS: Plant in moist, well-drained, humus-rich soil in partial shade to full sun. It will tolerate alkaline soil, but prefers a neutral to acid pH. Multiple suckers naturally form a small grove of trees, which is very effective at the edge of the woods. In the wild these trees form thickets that are valuable refuges for wildlife.

PROPAGATION: Pawpaw develops a long taproot and can be difficult to transplant. Purchase containerized plants or transplant self-sown seedlings when they are still very small. This plant suckers heavily, so if you plan to dig a wild Pawpaw, try to locate true seedlings to transplant or find a rooted sucker. Seeds planted in the fall may take up to two years to germinate unless cold-stratified for 2–3 months.

PLANTLORE: Native Americans and settlers prized the sweetish-pungent taste of the soft yellow fruit. *Asimina triloba* is currently being tested for use in chemotherapy for certain cancers. It also repels insects.

13.

Outlaw the Outlaws

A Look at Invasive Exotics

Russian Olive

When we moved from Idaho to Iowa in 1972, my husband and I inherited a Tree-of-Heaven *(Ailanthus altissima)*. It grew near our vegetable garden. Our young children played in the sandbox under its shade, and I always enjoyed its beautiful fall foliage. When we sold that home nine years later, the buyer added two requests to his purchase agreement. He asked me to bake him a blueberry pie, since each time he came to look at the house, I was baking brownies or fresh bread (on purpose, of course!). He also asked my husband to chop down the Tree-of-Heaven, which he knew to be invasive in his home state of Ohio. Our lawyer was appalled and considered these requests inappropriate in a legal document, but we laughed, signed, and complied with both.

This was probably the first time I ever really thought about possible negative characteristics of a nonnative species. After all, isn't it every homeowner's right and privilege to plant anything that suits his fancy in his own yard? Most nonnative plants, also known as aliens or exotics, which beautify public and private landscapes cause no problems. In their own native habitat, plants and animals are generally controlled and well-behaved. However, in areas where they are not native, they sometimes overstay their welcome, multiply, and become a grave threat to native wildlife and plants. In any society there are those who refuse to abide by the law and have total disregard for others. In the plant community, these are the aggressive nonnatives, commonly referred to as invasive exotics.

In the past few years, I have learned more about the havoc these plants can wreak in our fragile environment when they escape from cultivation into the wild and change ecosystems, threaten biodiversity, destroy habitats, and outcompete native plants. This problem affects agriculture and our economy as well as our environment, and becomes particularly worrisome when rare or endangered species are threatened, since invasive exotics respect neither plant nor place in their quest for space.

As I said at the beginning of this book, I am not against the use of nonnative plants. I have never been a total native plant gardener, nor am I a purist. I use a combination of natives and nonnatives in most of my gardens, and I often advise beginning native plant gardeners to add a few natives to an existing exotic perennial flower garden as a start. But as responsible gardeners, we also need to be aware of—and beware—those undesirable exotics that can compromise our environment.

This chapter will introduce you to some invasive exotics and their dangers, to encourage personal education, and hopefully, to increase your own sense of personal responsibility as you begin to garden with native plants and wildflowers. If there is one point to register, it is that we need to be responsible—each of us in our own small way. We need to understand and appreciate the dangers of irresponsible use of invasive exotics. A message on a friend's sweatshirt reads, "We will conserve only what we love, we will love only what we understand, we will understand only what we are taught." Only through education will we gain understanding.

When we lived in Iowa and Minnesota, long before I learned about the value and use of native plants in the landscape, I planted sun-loving perennials in my border gardens. At the back of these gardens grew large clumps of a tall, handsome plant that I had purchased at the local garden center. Neighbors would ask about this striking plant and request starts when I divided it. This beautiful garden plant, that I only knew as Lythrum, is currently destroying our nation's wetlands. Purple Loosestrife *(Lythrum salicaria)* blankets many of these areas and presents a solid sea of rosy-lavender in aerial photographs. It grows and spreads so rapidly that it eliminates open areas used by waterfowl and crowds out plant species used by wildlife for food and shelter.

Some exotic wildflowers are beautiful and have naturalized into large areas, so many people assume that they are native plants. Examples include Cornflower *(Centaurea cyanus)*, also known as Bachelor's Button, and Dame's Rocket *(Hesperis matronalis)*. Both of these species are commonly included in "Meadow-in-a-Can" or "Wildflower Mix" seed packets that are widely available in garden centers and grocery stores. Cornflower is becoming a widespread scourge, especially in native grasslands and prairies, where it threatens native plant diversity. Dame's Rocket, while not currently a serious threat as an invasive exotic, has recently become more prevalent, so it is on some state and federal "watch lists."

Dame's Rocket was probably the first wildflower I ever planted, and consequently it was responsible for my initial interest in photographing and learning more about the multitude of plants that grow without cultivation. I had just battled a ravine full of poison ivy and won, and a friend suggested I plant the area with wildflowers. A few days later, a construction worker agreed to let me lift several plants of Dame's Rocket blooming on a pile of topsoil near a house under construction. This phlox-like plant is a species in the Mustard Family, a family that typically seeds prolifically. Crucifers have four petals like a cross, while common garden phlox has five petals. Dame's Rocket can be observed flowering profusely along roadsides and ditches after early spring wildflowers have finished blooming, which was a characteristic I appreciated. It still blooms in that ravine along with woodland natives such as Bloodroot, Mayapples, Trillium, Celandine Poppy, Wild Geranium, and other spring wildflowers I planted so long ago, and the last time I visited, Dame's Rocket was still behaving itself.

Plants are expected to behave in our gardens, and if they get too aggressive, we simply share with friends or weed them out. However, problems occur when aggressive nonnative plants escape from our gardens or home landscapes to threaten our natural areas. Plants find many ways to escape from cultivation to the wild. Birds, animals, wind and weather, streams and waterways, car tires, clothing and shoes are only some of their means of transportation.

When gentle breezes riffle tiny new leaves, and warm, sunny days bring a promise of reemerging life, I pull on my jeans and waterproof duck boots to explore the local countryside. This season of rebirth is one of my favorites. In the spring, there seems to be a greater variety of shades of green in the landscape, and the fresh smell of earth and water is undeniably nostalgic. Nesting birds sing a special lilting song, and I can't describe the intense pleasure I feel as I walk through the peaceful woods, discovering each beautiful little wildflower, and greeting one "old friend" after another. On such days my step is light, my heart is happy, and my smile is constant.

In 1987, on one of these special kinds of days, I drove across Indiana to visit my friend Mary, who lives in a small town located on the border of Indiana and Ohio. I thoroughly enjoy finding and photographing wildflowers, and on this particular day, my friend had promised to take me to a hillside of Fire Pink in bloom. We set out burdened only with my camera and a picnic lunch. I had never found any large areas of native Fire Pinks, so to see the rocky hillside covered with the small brilliant red flowers was exciting. We spent a lovely, leisurely day walking, sitting on rocks or logs, talking, exclaiming, and taking photographs. Late in the afternoon, we headed down the hillside toward Mary's home, when she suddenly stopped the car near a bluff overlooking a wooded area below. Her face grew sad as she told me, "This whole valley used to be filled with wonderful wildflowers, and it is being overtaken and destroyed by Garlic Mustard. Soon there will be nothing but those horrid little white flowers covering the area."

I met Garlic Mustard again on a field trip to the Falls of the Ohio, a state park on the border of Indiana and Kentucky which boasts an incredible wealth of fossils. Garlic Mustard covered the woods, and looked ugly and menacing as it lay piled upon itself in layers, ripe with seed, along the trails. The following spring at Pokagon State Park in northeastern Indiana, not far from Ohio and Michigan, I was horrified to find a veritable sea of Garlic Mustard stretching as far as the eye could see. One small colony of Virginia Bluebells bloomed valiantly in an area where volunteers had pulled bushels of Garlic Mustard in order to give the bluebells a chance. Pokagon authorities are also battling an overpopulation of white-tailed deer, and the naturalist said dispiritedly, "The deer ate everything they could reach except Garlic Mustard. Wouldn't it be wonderful if they liked that nasty little plant?"

I began to see Garlic Mustard as we drove along the highways and country lanes in Indiana and Ohio and Illinois, and even found some in my own neighborhood as I walked along a road near a wooded area. When I found five plants in my own woods, I really began to get angry. In my President's message for the Indiana Native Plant and Wildflower Society newsletter, I wrote, "Aliens are invading our state and city parks, our roadsides and even our private gardens. They are marching through areas once considered pristine and safe and causing incredible havoc as they aggressively outcompete natives for a place and a space. No, I am not referring to aliens from outer space, but alien plants and animals that we introduce with great regularity to our landscape and to our environment."

Garlic Mustard (*Alliaria petiolata*) has been used as a potherb in Europe and was probably brought by early settlers. It was first recorded in the United States in 1868, and its presence was not noted in the Midwest until the 1960s. Only in recent years has this plant, with its interesting leaves and subtle scent of garlic, suddenly become an invasive exotic, threatening the very existence of our spring woodland wildflowers. A biennial, it produces thousands of viable seeds, and outcompetes any native plant brave enough to emerge from the forest floor.

Invasive exotic species are not limited to escaped potherbs or common garden plants. Nearly any garden center and mail order catalog has numerous plants for sale that also appear on current invasive exotic or noxious weed lists. Japanese Barberry (*Berberis thunbergii*), Burning Bush (*Euonymus alatus*), Japanese Spirea (*Spiraea japonica*), and Bush or Tatarian Honeysuckle (*Lonicera tatarica*) are widely used in landscaping. All four shrubs have escaped to the wild, outcompeting, overcrowding and shading out native species and disrupting plant diversity. Another escapee is the small landscaping tree Amur Maple (*Acer ginnala*). Large wild populations are found in Illinois and Missouri.

Landscape architects still recommend Japanese honeysuckle (*Lonicera japonica*) as a fast-growing vine to hide an ugly area. It is so fast-growing and aggressive that it also shades areas in the forest so densely that no other vegetation can survive. In addition, it forms large rhizomatous root systems which are nearly impossible to grub out.

Gardening and landscaping trends encourage the use of plants that may become troublesome when they escape. Butterfly gardens are extremely popular, but few gardeners realize that Butterfly Bush (*Buddleia davidii)*, originally from China, is spreading rapidly in the wild and may become a real pest. (Not all *Buddleia* species are aggressive. *B. globosa*, for example, does not currently appear to be as aggressive.)

Sometimes well-meaning government officials distribute misinformation. When we lived in Minnesota, city officials offered 3-inch-caliper "street trees" to homeowners for a reasonable price, and on their recommendation we planted two Norway Maples *(Acer platanoides)* in the grassy area between the street and the public sidewalk. Norway Maple was one of the most widely planted lawn and street trees across the United States.

The character of a woodland can be changed by escaped Norway Maples as they take over beech and Sugar Maple forests and affect diversity of woodland wildflowers because of their dense shade. 'Schwedler's Maple' and 'Crimson King' are two popular red-leaved cultivars of the Norway Maple still promoted by landscapers. City officials are now encouraged to promote native maples instead.

Two commonly used nonnative ground covers are Myrtle *(Vinca minor)* and English Ivy *(Hedera helix)*. These exotic ground covers blanket areas, causing the demise of native wildflowers and other native herbaceous plants.

Years ago, Department of Transportation administrators across our nation ordered plantings of Crown Vetch *(Coronilla varia)* on steep areas near overpasses and entrance ramps to control erosion, and these plantings still exist in many areas. Crown Vetch is still available through mail order catalogs and garden centers as a recommended ground cover. Department of Transportation employees in Missouri are warned not to try to seed wildflowers and native plants into areas where Crown Vetch exists, or even where it was seeded in the past, because of its highly invasive, aggressive nature. The only way to eradicate it is to sterilize the soil. Some authorities suggest that it is not even a very effective erosion control! Native prairie grasses and forbs, with their extensive and extremely deep root systems, would surely be a better choice.

The comic strip character Pogo stated, "We have met the enemy and they is us." At the beginning of this chapter, I wrote, "we need to be responsible—each of us in our own small way." This chapter relates only a few examples of invasive exotics. There are many more. Learn all you can about the plants you select for your landscape, and be responsible in choosing what to plant. The well-being of our gardens, our landscapes, our public places, our parks and natural areas is our responsibility. Irresponsible use of alien species can destroy habitats and existing native plant and animal populations, and eventually lead to the degradation of our environment. We all need to be better stewards of our environment. It is our responsibility and we can make a difference.

*   *   *

Descriptions of and eradication techniques for *Six Worst Invasive Exotics*

1. Garlic Mustard *(Alliaria petiolata)*

This aggressive biennial can be identified easily by bruising the plant. A light smell of garlic is exuded from crushed leaves or a broken taproot. In early spring, a cluster of scalloped basal leaves appears as a ground-hugging rosette. These leaves remain green throughout the winter. The alternate leaves of the second year are triangularly heart-shaped and sharply toothed. The plant grows from a thin, white taproot.

Flowering occurs in late spring of the second year. The four-petaled, small white flowers line a 12- to 30-inch stem in the spring. These are followed by long, thin capsules (silques) filled with seeds that split open and scatter widely. These second-year plants die and the cycle begins again.

ERADICATION TECHNIQUES: Cut the stem at ground level just before the plant sets seed in late spring or early summer. Pulling is also effective, but the entire taproot must be removed or the plant can resprout. Completely remove these plants from the area and solarize them in heavy plastic trash bags to destroy any viable seed.

Garlic Mustard has the ability to mature seed even when cut. I once left some cut plants lying beside a woodland path. I returned several days later to find they had simply turned their stems upward toward the light, continued flowering, and set seed!

In areas of large infestation, spray in late fall or early winter with a solution of glyphosate herbicide. Avoid hitting desirable semi-evergreen native species. A high-intensity burn can be effective, but must be repeated. An ongoing eradication program of up to five years may be necessary in order to destroy the entire seed population.

2. Amur Honeysuckle (*Lonicera maackii*)

Introduced from Asia in 1896, Amur Honeysuckle has been widely planted throughout the eastern and central United States. All across the Lower Midwest, these honeysuckle bushes line city roads and parks, creating solid hedges. When this shrub escapes to the wild, it quickly creates a monoculture. The middle story of an undeveloped wooded area not far from my home is exclusively honeysuckle. Naturalists, park rangers, government employees, and volunteers list it as one of the worst invasive exotics. *L. tatarica* and *L. japonica* are two other invasive honeysuckle "thugs."

Amur Honeysuckle is a highly adaptable plant. It will tolerate soil that is moist to dry, loam or clay, and will grow in sun or shade. It generally becomes 10 to 15 feet tall with an arching growth habit but can stretch as tall as 30 feet in a desirable environment. It can form a dense hedge or a nearly impenetrable thicket. It is one of the first plants to "green up" in the spring and one of the last to lose its leaves in the fall, so it is easy to spot in the woods.

Small white or pink-tinged flowers bloom in early spring, followed by bright red translucent berries in early summer. The berries appear in the axils of the opposite 2- to 3-inch dark green leaves and, although they are not a favored food source, are eaten by some birds. This results in the germination of hundreds of new seedlings each year throughout wooded areas.

ERADICATION TECHNIQUES: Pull or grub out young plants, or cut the woody shrub to the ground and paint the cut stems with glyphosate herbicide, which translocates to the roots and destroys the plant.

3. Multiflora Rose (Rosa multiflora)

A native of Japan and Korea, Multiflora Rose was introduced to North America in the 1860s and promoted as a "living fence" in both agricultural and urban settings. It was recommended as a food source and cover for wildlife in the 1930s, and was commonly used for roadside and ornamental plantings. This large, thorny plant forms impenetrable thickets. It can invade wetlands, destroy native plant environments, and disrupt pasture lands and agricultural sites. It has become a serious environmental problem in most Lower Midwest states. In a letter to Professor Daniel Den Uyl in the 1940s, Charles Deam wrote, "Please do not recommend the multiflora rose except to the bonfire."

Multiflora Rose has profuse clusters of small, fragrant, white five-petaled flowers in midsummer. The compound leaves have 5 to 7 opposite oval-shaped toothed leaflets that are each 1½ inches long. In fall and winter, birds feast on the small red rose hips and assist in its proliferation. This vigorous member of the rose family is used as understock for grafting. It is extremely hardy and relatively pest resistant. It grows 10 feet tall, and has long, arching branches.

ERADICATION TECHNIQUES: Cut large stems and spray or paint with glyphosate herbicide. Mow or dig to control seedlings.

4. Purple Loosestrife (Lythrum salicaria)

Purple Loosestrife was introduced in the early 1800s as a contaminant of European ship ballast and as a medicinal herb, used to treat diarrhea, dysentery, bleeding, wounds, ulcers, and sores. This beautiful plant has been a long-time favorite of gardeners. Unfortunately it escaped to the wild, where it has caused incredible havoc in the wetlands of North America. Each plant is capable of producing more than 2.5 million seeds annually. Purple Loosestrife is now listed as a noxious weed in many states, and the sale of this plant and even some of its cultivars is banned in many states of the Lower Midwest.

Experiments with biological control are currently being conducted in wetland areas. A root mining weevil *(Hylobius transversovittatus)* and two leaf-eating beetles *(Galerucalla calmariensis L.* and *Galerucella pusilla Duftschmid)* have been released in several states. Although this experiment will not eradicate Loosestrife in the treated areas, populations should be dramatically reduced.

Vivid magenta or rosy-lavender flowers bloom on long racemes. The opposite lance-shaped leaves feel slightly fuzzy. Each plant grows 2 to 3 feet tall and nearly as wide.

ERADICATION TECHNIQUES: Cut at ground level and treat cut stems with glyphosate herbicide.

5. Glossy Buckthorn *(Rhamnus frangula)*

Glossy Buckthorn is commonly used in foundation plantings or as a living privacy screen. Many landscapers and nurseries still recommend 'Columnaris', a cultivar of this invasive species, as "a fast-growing hedge." These shrubs are among the first to leaf out and the last to lose their leaves in the fall. In the wild, they aggressively crowd out other understory shrubs.

Also known as Smooth Buckthorn, this shrub reaches 10 to 25 feet tall with equally wide arching branches. Its shiny 3-inch dark green leaves turn bright yellow in the fall. The berries change from red to purplish-black and are devoured by birds and small mammals, which thus aid in its spread. This shade-tolerant plant has become a pest in woodlands as well as in wetlands as it displaces native plants.

Common or European Buckthorn *(R. cathartica)* is also a troublesome exotic, primarily invasive in woodland areas. This deciduous shrub grows 7 to 10 feet tall. It creates nearly impenetrable thickets because of the sharp thorns at the tips of the branches. Its black berries ripen in the fall and are eaten by birds and small mammals. The excreted seeds germinate readily and become widespread throughout the woodland.

ERADICATION TECHNIQUES: Cut woody stems to the ground in the fall and treat with glyphosate herbicide. Repeat the treatment if the shrub resprouts. Girdle larger specimens and pull or dig small seedlings.

6. Autumn Olive (*Elaeagnus umbellata*)

Gray-green foliage, fragrant spring flowers, and red fruits in the fall have made Autumn Olive a popular landscaping choice. Introduced from Asia in 1919 as a landscaping shrub, it flourishes in nearly any type of environment, even tolerating dry, infertile, shady areas. It has been spread widely by birds who relish the fall fruits and is rapidly crowding out more desirable native understory trees.

This large shrub grows 15 to 20 feet tall and equally as wide. It quickly forms thorny thickets. Its leaves are shorter and more rounded than the long thin leaves of Russian Olive, another undesirable. Autumn Olive seeds prolifically, and its only limitation is its inability to withstand temperatures below –20° F.

ERADICATION TECHNIQUES: Cut woody stems to the ground and treat with glyphosate. Pull or dig young seedlings. Established stands may have to be bulldozed and repeatedly treated with glyphosate herbicide to eliminate this invasive shrub.

If you are thinking a year ahead, sow a seed.
If you are thinking 10 years ahead, plant a forest.
If you are thinking 100 years ahead, educate
  people.   —*Ancient Chinese proverb*

14.

Some Final
Thoughts

But What Difference
Can I Make?

Botanist John Bartram planted the first botanical garden in America near Philadelphia in 1728. As he tramped along the banks of the Altamaha River in Georgia in 1765, he found a small, unique tree that he named *Franklinia alatamaha* in honor of his friend Benjamin Franklin. Today all known Franklin Trees are descended from the precious seeds he collected on his return trip to the site in 1770. A drawing of the spectacular flowers of the Franklin Tree serves as a handsome frontispiece in his son William Bartram's book, *Botanical and Zoological Drawings, 1756–1788*. Long extinct in the wild, this lovely tree still exists because of one man's foresight and dedication. One person *can* make a difference.

In 1922, Indiana naturalist and author Gene Stratton-Porter wrote, "If we do not want our land to dry up and blow

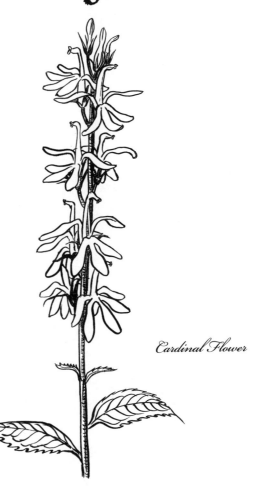

Cardinal Flower

away, we must replace at least part of our lost trees. We must save every brook and stream and lake . . . and those of us who see the vision and most keenly feel the need must furnish the motor power for those less responsive. Work must be done."

Native plants are our heritage, and the heritage of our descendants. Chief Charles Dawes of the Ottawa Tribe of Oklahoma wisely said, "What one may not be able to do alone, many have done together." Working together through education, proper plant selection, and responsible behavior, we can help to preserve this heritage for future generations to ensure a brighter future for our world. As Stratton-Porter concludes, "It is the time for all of us to get together and in unison make a test of our strength. All together, Heave!"

Resources

A definition is the enclosing a wilderness of ideas
within a wall of words.   —*Samuel Butler, 1912*

Glossary

Words change over time, and new ones are coined. My 1973 edition of Webster's Unabridged Dictionary *does not include such words as "ecosystem" and "forb," and a 1988* World Book Dictionary *gives the definition of "forb" as "any herb, excluding grasses and plants resembling grasses." An* Introduction to Plant Taxonomy *by George Lawrence and* A Dictionary of Botany *by R. John Little and C. Eugene Jones have been invaluable as I have attempted to write more precise, yet understandable, definitions and explanations for words used in the world of native plants. In this glossary, forb is described as "An herbaceous plant that has showy flowers; not a grass or sedge." And so we continue to learn and grow.*

Achene: A dry, thin-walled fruit that does not split open at maturity, containing only one seed.

Acid Bath: A mild acid (like muriatic acid) used to cover and soak hard-coated seeds so as to scarify the seed and allow germination. Some thinner-coated seeds may be scarified in pure white vinegar.

Acid soil: Soil that has a pH below 7.0.

Aggressive: Growing rampantly without restraint.

Alien: A resident foreigner; not a native.

Alkaline soil: Soil that has a pH above 7.0.

Allelopathic: The production of chemicals by one plant to inhibit the growth of another. *Allelon* is a Greek word for "of each other" and *pathos* for "suffering."

Alternate: Each leaf or branch appearing at different heights and on different sides of a stem, branch, or trunk; not opposite or whorled.

Annual: A plant that produces flowers, sets seed, and dies in one growing season.

Anther: The part of the stamen that produces pollen; male.

Aquatic plant: A plant that grows in water.

Awn: A slender bristle; part of a grass or sedge flower.

Axil: The angle above the spot where a leaf petiole attaches to a stem; where a branch attaches to a main stem.

Balled and burlapped: Describes a woody plant whose roots are encased in a ball of soil, wrapped in burlap, and tied to facilitate transplanting.

Bare root: Refers to a plant that has been dug out of the ground, but has no soil left around its roots.

Berry: A fleshy fruit which develops from a single ovary, with one or more hard-coated seeds.

Biennial: A plant that completes its life cycle in two growing seasons; during the second season the plant produces flowers, sets seed, and dies.

Biohedge: A combination of trees and shrubs of varying sizes and shapes with different flowering and fruiting habits, planted closely as a hedge to create a wildlife habitat.

Bog: A wetland filled with decaying organic matter; spongy earth.

Botanical names: Scientific designation to provide specific identification and origin.

Bract: A modified leaf immediately below a flower or flower cluster.

Bramble: A prickly shrub or vine.

Breast height: The diameter of a tree measured

4½ feet above ground level; diameter breast height (DBH).

Bud: A small swelling on a plant that develops into a flower, stem, or leaf.

Building envelope: The walls of the proposed building inward; the footprint of a building.

Bulb: A short underground stem, covered by onion-like, fleshy, overlapping scales which store food for the plant; e.g., a daffodil bulb.

Bunch grasses: Grasses that form well-defined clumps; not spreading by rhizomes or stolons.

Canopy: The area from the main stem to the outer limits of branches and leaves of a tree.

Capsule: A dry, slender seedpod, with two or more chambers, that splits opens to release its multiple seeds.

Catkin: An elongated cluster of unisex flowers with no petals; e.g., Pussy Willow.

Chaff: Floral parts or small bracts on the seed receptacle that are removed by cleaning the seeds.

Chlorotic: Yellowing as a result of loss of chlorophyll due to extremely stressful conditions; often caused by high pH, which will not allow the plant to utilize existing elements (such as iron) in the soil.

Colony: A large group or mass of a single species.

Common name: Nonscientific name for a particular plant or animal. These names may be legion.

Community: Populations of different species living and interacting with each other in the same environment.

Composite: Plants with ray and disc flowers; e.g., *Aster* spp.

Compound leaf: A leaf with two or more similar parts; divided into two or more separate leaflets.

Conifer: A cone-bearing tree or shrub; e.g., pine, fir, spruce, juniper, cypress; usually evergreen.

Contractile roots: Specialized roots that contract to pull a plant deeper into the soil.

Corm: An underground bulb-like structure composed of stem tissue and membranous scales for storing food, generally oval-shaped rather than round, with fibrous or contractile roots.

Creeper, creeping: A trailing plant or shoot which roots along most of its length or at the nodes.

Crosier: The coiled top of an emerging fern.

Crown: The base of a plant where stems and roots join, usually just beneath the soil level.

Crucifer: A plant with four petals in the form of a cross; a member of the Mustard Family.

Culm: The stem of the flowering part of grasses or sedges.

Cultivar: A contraction of "cultivated variety."

Cutting: A stem or branch cut from a plant for the purpose of propagation.

Cyme: A broad, flat-topped flower cluster, with the flowers in the center opening first.

Damping off: A fungal disease that causes seedlings to die before they emerge from the soil, or rots their stems at soil level.

Deciduous: Trees and shrubs that drop their leaves in the fall; not evergreen.

Defoliation: The loss of leaves.

Dioecious, dioicous: Having the male and female flowers located on different, separate plants of the same species. *Di* is from the Greek meaning two, and *oecious* means households. Thus it takes two plants to house both sexes.

Disc flower: Small tubular flowers in the center of the heads of composites; e.g., asters, coneflowers.

Diversity: The number of different species in a particular area.

Doctrine of Signatures: A belief, introduced during the Middle Ages, that God had provided man with a signature or clue in the appearance of each plant to indicate what diseases it could cure; e.g., the Hepatica leaf looked like a liver; Bellwort resembled the uvula in the throat; yellow Celandine Poppies were used to treat jaundice.

Dormancy, dormant: A time when active growth temporarily ceases due to unfavorable environmental conditions; resting in the winter.

Drupe: Fleshy fruit that is covered by an outer skin, and encloses a hard single seed, like peaches or cherries.

Duff: The layer of leaves and other plant debris, in various states of decomposition, lying on the ground.

Ecology: The study of the relation of living organisms to their environment and to each other.

Elaiosome: A tail-like appendage on a seed or fruit that stores oil and serves as food for ants, which aid in seed dispersal.

Environment: All of the external conditions affecting the growth and development of living things.

Ephemeral: Those spring woodland wildflowers

that emerge, bloom, set seed, and become dormant in only a few weeks, such as Toothwort, Virginia Bluebells, and Dutchman's Breeches.

Epithet: The descriptive Latin name given to a species; the second part of the scientific name; also called the specific epithet.

Erosion: The loss of soil from an area, generally due to wind or moving water.

Evergreen: Plants that do not drop their leaves in the fall and remain green during the winter.

Exfoliating: Peeling off in small pieces or thin layers, like the bark of a River Birch.

Exotic: Foreign, not native.

Fibrous roots: Roots that are similar in length and thickness, growing from a crown; not aggressive.

Flower: The reproductive structure of a flowering plant that produces the seeds.

Forb: An herbaceous plant that has showy flowers; not a grass or sedge.

Friable: Soil that crumbles easily; rich in humus.

Frond: A fern leaf.

Fruit: The ripened ovary, generally containing the seeds.

Fungicide: A chemical used to treat and control fungi.

Germination: To sprout from a seed or spore and begin to grow.

Girdling: Cutting and removing a complete ring of bark from a tree. Food cannot reach the roots and the tree dies.

Glyphosate: A non-selective herbicide that does not remain in the soil, used to eradicate undesirable plant material.

Habitat: The natural home or location of a plant or animal, where it is usually found.

Hardiness Zones: Established by the United States Department of Agriculture (USDA) to indicate the ability of plants to withstand winter temperatures. The formula created ten hardiness zones, rising in 10° increments from one to the next. Zone 1 plants can tolerate –50° F.; Zone 10 can tolerate temperatures above 30° to 40° F.

Herbaceous: A non-woody plant that dies to the ground at the end of the growing season. It may be an annual, a biennial, or a perennial.

Humus: leaves, wood, and other decomposing organic matter.

Indigenous: Native to a region or country; origi-

nating in that location; not exotic.

Inflorescence: A terminal flower cluster; the flowering seed heads of grasses and sedges.

Invasive exotic: An aggressive plant from another country or geographical area that rapidly colonizes a growing area, crowding out native plants.

Joint: The node of the stem of a grass or sedge.

Landscape architecture: The manipulation and management of outdoor space to bring harmony between living things and their environment.

Layering: Covering a portion of a stem or branch, still attached to the parent plant, with soil to induce roots to form in order to propagate a new plant.

Leaflet: A single part of a compound leaf.

Loam: Soil that is rich in organic matter, absorbs water readily, drains well, and crumbles easily; composition is approximately 10 percent clay, 45 percent sand, and 45 percent compost.

Lower Midwest: Those portions of Ohio, Indiana, Illinois, Iowa, Missouri, Michigan, Wisconsin, Kentucky, and Tennessee located within Zones 5–6.

Mesic: Containing a moderate amount of moisture; moist.

Metamorphosis: A change in form, structure, or function as a result of development; a transformation; e.g., a caterpillar to a chrysalis to a butterfly.

Monoculture: A population of only one species.

Monoecious: Separate male or female flowering reproductive structures appearing on the same plant; one plant that houses both sexes.

Native: A plant or animal that originated in a particular place or region and was not introduced; plants that existed in a particular location prior to the arrival of the settlers.

Naturalize: A foreigner that moves into a new environment and establishes itself as if it is native; e.g., Queen Anne's Lace, Chicory.

Nature's envelope: That part of the building lot from the outside of the proposed building's footprint to the boundaries of the lot.

Nectar: A sweet liquid produced by a plant, which contains up to 75 percent sugar. Insects and birds that seek the nectar as a source of food help to pollinate the plants.

Neutral soil: Soil which has a pH of 7.0 and is neither acid nor alkaline.

Node: The spot where the leaves are attached to the stem; stems have nodes, roots do not.

Nonnative: Alien, exotic, foreign; not originating in the area.

Nutlet: A small nut; one of a group of small seeds.

Nutrient: Substance which nourishes; promotes growth; nutritious.

Old-fields: abandoned agricultural land.

On-center: Measuring from the main stem of one plant to the main stem of the next when planting.

Opposite: Leaves or branches appearing in pairs on opposite sides of a stem.

Palmate: Shaped like the palm of the hand and having lobes, veins, or divisions arising from a common point.

Panicle: A branched flower head that is usually longer than it is wide.

Perennial: A plant which lives for more than two years.

Perfoliate: The base of a leaf completely surrounding the stem, giving the appearance of "stitching" the stem through the leaf.

Persistent: Remaining attached during the dormant season.

Petal: The colored parts of a flower.

Petiole: The stem of a leaf.

pH: A measure of the acidity or alkalinity of soil. pH values range from 0 to 14; pH 7.0 is neutral, less than 7 is acidic, and greater than 7 is alkaline.

Plugs: A method of propagation by planting individual seeds in specially designed trays with small indentations. The root system of the seedling fills the hole, forming a plug, and can be easily removed and planted where desired.

PLS: Pure live seed.

Population: A group of one species living in a particular area at the same time.

Propagation: Increasing the number of plants through seed germination, cuttings, or division.

Provenance: The origin of a seed. Seed that was developed on plants which have originated, matured, and are growing in a particular region or zone produces seedlings that are hardier in that region or zone than are the seedlings from seed grown in another part of the country.

Prune, pruning: Cutting off stems or branches of a woody plant to control size or shape, or to influence fruiting or flowering.

Pubescent: Covered with soft, rich hairs or scales.

Raceme: An unbranched cluster of individual flowers on short stalks along a main stem.

Ray flower: The petals that surround the center or disc flowers of a composite, like rays; e.g., coneflowers, asters.

Rhizome: Not a true root, but a fleshy, horizontal, underground stem with roots underneath. It has buds, nodes, and scale-like leaves.

Root: The underground portion of a plant that absorbs water and minerals, sometimes stores food, and anchors the plant. Roots have no nodes.

Rootlet: A small root

Rootstock: A rhizome.

Runner: A thin, creeping stem or stolon that emerges from the crown of a plant and grows horizontally along the ground, forming small roots and shoots at its nodes, like a strawberry plant.

Scarification: Abrasion of the hard seed coat by scratching, breaking, roughening, or treating with acid or hot water to hasten germination.

Sedge Meadow: A wet place with peat or saturated, mucky soil that is dominated by sedges of some kind (Carex, Scirpus, etc.). Forbs and grasses can also be found in a sedge meadow.

Sepal: Green floral parts (calyx) which normally enclose the flower bud that are found at the base of the flower. Sometimes sepals are colored and resemble petals, as in Rue Anenome or Dogwood.

Sessile: Without a stalk or stem.

Shrub: A perennial woody plant usually with several main stems arising from or near the ground; a bush.

Sod grasses: Grasses that spread by stolons or rhizomes forming a dense mat of grass, as opposed to bunch grasses.

Solarize: To cover with clear or dark plastic in order to create intense heat from the sun so as to injure or kill vegetation.

Specimen: An individual plant; a prime example of a particular species; an accent plant.

Spike: An unbranched elongated cluster of flowers with no stalks (sessile).

spp.: Plural abbreviation for species; used when referring to a number of different plants; e.g., *Aster* spp.

Sterile: Infertile; not having any reproductive structures.

Stoloniferous: Producing or bearing thin, underground runners or stolons that grow horizontally above or below the ground, and form roots at the nodes, producing new plants.

Stratification: Placing ripened, dormant seeds into moist soil or sand in cold or warm temperatures, as is required by the particular seed to break dormancy.

Sucker: A shoot from a root or from the lower part of a stem.

Tannin: Astringent phenol derivatives in plants that are used for tanning, dyeing, and the manufacture of ink.

Taproot: A stout, carrot-like root with smaller rootlets.

Tendril: A modified leaf or stem used by a climbing plant to twine around a support.

Terminal bud: A bud found at the top of the main stem.

Tissue culture: The technique of propagating plants from tissue taken from an organism and grown in a sterile, synthetic media.

Tomentose: Covered with dense, matted woolly hairs.

Trailing: Lying on the ground, but not rooting.

Transplanting: Relocating a plant from one place to another.

Tuber: A thickened, potato-like underground stem that provides food and water storage, and which has nodes, called eyes, for propagation.

Umbel: A flat-topped or convex flower cluster with branching stems attached to a single point, like an umbrella.

Understory: Medium-sized or small trees in a forest that grow beneath the level of the main canopy.

Vegetative propagation, vegetative reproduction: Propagation by leaves, stems, tubers, rhizomes, stolons, and other non-reproductive parts of the plant to duplicate the original plant.

Wetland: Low-lying land where the soil is submerged in water, or wet for a significant portion of each year.

Whorl: Three or more leaves or branches clustered around a stem at a single spot.

Wildflower: An herbaceous plant that grows without cultivation.

Winter hardiness: The ability of a plant to tolerate severe winter conditions.

Winter-kill: When a plant dies because of extremely low temperatures or severe winter weather conditions.

Witches' Broom: Bunches of twiggy branches growing from the end of a branch not pruned near a node; a disease that causes excessive broom-like branching, similar to a witch's broom.

Woody: Hard titrossues that persist, and also increase in diameter, from year to year, like trees and shrubs.

Collecting from the wild has seriously depleted stands of many species in areas where collectors are concentrated.   —*Jim Wilson, 1992*

Native Plant Sources

NATIVE PLANT NURSERIES

Nurseries are listed here by state so that you can visit or order from those closest to you. When provenance is important, ask where the stock originated. As you begin acquiring native plants, be a responsible consumer and purchase only from those nurseries that propagate by seed, division, tissue culture, or vegetative reproduction. Ask questions. Wild collection of plants from undeveloped natural areas is unethical for individuals and businesses alike.

I have contacted each nursery by telephone or e-mail or through a mailed questionnaire. Fax and telephone numbers, and e-mail and website addresses, change frequently, so only the postal address is given below. Mail-order companies often charge a small fee for their catalog, which is credited to the first purchase. While some of these nurseries are well-established, others are just beginning, so enclosing a stamped, self-addressed legal-sized envelope when you write for information is usually appreciated.

Illinois

Absolutely Wild Inc.
25310 S. Stoney Island Avenue
Crete, IL 60417

Bluestem Prairie Nursery
13197 E. 13th Road
Hillsboro, IL 62049
Seeds and bare-root plants; wildflowers and grasses (Illinois ecotype, prairie, & some savanna)

Enders Greenhouse
104 Enders Drive
Cherry Valley, IL 61016
Container-grown Midwest natives for woodland, prairie, & wetland (over 250 species, most native to No. IL)

Genesis Nursery
23200 Hurd Road
Tampico, IL 61283
Plants, seeds

Greenview Nurseries
2700 W. Cedar Hills Drive
Dunlap, IL 61525
Native and exotic species

H. E. Nursery
1200 Old Route 66 North
Litchfield, IL 62056

Lafayette Home Nursery, Inc.
1 Nursery Lane
Lafayette, IL 61449

Grasses, sedges, forbs, woody plant and wildflower seeds

Lee's Gardens
P.O. Box 5
Tremont, IL 61568
Wildflowers, perennials

Midwest Wildflowers
P.O. Box 64
Rockton, IL 61072
Native forb seed only

The Natural Garden
38 W443 Highway 64
St. Charles, IL 60175
Wildflowers, grasses, sedges, seeds (origin 90-mi. radius)

Purple Prairie Farm
P.O. Box 176, Route 2
Wyoming, IL 61491
Native grass and wildflower seeds

Indiana

AgVenture D.&M. Seeds, Inc.
P.O. Box 102
Kentland, IN 47951
Native grass and wildflower seeds

Crystal Palace Perennials
P.O. Box 154
St. John, IN 46373

Earthly Goods, Ltd.
P.O. Box 614
New Albany, IN 47151
Seeds only

Heartland Restoration Services, Inc.
349 Airport N. Office Park
Ft. Wayne, IN 46825

Indiana Propagation Nursery
3 Lyon Block
Salem, IN 47167
Native trees

J. F. New & Associates
P.O. Box 243
708 Roosevelt Road
Walkerton, IN 46574

Jasper-Pulaski State Nursery
Indiana Division of Forestry
15508 W. 700 N.
Medaryville, IN 47957

Munchkin Nursery
323 Woodside Drive N.W.
Depauw, IN 47115
Woodland wildflowers

Spence Restoration Nursery, Inc.
P.O. Box 546
2220 E. Fuson Road
Muncie, IN 47308
Wetland, woodland, prairie, grasses; prairie, wetland restoration

Vallonia State Nursery
Indiana Division of Forestry
2782 W. County Road 540 S.
Vallonia, IN 47281

Iowa

Allendan Seed
1966–175th Lane
P.O. Box 625, Route 4
Winterset, IA 50273
Native grass, wildflower seeds, plants (local ecotype 50-mi. radius)

Carl Kurtz
1562 Binford Ave.
St. Anthony, IA 50239
Mixed local ecotype native tall-grass prairie forbs and grasses

Cascade Forestry Nursery
22033 Filmore Road
Cascade, IA 52033
Native trees, shrubs; specialize in nut-bearing trees

Heyne Custom Seed Services
26420–510th Street
P.O. Box 78, Route 1
Walnut, IA 51577

Ion Exchange
1878 Old Mission Drive
Harpers Ferry, IA 52146
Seeds, plants; mail order, wholesale/retail

McGinnis Tree and Seed Co.
309 E. Florence
Glenwood, IA 51534
Herbaceous plants, grasses, trees, shrubs,
wildflower seed

Rose Hill Nursery
2282 Teller Road
Rose Hill, IA 52586
Grass and wildflower seed

Smith Nursery Co.
P.O. Box 515
Charles City, IA 50616
Trees and shrubs, also seed

Kentucky

J & M Seed Distributors
P.O. Box 550
London, KY 40743

Shooting Star Nursery
444 Bates Road
Frankfort, KY 40601
Seeds and propagated plants; wildflowers,
grasses, sedges, rushes, shrubs, woody vines,
ground covers, trees

Michigan

Arrowhead Alpines
P.O. Box 857
Fowlerville, MI 48836
Wildflowers, perennials and rock plants, conifers,
shrubs

Cold Stream Farm
2030 Free Soil Road
Free Soil, MI 49411
Trees, shrubs

Grass Roots Inc.
P.O. Box 4001
E. Lansing, MI 48826

Grow Wild Nursery
P.O. Box 401
Byron, MI 48418

Michigan Wildflower Farm
11770 Cutler Road
Portland, MI 48875
Native wildflower seeds

Nesta Prairie Perennials
1019 Miller Road
Kalamazoo, MI 49001
Herbaceous plants/grasses

Oikos Tree Crops
P.O. Box 19425
Kalamazoo, MI 49019

Owl Ridge Alpines
5421 Whipple Lake Road
Clarkston, MI 48016
Alpine, woodland species

Vans Pines Nursery, Inc.
7550–144th Avenue
West Olive, MI 49460
Grasses, trees, ground covers, and shrubs

**Western Regional Environmental Network
(WREN)**
Muskegon Conservation District
1001 E. Wesley Ave.
Muskegon, MI 49442
Provides educational information (only) on use of
native plants and seeds; works closely with
nurseries to ensure availability

Wetlands Nursery
P.O. Box 14553
Saginaw, MI 48601

Wildtype Native Plants and Seeds
900 Every Rd.
Mason, MI 48854

Minnesota

Prairie Moon Nursery
Rural Route 3, Box 163
Winona, MN 55987
Over 450 species of seeds/plants native to
Midwest, seeds IL

Missouri

Bowood Farms Wholesale only
Fox Creek Lane
Clarksville, MO 63336

Elixir Farm Botanicals
General Delivery
Brixey, MO 65618
Chinese & indigenous medicinal seed, plants,
roots, books; catalog available

Gilberg Perennial Farms
2906 Ossenfort Road
Glencoe, MO 63038
Prairie, woodland (MO ecotypes)

Hamilton Seeds and Wildflowers
16786 Brown Rd
Elk Creek, MO 65464
Seeds and plants: wildflowers and grasses

Mangelsdorf Seed Co.
P.O. Box 327
St. Louis, MO 63166

Missouri Wildflowers Nursery
9814 Pleasant Hill Road
Jefferson City, MO 65109
Shrubs, grasses, wildflowers, plants, seeds

Rock Post Wildflower Nursery
5798 Windy Meadows Lane
Fulton, MO 65251
Ferns, wetland plants, shrubs

Sharp Bros. Seed Co.
396 SW Davis-Ladue St.
Clinton, MO 64735
Wildflower and native grass seeds

Vermont Wildflower Farm
P.O. Box 1400
Louisiana, MO 63353
Seeds

Ohio

Cattail Meadows, Ltd.
5975 Liberty Rd.
Solon, OH 44139
Woodland, bog, prairie perennial plants

Companion Plants
7247 North Coolville Ridge
Athens, OH 45701
Wildflowers, medicinals, and herbs

Land Reformers
35703 Loop Road
Rutland, OH 45778

Mary's Plant Farm & Landscaping
2410 Lanes Mill Road
Hamilton, OH 45013
Native perennials, ferns, shrubs, trees, grasses,
seeds

Trennoll Nursery
3 West Page Avenue
P.O. Box 125
Trenton, OH 45067
Wildflowers, ferns, native plants

Valley Creek, Inc.
P.O. Box 475
Circle Drive
McArthur, OH 45651
Wildflower seeds

Tennessee

Beaver Creek Nursery
7526 Pelleaux Road
Knoxville, TN 37938
Trees, shrubs, grasses, rare and unusual plants

Growild Inc.
7190 Hill Hughes Road
Fairview, TN 37062
Landscape design, native trees, shrubs, wildflowers, grasses

Native Gardens
5737 Fisher Lane
Greenback, TN 37742
Native plants, seed packets

Sunlight Gardens, Inc.
174 Golden Lane
Andersonville, TN 37705
E. North America only (list)

Wisconsin

Applied Ecological Services
Taylor Creek Restoration Nurseries
P.O. Box 256
Brodhead, WI 53520
Seed propagation/plant division

Bauer's Garden Center
1559 W. Forest Home Ave.
Milwaukee, WI 53204

Bluestem Farm
S. 5920 Lehman Road
Baraboo, WI 53913
Prairie, savannah, woodland-plants/seeds (So. WI natives)

Country Wetlands Nursery & Consulting Ltd.
Box 126
575 W. 20755 Field Drive
Muskego, WI 53150
Wetland, woodland plants, seeds

Great Lakes Wildflowers
Box 1923
Milwaukee, WI 53201
Wildflowers, grasses

Hild & Associates
326 Glover Rd. So.
River Falls, WI 54022

J&J Transplant Aquatic Nursery
W4980 Hwy W
Wild Rose, WI 54984
Aquatic & prairie plants/seeds, ferns, shrubs, trees

Johnson's Nursery
W180 N6275 Marcy Rd
Menomonee Falls, WI 53051
Woody plant material

Kester's Wild Game Food Nurseries, Inc.
P.O. Box 516
Omro, WI 54963
Specialize in plantings for wetlands, ponds for wildlife

Kettle Moraine Natural Landscaping
W996 Birchwood Drive
Campbellsport, WI 53010
Consulting/restoration/seed sales only in 75-mi radius; no plant sales

Little Valley Farm
5693 Snead Creek Road
P.O. Box 544, Route 3
Spring Green, WI 53588
Prairie, wetland, woodland

Marshland Transplant Aquatic Nursery
P.O. Box 1
Berlin, WI 54923
Aquatic, prairie, woodland plants/seeds; restoration, water gardening

Milaeger's Gardens
4838 Douglas Ave.
Racine, WI 53402
Plants, trees, shrubs, grasses

Murn Environmental, Inc.
11643 E. Minkey Rd.
Darien, WI 53114

Natural Lawn & Landscape Ltd.
3522 W. Kilbourn Ave
Milwaukee, WI 53208
Design, installation, maintenance: uses native
plants only

Nature's Nursery
6125 Mathewson Road
Mazomanie, WI 53560
Wildflowers, seeds, grass seeds

Oak Prairie Farm
W4642 Highway 33
Pardeeville, WI 53954

Prairie Future Seed Co.
P.O. Box 644
Menomonee Falls, WI 53052

Prairie Nursery, Inc.
P.O. Box 306
Westfield, WI 53964
Wildflowers, grasses, seeds, plants

Prairie Ridge Nursery/CRM Ecosystems
9738 Overland Rd
Mt. Horeb, WI 53572
Woodland, wetland, prairie

Prairie Seed Source
P.O. Box 83
North Lake, WI 53064
SE WI grass, forbs, seeds, some shrubs

Reeseville Ridge Nursery
P.O. Box 171
Reeseville, WI 53579
Trees, shrubs, vines, woody plant seeds, ground
covers

Rohde's Nursery
N8098 Duck Creek Ave.
Neshkoro, WI 54960
Woodland, wetland, prairie plants; design,
consultation, restoration

Wehr Nature Center
9701 W. College Ave.
Franklin, WI 53132
Prairie seed mix—75% forbs, 25% grass-clay-
loam mesic prairie

Wildlife Nurseries (wholesale only)
P.O. Box 2724
Oshkosh, WI 54903
Water plants, wild rice, annuals, bare-root
hardwood seedlings

Woodland Gardens
W140N 10829 Country Aire Road
Germantown, WI 53022
Native marsh, woodland perennials

STATE FORESTERS

*These addresses are included as a resource for
individuals who need information or who may want
to purchase bundles of trees or shrubs for windbreaks,
wildlife habitats, or naturalizing.*

Illinois

Stewart Pequignot
Division of Forest Resources
524 S. Second Street (62701)
P.O. Box 19225
Springfield, IL 62794
(217) 782-2361
Fax: (217) 785-5517
e-mail: spequignot@dnrmail.state.il.us

Indiana

Burnell C. Fischer
Division of Forestry
Dept. of Natural Resources
402 W. Washington St.
Room W296
Indianapolis, IN 46204
(317) 232-4015
Fax: (317) 233-3863
e-mail: bfischer@dnr.state.in.us

Iowa

William Farris
Dept. of Natural Resources
Wallace Office Building
East 9th & Grand Ave.
Des Moines, IA 50319
(515) 281-8656
Fax: (515) 281-6794
e-mail: wfarris@max.state.ia.us

Kentucky

Mark Matuszewski
Kentucky Division of Forestry
627 Comanche Trail
Frankfort, KY 40601
(502)564-4496
Fax: (502)564-6553
e-mail: matuszewski@nrepc.nr.state.ky.us

Michigan

Gerald Thiede
Forest Management Div.
Michigan Dept. of Natural Res.
Mason Bldg.8th Floor
Box 30452
Lansing, MI 48909
(517) 335-4225
Fax: (517) 373-2443
e-mail: thiedeg@dnr.state.mi.us

Missouri

Marvin Brown
Missouri Dept. of Conservation
2901 West Truman Blvd.
P.O. Box 180
Jefferson City, MO 65102
(573) 751-4115 ext. 115
Fax: (573) 526-6670
e-mail:
brownm@mail.conservation.state.mo.us

Ohio

Ronald Abraham
Division of Forestry
1855 Fountain Sq. Ct. H.1
Columbus, OH 43224
(614) 265-6890
FAX: (614) 447-9231
e-mail: Ron.Abraham@dnr.ohio.gov

Tennessee

Ken S. Amey
Tennessee Dept. of Agriculture
Division of Forestry
P.O. Box 40627
Melrose Station
Nashville, TN 37204
(615) 837-5520
Fax: (615) 837-5003

Wisconsin

Charles Higgs
Dept. of Natural Resources
P.O. Box 7921
Madison, WI 53707
(608) 266-0842
Fax: (608) 266-8576
e-mail: higgsc@dnr.state.wi.us

NATIVE PLANT SOCIETIES

Illinois

Illinois Native Plant Society
Forest Glen Preserve
20301 East North Road
Westville, IL 61883
(217) 662-2142

Southern Illinois Native Plant Society
Botany Dept.
Southern Illinois University
Carbondale, IL 52901

Indiana

Indiana Native Plant & Wildflower Society
6106 Kingsley Dr.
Indianapolis, IN 46220

Kentucky

Kentucky Native Plant Society
c/o Dept. of Biological Sciences
Eastern Kentucky University
Richmond, KY 40475
(606) 662-2258

Michigan

Wildflower Association of Michigan
6011 West Joseph St.
Suite 403 P.O. Box 80527
Lansing, MI 48908

Missouri

Missouri Center for Plant Conservation
Missouri Botanical Garden
P.O. Box 299
St. Louis, MO 63166

Ohio

Ohio Native Plant Society
6 Louise Dr.
Chagrin Falls, OH 44022
(216) 338-6622

Tennessee

Tennessee Native Plant Society
Susan Sweeter
Dept. of Botany
University of Tennessee
Knoxville, TN 37996

Wisconsin

Wild Ones
Natural Landscapers, Ltd.
P.O. Box 23576
Milwaukee, Wisconsin 23576

I suggest that the only books that influence us are those for which we are ready, and which have gone a little farther down our particular path than we have yet got ourselves.

—*E. M. Forster, 1951*

References

Anon. *A Merry Briton in Pioneer Wisconsin.* Madison: State Historical Society of Wisconsin, 1950.

Augarde, Tony. *The Oxford Dictionary of Modern Quotations.* Oxford: Oxford University Press, 1991.

Bailey, Liberty Hyde, and Ethel Zoe Bailey. *Hortus Third, A Concise Dictionary of Plants Cultivated in the United States and Canada.* Revised and expanded by the staff of the Liberty Hyde Bailey Hortorium. New York: Macmillan, 1976.

Bales, Suzanne Frutig. *Vines.* Burpee American Gardening Series. New York: Macmillan, 1995.

Bartram, William. *William Bartram, Botanical and Zoological Drawings, 1756–1788.* Independence Square, Philadelphia: American Philosophical Society, 1968.

Beach, W. M. D. *The American Practice of Medicine.* New York: Betts and Anstice, 1832.

Bremer, Fredrika. *The Homes of the New World: Impressions of America.* Vols. 1 & 2. New York: Harper & Brothers, 1853.

Britton, Nathaniel Lord, and Hon. Addison Brown. *Illustrated Flora of the Northern United States, Canada and the British Possessions.* New York: Charles Scribner's Sons, 1896.

Brooklyn Botanic Garden. *Invasive Plants.* Handbook #148. Brooklyn, N.Y.: Brooklyn Botanic Garden, Winter, 1996.

Burrell, C. Colston. *A Gardener's Encyclopedia of Wildflowers.* Emmaus, Penn.: Rodale Press, 1997.

Collingwood, G. H., and Warren D. Brush. *Knowing Your Trees.* Washington, D.C.: American Forestry Association, 1984.

Davitt, Keith. "New Soil-test Kits Yield Reliable Results." *Fine Gardening* 64 (December 1998), pp. 32–35.

Deam, Charles C. *Flora of Indiana.* Indianapolis: Department of Conservation, Division of Forestry, 1940.

Deam, Charles C. *Trees of Indiana.* First revised edition. Publication No. 13. Indianapolis: Department of Conservation, State of Indiana, 1921.

Densmore, Frances. *How Indians Use Wild Plants for Food, Medicine and Crafts.* First published in the Forty-fourth Annual Report of the Bureau of American Ethnology to the Secretary of the Smithsonian Institution, 1926–27. Washington: United States Government Printing Office, 1928. Article printed as a booklet, New York: Dover, 1974.

Diekelmann, John, and Cathie Bruner. *An Introduction to Naturalized Landscapes: A Guide to Madison's "Natural Lawn" Ordinance.* Second revision. Madison, Wisc.: City of Madison, Wisconsin, 1991.

Dirr, Michael A. *Dirr's Hardy Trees and Shrubs.* Portland, Ore.: Timber Press, 1997.

Dirr, Michael A., and Charles W. Heuser, Jr. *The Reference Manual of Woody Plant Propagation.* Athens, Ga.: Varsity Press, 1987.

Doane, Nancy Locke. *Indian Doctor Book.* Charlotte, N.C.: Nancy Locke Doane, 1985.

Druse, Ken. *The Natural Habitat Garden.* New York: Clarkson N. Potter, 1994.

Druse, Ken. *The Natural Garden*. New York: Clarkson N. Potter, 1989.

Dunglison, Robley, M.D., LL.D. *A Dictionary of Medical Science*. Philadelphia, Penn.: Blanchard and Lea, 1854.

Foster, F. Gordon. *Ferns to Know and Grow*. Portland, Ore.: Timber Press, 1993.

Greenlee, John. *The Encyclopedia of Ornamental Grasses*. Emmaus, Penn.: Rodale Press, 1992.

Greenoak, Francesca. *Water Features for Small Gardens*. North Pomfret, Vt.: Trafalgar Square, 1996.

Grimm, William Carey. *The Book of Trees*. Harrisburg, Penn.: Stackpole, 1957, reprinted 1966.

Gunn, John C., M.D. *Gunn's New Domestic Physician*. Cincinnati, Ohio: Moore, Wilstach & Baldwin, 1864.

Haggard, Ezra. *Perennials for the Lower Midwest*. Bloomington: Indiana University Press, 1996.

Heilenman, Diane. *Gardening in the Lower Midwest*. Bloomington: Indiana University Press, 1994.

Henderson, Carrol L. *Landscaping for Wildlife*. St. Paul, Minn.: Department of Natural Resources, 1981.

Henn, Robert L. *Wildflowers of Ohio*. Bloomington: Indiana University Press, 1998.

Hightshoe, Gary. *Native Trees for Urban and Rural America*. Ames: Iowa State University Research Foundation, 1978.

Hubbard, Juliet Alsop. *Wildflowers*. American Gardening Series. New York: Macmillan, 1995.

Jackson, Marion T., ed. *The Natural Heritage of Indiana*. Bloomington: Indiana University Press, 1997.

Johnson, Howard. *A Home in the Woods*. Indianapolis: Indiana Historical Society, 1951.

Jones, Samuel B., Jr., and Leonard E. Foote. *Gardening with Native Wild Flowers*. Portland, Ore.: Timber Press, 1990.

Kuttruss, Jenna T., DeHart, S. Gail, O'Brien, Michael J. 2500 Years of Prehistoric Footwear from Arnold Research Cave, Missouri. *Science*. 281, issue 5373 (July 3, 1998), p. 72.

Ladd, Doug. *Tallgrass Prairie Wildflowers*. Helena and Billings, Mont.: Falcon Press, 1995.

Lawrence, George H. *An Introduction to Plant Taxonomy*. New York: Macmillan, 1955.

Little, R. John, and C. Eugene Jones. *A Dictionary of Botany*. New York: Van Nostrand Reinhold, 1980.

Loewer, Peter. *Step-by-step Wildflowers & Native Plants*. Des Moines, Ia.: Better Homes and Gardens Books, 1995.

Malecki, Richard A., Bernd Blossey, Stephen D. Hight, Dieter Schroeder, Loke T. Kok, Jack R. Coulson. "Biological Control of Purple Loosestrife—A Case for Using Insects as Control Agents, after Rigorous Screening, and for Integrating Release Strategies with Research." *BioScience* 43, No. 10 (November 1993), pp. 680–86.

Marryat, Captain Frederick. *Diary in America*. 1839. Rpt. London: Nicholas Vane, 1960.

Mitchell, Henry. *The Essential Earthman*. Bloomington: Indiana University Press, 1981.

Moody, Mary. *Creating Water Gardens*. Better Homes and Gardens Books. Sydney, Australia: Lansdowne, 1993.

Museums at Prophetstown, Inc. "From the Hearts of This Generation to the Hands of the Next . . . We Must Pass on Our Heritage." Brochure, Tippecanoe County, Indiana, 1998.

Nash, Helen, and C. Greg Speichert. *Water Gardening in Containers*. New York: Sterling, 1996.

Newcomb, Lawrence. *Newcomb's Wildflower Guide*. Boston: Little Brown, 1977.

Oakes, A. J. *Ornamental Grasses and Grasslike Plants*. New York: Van Nostrand Reinhold, 1990.

Oliver, Martha. "Native Ground Covers for Sun." *Fine Gardening* 43 (May-June 1995), pp. 54–57.

Peterson, Roger T., and Margaret McKenny. *A Field Guide to Wildflowers of Northeastern and North-central North America*. Boston: Houghton Mifflin, 1968.

Phillips, Harry R. *Growing and Propagating Wild Flowers*. Chapel Hill, N.C.: University of North Carolina Press, 1985.

Phillips Petroleum. *Pasture and Range Plants*. Bartlesville, Okla.: Phillips Petroleum, 1963.

Rishel, Dr. Jonas. *The Indian Physician*. New Berlin, Penn.: Joseph Miller, 1828.

Runkel, Sylvan, and Alvin Bull. *Wildflowers of Iowa Woodlands*. Ames: Iowa State University Press, 1979.

Runkel, Sylvan, and Dean Roosa. *Wildflowers of the Tallgrass Prairie*. Ames: Iowa State University Press, 1989.

Shelton, Ferne. *Pioneer Comforts and Kitchen Remedies*. High Point, N.C.: Hutcraft, 1965.

Shirreff, Patrick. *A Tour through North America*. First published in 1835, Edinburgh, Scotland. Reprinted, New York: Benjamin Blom, 1971.

Shull, Ernest M. *The Butterflies of Indiana*. Bloomington and Indianapolis: Indiana University Press/Indiana Academy of Science, 1987.

Snyder, Leon C. *Native Plants for Northern Gardens*. Chanhassen, Minn.: Anderson Horticultural Library, 1991.

Sperka, Marie. *Growing Wildflowers: A Gardener's Guide*. New York: Harper and Row, 1973.

Stein, Sara. *Planting Noah's Garden: Further Adventures in Background Ecology*. Boston and New York: Houghton Mifflin, 1997.

Sternberg, Guy, and Jim Wilson. *Landscaping with Native Trees*. Shelburne, Vt.: Chapters, 1995.

Stone, Norma M., translator. *Letters of Jakob Schramm and Family from Indiana to Germany in 1836*. Hanover, N.H.: Dartmouth Printing, 1951.

Stratton-Porter, Gene. *A Girl of the Limberlost*. New York: Grosset & Dunlap, 1909. Reprinted, Bloomington: Indiana University Press, 1984.

Swink, Floyd, and Gerould Wilhelm. *Plants of the Chicago Region*. Fourth ed. Morton Arboretum, Lisle, Ill. Indianapolis: Indiana Academy of Science, 1994.

Taylor, Norman. *The Guide to Garden Shrubs and Trees*. Boston: Houghton Mifflin, 1965.

Taylor, Patricia A. *Easy Care Native Plants*. New York: Henry Holt, 1996.

Time-Life Gardener's Guide. *Wildflowers*. Alexandria, Va.: Time-Life Books, 1989.

Time-Life Gardener's Guide. *Evergreen Shrubs*. Alexandria, Va.: Time-Life Books, 1989.

Trollope, Frances. *Domestic Manners of the Americans*. Fifth ed. London: Richard Bentley, 1839.

Wallace, Mervin, and John Logan. *Methods of Establishing Wildflowers on Missouri Highway Rights-of-Way*. Prepared for the Missouri Highway & Transportation Department in cooperation with the U.S. Department of Transportation, Federal Highway Administration, 1991.

Warren, Robert Penn. *Audubon: A Vision*. New York: Random House, 1969.

Wasowski, Andy. "The Building Envelope." Alexandria, Va.: *The American Gardener* (American Horticultural Society). January/February 1997, pp. 26–33.

Wasowski, Andy. "Building in Nature's Envelope." Springfield, Ore.: *Wild Garden*, premiere issue, January 1998, pp. 18–22.

Weed, Clarence, D.Sc. *Our Trees: How to Know Them*. Fifth ed. Reprint, New York: Garden City, 1946.

White, Hazel. *Growing Wildflowers*. Northrup King Lawn & Garden Books. New York: Avon Books, 1994.

Wilson, Jim. *Landscaping with Wildflowers*. Boston: Houghton Mifflin, 1992.

Wilson, William. *Landscaping with Wildflowers & Native Plants*. San Ramon, Calif.: Ortho Books, Chevron Chemical, 1984.

Author's Note: The epigraph in chapter 12 is taken from a song by Verlene Schermer, "Equal to the Task," written in 1995. It is on a 1996 CD entitled "Dreamtime," published by Karmalu Records, San Jose, California

Index

Carolyn Harstad is one of the founders of two successful organizations—the Indiana Native Plant and Wildflower Society (1993) and the Indianapolis Hosta Society (1986). She is a popular garden lecturer, nature photographer, certified Landscape Design Critic, and a regular contributor to several gardening newsletters. In 1990, Harstad wrote the wildflower guidelines, still used by 4-H members, to complete her certification as Advanced Master Gardener, Purdue University.

Jeanette Ming has been Art Editor at Worrall Community Newspapers in Union County, New Jersey. She is currently employed by the Metropolitan Museum of Art in New York City.